Searching for Unique

Jay,
Wishing you
many happy travels!

Searching for Unique

A Traveller's Guide to Extraordinary Experiences

Nancy O'Hare

Published by Nancy O'Hare at IngramSpark

ISBN: 978-1-775039068

First published: 2018

Editor: Susan Fitzgerald

Proofreader: Mirror Image Publishing

Cover designer: Ingrid Paulson

Photography: Chad O'Hare

bynancyohare.com

The information in this book is true and complete to the best of the author's knowledge. All recommendations are made without guarantee on the part of the author. The author disclaims any liability in connection to the use of this information. None of the establishments or services mentioned or reviewed in this book have provided compensation to the author.

Contents

	Acknowledgements	ix
	Preface	xi
	Introduction	1
1.	Wilderness Treks	*5*
	Bhutan—Tackling the Snowman Trek	*9*
	Bhutan—Treading Mystical Lands along the Merak to Sakteng Cultural Trek	*37*
	Iceland—Finding Solitude in Eastern Iceland	*48*
2.	Little-Known Hikes	*59*
	Colombia—Entering the Home of the Sun God in the Páramo de Ocetá	*62*
	Cuba—Uniting Sierra, Cigars and Solitude in Parque Nacional Viñales	*70*
	Faroe Islands—Dodging Wind and Rain across Vágar and Gjógv	*78*
	Portugal—Capturing the Milky Way in Madeira	*89*

3. Ancient Temples 100

Bhutan—Chasing Demons in Chimi Lhakhang 103
Myanmar—Biking through Bagan's Four Thousand Temples 112
Myanmar—Meeting Monks in Nyaungshwe 125
Myanmar—Behold Gold and Treasure at Yangon's Shwedagon Paya 135
Sri Lanka—Walking with Pilgrims at Mihintale 143
Sri Lanka—Scrambling Up the Boulder Temple of Pidurangala 155

4. Rare Festivals 161

Bhutan—Unmasking the Yak Cham 164
Bhutan—Glimpsing Sakteng's Secluded Ceremonies 173
Bhutan—Burning Arches and Masked Dancers at the Tamshing Phala Choepa 186
Bhutan—Translating Sutras inside Thimphu's Buddha Dordenma 198
China—Unrolling Tibet's Oldest Thangka at the Gyantse Festival 204
Malawi—Dancing the Malipenga on the Shores of Lake Malawi 213

5. Fallen Kingdoms 220

Estonia—Unravelling Tragedy and Myth at Kuressaare Castle 224
Latvia—Finding Rugged Simplicity at Cēsis Castle 231
Lithuania—Mingling with the Old and New in Refined Vilnius 237
Sri Lanka—Delving into the Spiritual Past of Anuradhapura 246
Sri Lanka—Shifting Waters at the Kingdom of Polonnaruwa 257

6. Modern Metropolises 267

Bhutan—A Trickle of Change Enters the Secluded Capital of Thimphu 270

Brunei Darussalam—Discover Bandar Seri Begawan's Pulse beneath its Formal Facade 279

Cuba—Losing Yourself in Havana's Tangle of Art, History and Authority 285

Myanmar—Mandalay's Shimmer and Serenity 297

About the Author 311

Other Books by the Author 313

Bibliography 316

Acknowledgements

To my indubitably inspiring partner and closest friend, **Chad O'Hare**, who has not only shared every adventure with me but transformed them through the camera lens into his own particular style. A few of my stories have even emerged from our late-night endeavours to capture that stunning shot. Why else would we hike to a lonesome peninsula on Portugal's island of Madeira at one o'clock in the morning? This unforgettable night, depicted in Chapter Two, was worth every lost minute of sleep. Thank you for making dinner to remind me we still had to eat when I became too absorbed in my writing and for gently encouraging me to refocus when I became distracted.

To my unwaveringly supportive parents, who have stood by me and have visited me nearly everywhere I lived around the world. My dad, **Brian Veale,** read and reread early drafts to help refine the writing and build interest. He somehow retains facts about almost everything: the Carpathian Mountains, Spanish forts, old cars, general history, geography, politics—just about anything you might ever want to talk about. And if he does not know something, there is always, in his words, "Mr. Google." Dad has the finesse to point out areas to tighten and improve while adding words of encouragement to carry on. My mom, **Millie Veale**, also an avid reader, never tired of reviewing draft versions, sharing my work with friends and family and following my progress, both in writing and when travelling the globe. Thank you both for being such positive influences.

To my dear friends and neighbours who read early chapters and provided fresh angles. Their insight helped to sharpen storylines and highlight nuances otherwise trapped inside my head. Thank you to **Nancy McNair**, **Jim Schram** and **Caroline Smith**, who all helped to ensure the stories carried the reader along on a worthwhile yet focused journey.

Thank you for sharing your perspective and time. This book is better because of your contributions.

Preface

I am often asked why I decided to write. I gave up a successful career in finance for which I had earned an executive MBA and a professional designation, a career that allowed me to live abroad and get paid for it. Simply, I wanted to refocus my energy towards a simpler, healthier lifestyle. And discovering new cultures has proven to me over and over how much I have yet to learn about our planet and how we are all connected.

Yet shards of animosity have surged in the current climate and have transformed into a virtual hailstorm pummelling our world. You can see the tension wearing people down. People with opposing views are becoming more isolated from each other and are unable to bridge or even discuss their misunderstandings with one another. At times it seems there is no common ground. Still, the more I travel and meet people from different backgrounds, religions and countries, the stronger my belief that we are more alike than not. So I ask myself, "How can I help bring people together and make the world a better place?"

This quest is an unanswered puzzle to which I cannot quite see all the pieces. For now, I will continue to travel. I will continue to write about these experiences in a way that presents a different perspective on a place or a population than what people might expect. I want to pull apart the walls of bias that shift and morph general perception. Instead of overlaying assumptions from our own culture, let us try to delve in and better understand why someone somewhere else does things differently.

In any case, why is being different considered so scary? Bananas have over a thousand different varieties. Are you scared of a banana? Orchids alone split into more than 25,000 species. Yet do florists wince when a mixed bouquet is placed on a table? When we set the dining table, we give each setting a fork, a spoon, a knife and maybe even a butter knife or soup spoon. Each utensil has its use, yet I have never heard someone say a knife is less worthy than a fork or try to ban a setting of teaspoons. People realize that these tools each offer value and it would be senseless to consider one better or worse than another. Difference is a necessity. It helps society function, to be more efficient and to have depth.

So peel away your assumptions and get ready to unwrap secluded places and far-off cultures. In the following pages, find contradiction that captivates and uniqueness that inspires.

Introduction

My neighbour once asked me an important question about this book, a basic yet crucial perspective: "Who is your intended readership?" We sat down over a glass of wine, and after a few minutes of my rambling about discovering places most people do not consider venturing to, about the satisfaction of finding an awe-inspiring vista or unwrapping an ancient sight few have heard of, he summed it up magnificently. It is a book for travellers, not tourists.

I had two criteria for the stories and places included in this book. First, the destination had to be away from the main tourist track. Second, the experience had to have left a lasting impression. I was looking for unforgettable memories in incomparable places that most people never see. Thousands of people a year visit Iceland's Skaftafell National Park, which showcases stunning natural glaciers, yet a day's hike away lies the virtually vacant Lónsöræfi region. Sri Lanka's old centre of Galle packs visitors inside its stony walls, but travel farther north and you can watch while history replays itself. At the rock temple of Mihintale—the same hilltop location where Buddhism was first introduced to Sri Lanka—we were the only foreigners to join pilgrims practising century-old traditions during a *poya* ("full moon") ceremony. *Searching for Unique* helps travellers uncover such enigmatic experiences in distant lands.

Whether you prefer active adventure or more subdued cultural encounters, the themes covered in these chapters are sure to ignite your desire to get out and explore our wondrous world. Chapters One and Two are targeted for the active traveller who enjoys trekking and hiking. The third chapter explores ancient temples that have come alive with modern-day devotion. Rare festivals that pushed the boundaries of our expectations are captured in Chapter Four. The book then unveils fallen kingdoms, some of which have been brought back to life, while others remain dormant. The last chapter is for those who like the action of cities but still crave a vacation that feels a little obscure. Overall, these six chapters will take you across five continents, fourteen countries and over twenty-five specific destinations.

Every section recreates the essence of a place and concludes with on-the-ground travel advice. So whether you are an armchair traveller or you are planning your next trip abroad, this book will explore unexpected destinations that feed your traveller's spirit.

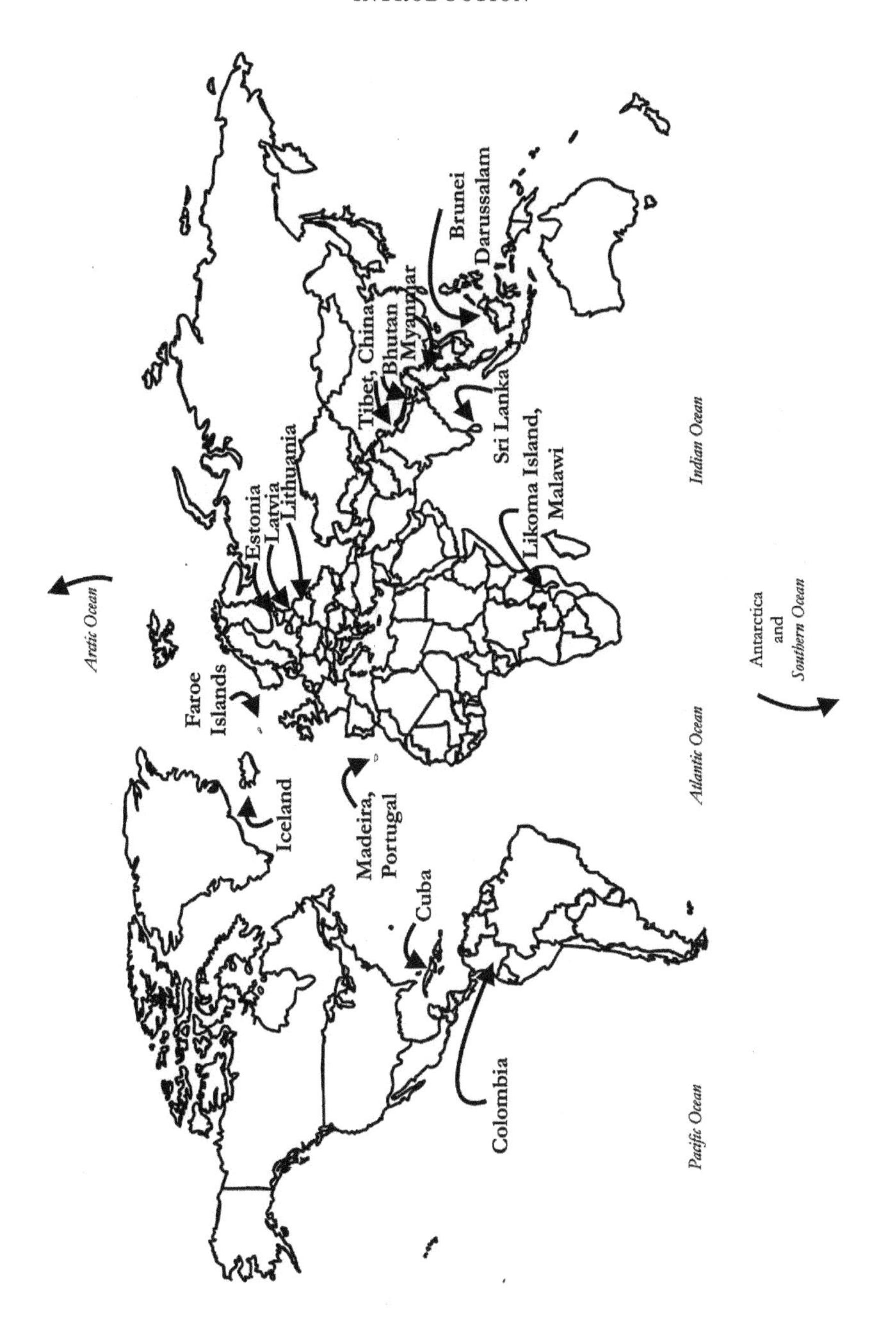
Artic Ocean
Faroe Islands
Estonia
Latvia
Lithuania
Tibet, China
Bhutan
Myanmar
Brunei Darussalam
Sri Lanka
Likoma Island, Malawi
Indian Ocean
Antarctica and Southern Ocean
Atlantic Ocean
Iceland
Madeira, Portugal
Cuba
Colombia
Pacific Ocean

1

Wilderness Treks

Trekking over multiple days is not for everyone. There are no showers, running water or fresh clothing to snuggle into on cool mornings. Gone are the evenings when you can tiptoe barefoot to the bathroom in the middle of the night. Instead you have to pull on musty hiking boots and grab a headlamp to scurry outside to the toilet tent. But the payoff is mighty impressive. This chapter will take you along on three unforgettable treks through the wilderness of Bhutan and Iceland. In the first section we tackle Bhutan's highest and longest trek, the Snowman trek. Then we shift eastward to the country's most secluded and protected region to traverse between the alpine villages of Merak and Sakteng. The third section explores the eastern Lónsöræfi region of Iceland, a glacial wasteland where we escaped the crowds.

Let us start by exploring the enigmatic country of Bhutan. It lies in the Himalaya Mountains, with China to its north and India to its south. The country places top priority on its traditional culture and pristine environment. In fact, Bhutan's constitution holds every citizen accountable as a trustee of the country's natural resources for future generations, and holds the Royal Government responsible for conserving and protecting the environment. Foreign tourists must come with an approved local tour company and pay a fixed day rate as set by the government. This approach helps ensure high-quality, low-impact tourism. It seems to be working. The country ranks as one of the ten most bio-diverse regions in the world, and it is the only carbon-negative nation on the planet. Sixty percent of Bhutan's land is protected, and logging for export is prohibited. This small kingdom makes a big impact.

During the first trek in this chapter, we traversed the northwestern corner of Bhutan. We crossed a route that had enticed us ever since we first visited the country in 2010. At that time, we learned of Bhutan's most difficult trek, the Snowman trek. Due to high altitude, unpredictable weather and lack of infrastructure, only fifty percent of trekkers who attempt the journey actually complete it. The Snowman daunted us as much as it inspired us. In 2017, we tackled the trail ourselves. Between the summer monsoon rains and shifting winter snows, a sliver of opportunity opens from mid-September to early October to attempt this legendary track.

For me, the effort required to reach such isolated spaces made it all the more worthwhile. I would not give up an evening spent at five thousand metres on a Himalayan plateau beneath black boulders, creaking glaciers and the shadow of Gangla Karchung's serrated ridge. Nor will I forget an encounter with a herd of takin, the national animal of Bhutan, foraging along a yak herders' trail in northwestern Bhutan. These odd-looking Himalayan creatures resemble a cross between goats and muskox and gave us a quintessential Bhutanese welcome before they scurried away in the dense undergrowth.

That said, there are always moments of weakness. I recall the sixteenth night of our seventeen-day trek. We had camped next to a creek, alongside a picturesque valley overflowing with vegetation. It had been raining on and off for days. Streams became "boot cleaners," a nickname earned after we had walked through a special blend of mud formed from dirt, rain, yak droppings and horse dung. As I slapped my hiking boots together before bringing them inside the tent, bits flicked across my face and into my eyes. I initially swore with disgust and aggravation. Then I caught myself. I had chosen this path. After a slow inhale, I grabbed one of my last wet wipes and eased back into our cozy, though slightly dank, tent. Life could certainly be worse.

During our second trek, we shifted to the far eastern region of Bhutan, which opened its borders to foreigners only in 2010. Our route stretched from the town of Merak to Sakteng, a village that can be reached only by walking for one to two days, depending on your route. We passed through highland forests where thirty-five species of rhododendron grew among broadleaf and coniferous trees. Rare red pandas and, according to local legend, the fierce yeti are known to lurk in these forests. In the words of the Tourism Council of Bhutan, the Sakteng Wildlife Sanctuary is a "lost world of biodiversity waiting to be discovered."[1] This protected alpine is also home to a semi-nomadic people, the Brokpas, who welcomed us to share in their sacred ceremonies and local dances, brought alive in Chapter Four: Rare Festivals.

While just over two hundred thousand tourists visited Bhutan in 2017,[2] ten times that many people—over two million—travelled to Iceland during the same period.[3] A ring road circles Iceland and directs visitors to the island's most popular sites. Icebergs bob in

1. bhutan.travel/national-park/sakteng-wildlife-sanctuary
2. tourism.gov.bt/uploads/attachment_files/tcb_buHnrvHE_BTM 2017.pdf
3. grapevine.is/news/2018/01/16/number-of-tourists-to-iceland-surpasses-2-million-in-2017

lagoons, glaciers groan and geothermal pools ease travellers' muscles, achy after a day spent exploring. These are the images most people take from Iceland. Our target was something different, a lesser-visited part of the country. We wanted remote and rugged. We wanted unique.

East Iceland, the last of our three treks covered in this chapter, answered our call. We spent four days in the eastern Lónsöræfi region, encountering no one until our last night, when we met the caretaker of that evening's hut. We found solitude in a barren expanse, brightened in places by colourful rhyolite canyons that looked as if they had been transplanted from a strange metallic world. The apparently empty *öræfi*—meaning an untouched wasteland or desert wilderness—of East Iceland showed its personality through tiny mosses and colourful rhyolite. Here we met Iceland's exquisite emptiness, and it was an honour to glimpse it.

So, when this world feels too small, too connected by global networks and more chaotic by the hour, consider lacing up your hiking books and going far, far away. The minor hardships encountered on the way wash away from memory soon after the first warm shower. What remains are memories stuck in your mind forever. Those endearing moments are what I focus on in the upcoming sections, the glory beneath the grit.

~~~
~~~

BHUTAN—TACKLING THE SNOWMAN TREK

Challenge yourself to Bhutan's highest, longest and toughest trek, climbing passes of over five thousand metres in elevation

The Experience

I tried to gently close our room's heavy wooden door, but its shrill squeal shattered the silence of the guesthouse. "Did the local wildlife wake you up, too?" our friend casually asked. It turned out that minutes before, a mouse had leapt from its crevasse in the stone wall and landed in a bellyflop squarely on her face. I was not sure how she remained so calm. Rodents are my nemesis, the one type of creature that invariably send chills of disgust sweeping across my shoulders. For the next hour, my husband and I shot beams from our headlamps at every scuffle we heard, each tremble of dust, which occurred far too frequently in our close-quartered room.

Two friends, my husband and I were staying in the Koina guesthouse, a rustic stone building located in one of Bhutan's most isolated Himalayan regions. In our room, four foam mattresses covered most of the ground, leaving just enough space for our packs and hiking boots. I tried, unsuccessfully, to ignore the mental image of a mouse settling down inside one of my boots or gnawing into my pack. Finally, I tucked my head underneath my sleeping bag and fell into a restless slumber. Sometime during the night, our friend was woken a second time when the aspiring Olympic mouse once again dived off the wall and landed smack onto her head. Our upcoming sixteen nights in tents were looking better by the minute. The next morning brought the appearance of another rodent, but of a different sort. When we visited the attached outhouse, an unmoving waterlogged rat sprawled beside the squat toilet's water bucket. Not long after, we heard the caretaker giggle—and that was the last anyone saw of the unfortunate critter.

The primary caretaker was away, likely organizing supplies, so his wife managed the guesthouse by herself. The rock building was used mainly by traders and yak herders from villages higher in the mountain range, typically transiting supplies they had bought or were going to sell in the more populous town of Gasa, where we had started our trek. This hut was a busy transit point. We had heard stories of the guesthouse filled with up to one hundred travellers at a time. They would sleep on a stone floor, perhaps with a foam mattress if the traveller was lucky enough to nab one, snuggled tightly together so everyone could fit inside. Luckily during our stay, our trekking crew was the only group spending the night. Four rooms fanned out on either side of one central area, each approximately three metres by four metres. One of these was the caretaker's kitchen-cum-shop-cum-bedroom.

We watched as she carried another supply of branches into her room to keep the old wood stove alight. She was a welcoming lady and a tough lady. She had little privacy, with the door to her room open for much of the day. The battered stove kept her niche warm and ensured that someone could usually be found huddled on the floor, more than likely rocking a warm mug of tea. She did not seem to mind our company inside her cozy space. Her sturdy but well-worn wooden stool sat behind the stove. A formerly silver-coloured kettle shared the stovetop with a large blackened pot, now a matched set tarnished by smoke and flames. She occasionally stirred the pot of steaming goodness. Before long, she filled a mug of the creamy masala *ja* (spicy tea with milk) and handed it to me. With my first sip, visions of the day's mud faded, and I felt a subtle smile settle across my face.

It rained all night on that first night of our seventeen-day trek. We were in northwestern Bhutan, not far from the Tibetan border. The full Snowman trek can take up to twenty-five days along yak herder trails, but we had lopped off the initial section, as we had covered it in 2010 as part of the Jomolhari trek. We would camp in wilderness most of the time because only a handful of basic villages exist at these high elevations. Most inhabitants are yak herders who move to lower ground for the winter. For now, the rainy season was still upon us, but the winter snows would soon arrive and could make the passes uncrossable. With full Gore-Tex rain pants and jackets, we left the relative dryness of the hut and launched into day two.

Soon after we left the Koina guesthouse, the trail turned narrow. A steep scree edge sliced down the slope to our right. Some sections looked freshly washed away, but the trail remained relatively intact. A lone backpack lay on the gravel ahead of us. Two shiny rolls of corrugated sheet metal had come to a rest about twenty metres below. We noticed a stranded horse among the dirt and thickets, relatively unscathed. His harness hung useless as he shifted slightly and peered up at us. We heard his handler, the owner of the abandoned backpack, before we saw him behind a clump of bamboo stalks. Reeds crumpled as he slashed a pathway back up to the trail for the horse.

Most buildings in this region have zinc-coated metallic roofs. They offer durable, waterproof shelter. But without roads to supply such materials, rolls of the metal have to be hauled in on the backs of horses. This particular horse had been carrying just such a roll, as long as his back and practically touching his eyelashes. We had passed many strings of similar horses, all carrying rolls balanced lengthwise between their ears and tails. A few carried other necessities packed inside canvas sacks. It was a difficult balancing act. The horses needed to hold their heads down to avoid the sharp edges since the metal rolls jiggled with every step. It was not uncommon to see drops of blood splattered along the metal's rim or scrapes near a horse's ears or mouth. For the horse at the bottom of the scree, it was a lucky day. He could walk away. We thought of the horses carrying our trekking supplies. They were behind us and still had to cross this loose path. Fifteen horses in total were needed to carry our tents, food, gear and cooking equipment—enough to last seventeen days for our team of ten people. We were currently short three horses, which would join us from the town of Laya, a few days' walk ahead.

We later learned that the royal family was planning to visit Laya in a few weeks. New tents and buildings were being constructed for the grand affair, which explained the stream of horses bringing supplies. Later that day, we met two young men who each carried a two-metre-long steel post on his back. The first man's pole balanced against a pine tree as he took a break. It was not an easy feat to wield such a piece on your shoulders along a windy, slippery and arduous pathway. It made me feel like a novice as I watched each step closely to avoid slipping, with only a day pack to carry.

We heard stories of how Bhutan's present king would visit similarly remote villages unexpectedly and in disguise. He wanted to see the real life of his subjects without the superfluous facade that comes with a typical royal visit. Perhaps it was these wanderings that spurred the improvements to the quality of life in remote Himalayan communities that we had heard so much about. For example, the road where we had started our trek was newly constructed. I use the past tense softly, as it was a work in progress rather than a work completed. A four-wheel-drive vehicle was still required to get through, and even our truck struggled through the thick sludge, ruts and rocks that formed the road. Huts made of canvas and tin had been strung along the edges of the work zone to house construction workers, mostly from India. I felt guilty walking past with moisture-wicking clothing and carbon hiking poles, frivolous luxuries compared to their basic conditions.

Kobelco excavators were the most commonly used equipment along these treacherous ravines. At times, we would come around a corner and find an excavator teetering on the edge of the road while its bucket chipped away rock and dirt. A few machines had been abandoned, many of them missing some critical part or listing at an awkward angle. We were told that two drivers had recently lost their lives on a section of the road we had passed through. The locals had mixed feelings about the road. It would ease access and hopefully bring prosperity to residents, yet such negative signs indicated the valley's local deity, or "protector god," was unhappy. Apparently, plans for a lama to conduct a cleansing ceremony were progressing, but bringing lamas to such a remote area was a costly affair. It was thought that a religious ritual would change the deity's disposition and, in turn, protect workers from further accidents. Basically, it was an attempt to get the gods on their side. I was certainly glad to have left the construction zone after our first morning.

On the afternoon of our second day, the gods showed us their favour. After a steep, slick section, the trail flattened and transformed into a dry, leaf-strewn pathway. Not far ahead, we spotted a herd of odd-looking creatures. The esteemed Lama Drukpa Kunley allegedly conceived of these species in the fifteenth century. Folklore recounts how he stuck a goat's head onto a cow's body after a particularly delectable meal of goat meat and beef. This incredulous act created what is now Bhutan's national animal, the takin. Eight of these peculiar animals sauntered through the trees towards us, munching grass and sniffing the ground. Their carefree pace abruptly stopped as they stared at us while we gawked back at them. Their muzzles were rounded like a moose's. Their horns were small, more similar to a water buffalo's curved crown than the straight pointed horns of a goat. The colour of their fur ranged from a golden hue to tones of dark chocolate, melding with the shadowed forest. Within moments, the lead animal veered into low shrubs and headed uphill where the trees thickened. Two young takins disappeared as soon as they stepped off the path and into the scrubby bush.

That night, we camped near an army post, down the valley from the village of Laya. A river raged below our campsite, and dense forest spread above us. We had passed the three-thousand-metre mark. While we were enjoying what we felt was a well-deserved cup of ja, two strangers popped through our dining tent's doors. One man wore a light-grey down jacket, not the fatigues one might expect from a soldier. We listened to the man's clear English with an Indian lilt as he explained that the pair were from a team of four men posted in the valley. Bhutan, being a small nonviolent Buddhist country, relies heavily on India's military protection. Curious to see their camp, we readily accepted their offer to follow them. The Indian military camp lay just beyond the Bhutanese army camp, where we had earlier plugged in our rechargeable camera batteries, grateful for such a rare luxury in this remote valley. Otherwise, we relied on solar panels with a compatible battery pack.

The Indian base turned out to be different than my image of an army base. Inside the gate, a well-tended garden was cultivated in perfectly aligned rows. The quieter man pointed out bunches of coriander, spinach and garlic sprouting through the soil. Before long, they brought steaming mugs of masala chai to a picnic table. Four wee puppies then bounded into the yard, tumbling over one another. They were one month old and had definitively embedded themselves in camp life. As we sat around the table, our second day felt rather surreal. I had not expected to be enjoying flavourful tea with soldiers in an idyllic setting of lush forests, babbling rivers and cheerful puppies. After chatting for a while, we strolled back towards the Bhutan army barracks. By now, a few army families were working at various chores around their post. We talked with them as much as we could in our limited Dzongkha, declined to buy a woollen hat from an entrepreneurial army wife and collected our fully charged camera batteries.

Our third day was a rest day, or down day. We climbed four hundred metres to the town of Laya. The path was well used; after all, it provided the only access in or out of the village. Shaggy yaks stood off-duty and watched us walk past. They barely moved, raising questions about their reputation as skittish creatures. Cattle grazed in fields closer to town. For such an isolated community, there was a surprising number of new homes under construction. We soon learned that not only was the royal family coming for a visit, but the residents of Laya were also building new homes for themselves. Local entrepreneurs had mastered a rather unique livelihood—they harvested caterpillar fungus—and business was booming. The coveted cordycep mushroom had earned the people of Laya much more than their traditional yak herding or cheese making ever had.

The cordycep fungus attaches itself to young caterpillars. When the caterpillars hibernate, the cordycep infiltrates their bodies and essentially mummifies the unlucky larvae. The fungus continues to live inside its host and eventually emerges as a spike on top of the caterpillar's head. This spike is the target of cordycep pickers. The fungus thrives in the high-altitude ranges of the Himalaya, like those surrounding the village of Laya, and has become a lucrative commodity over the last decade. Prices have soared as demand for this traditional medicine has shot up, particularly in China. The shrivelled mushrooms have been dubbed the Viagra of the Himalaya. Prices are reported to range from US$10,000 to US$50,000 for one kilo of the precious mushrooms. Our assistant cook had his own bag, which he was filling with the traditional love elixir in hopes of earning some extra cash when he returned to the city. I have since read that supply has started to subside, blamed on either warming temperatures or overharvesting, so the windfall gained by so many remote communities like Laya over the last decade may start to wither.

The greatest demand for caterpillar fungus came from China, and both the Laya and Lunana regions, which we were crossing, bordered Tibet. A busy trade route had developed between these mountainous districts. However, a few months earlier the government of Bhutan had closed its borders with China. Tensions with its massive neighbour were mounting. News reports focused on the Doklam plateau, a no man's land between China and Bhutan that sits near India's Sikkim territory. In June 2017, China had begun to construct a road leading up and into the disputed territory. Because India provides Bhutan's military protection and because their own sovereign border lies close by, they played a key role in the situation. *The Diplomat* newspaper delved into this issue in their article "The Political Geography of the India-China Crisis at Doklam."[4] Chinese armed soldiers were also rumoured to be crossing into Bhutan's western region of Ha, which we had visited in 2010. The government of Bhutan warned that anyone trying to cross the border into China would be shot, quickly stifling the cordycep market.

As far as alternative industry, Laya had one guesthouse when we visited. Piles of wood created a low fence around the house, a stockpile for heating and cooking that should last the winter. Inside the yard, a cement basin supported the single water tap used by the guesthouse, with a bar of soap set conveniently beside it. The rest of the yard was filled with an assortment of black cable, metal bowls and plastic tubs. The owner led us up a ladder-like staircase to a small open-air landing. Before we turned a corner, I noticed the white skull of a yak resting on the floorboards. My eyes slowly adjusted to the dim room. Sunlight entered through a couple of small windows, which did little to brighten the low-ceilinged room. Beyond the wooden table and plastic chairs where we were served butter tea, a traditional hat hung on the wall. The women of Laya prefer this thatch hat, which is woven into a conical shape. It may not be warm or cozy, but it certainly exudes a distinctive fashion sense. As we sat around the wooden table, the drizzle outside turned heavy. Steep hills in the distance faded behind an opaque mist while droplets dripped off the guesthouse's metal roof. Butter tea is not my favourite drink,

4. thediplomat.com/2017/07/the-political-geography-of-the-india-china-crisis-at-doklam

but the warmth and dry location made it enticing enough to stay awhile.

The streets of Laya meandered along a course that had naturally evolved as each house was built or a family's needs expanded. Recent steady rains had turned the narrow tracks into a gooey mess of mud mixed with animal droppings. At one point, the pathway split. One direction wrapped down through a home's front entrance while the alternative connected with a few neighbouring houses. If we wanted to reach the fifteenth-century *dzong* ("fort monastery") at the end of town, we would have had to climb over a fence and onwards through someone's buckwheat field. Instead of intruding, we watched from afar. From the small temple, freshly painted boards flashed in the sunlight, and echoes of hammering drifted our way. The dzong had been damaged in a recent earthquake, but we were assured its original foundation stood strong.

Before heading back to our campsite, we passed through Laya's schoolyard. The school was built in the shape of a U with doors facing towards the centre field where we stood. Posters with English phrases hung on the walls. A few brave kids said "Hello," and we answered back in the local Dzongkha, "*Kuzuzangbola.*" About two hundred children attended this primary school, although we could see only a handful as we walked past. They travelled from their home villages across the entire Laya and Lunana regions to board at Laya's school. Older kids went farther south to attend a senior boarding school in Gasa, the town where we had started our trek.

Back in camp, a new tent had been raised while we were away. It was not large, perhaps half a metre square, but high enough to stand in. This was our shower tent. Even though we were only three days into our trek, the thought of a cleansing shower was tantalizing. Wet wipes were fine, but a sudsy shower would be sublime. I slipped open the tent's door flap. There stood a stick, stuck relatively firmly into the ground. A plastic sack hung from a notch of a broken branch. A hose ran from its base and ended at a spray nozzle. The concept seemed solid. It relied on gravity to force the water out once a release valve was opened.

In practice, the contraption did not function so smoothly. Once I turned the cap to open the water flow, water spilled out of the base of the water bag instead of funnelling through its hose. After several futile attempts to tighten and adjust the contraption or to squat on the ground underneath the bag of dripping water, I decided to try a more basic approach. A tin bowl of warm water had been set on the ground in the shower tent, and this turned out to be a far more effective way to splash and scrub. After bathing I felt slightly better, but left the tent with more grass and mud on my feet than when I had entered. And my enthusiasm for another shower on the trek quickly dissipated. The jumbo-sized baby wipes that I had stuffed inside a Ziploc bag would have to suffice.

Over the next few days, we continued our climb. Tall pine trees and billowing rhododendrons gave way to scrubbier bushes. Boulders emerged from thickets, their hard edges softened by patches of moss and splotches of white lichen. The path followed the Rhodu Chhu, a frothy river beside which yak herders had built the occasional stone hut. For one night, we camped on a grassy bank near the water's edge. Our cooks used one of the huts for their kitchen and turned its spacious dry interior into our dining room.

By our fifth day, Tsomo La beckoned us. In Dzongkha, *la* refers to a mountain pass, and we would cross several high passes along the Snowman trek. Throughout the Himalaya, prayer flags are hung across passes to catch the wind. Each string of flags has five swatches of cloth that correspond with the five elements: blue for sky, white for clouds or wind, red for fire, green for water and yellow for earth. The flags are imprinted with prayers or mantras, which are believed to be carried by the wind and scattered as blessings to whomever they touch.

We climbed two false summits before reaching the actual Tsomo La at 4,900 metres. My husband and I were the first to arrive. The wind was eerily calm for such a high ridge. I clambered on top of some rocks for a better view. Farther west, the domineering Mount Jomolhari rose to a height of 7,314 metres. We had hiked to its base camp, Jangothang, in 2010.

As is the custom, we had brought a string of prayer flags.[5] We pulled it out and tied one end of the string to a rock and the other to an existing flag already tethered securely. Piles of flat rocks had been stacked at the pass, and their pointed tips provided convenient anchors for fastening flags. A muddied old yak horn was also wedged into one of the larger piles. The wind whipped the splashes of colour in an endless flutter, embodying the music of the passes. It also brought mist, a damp thickness that soon condensed into droplets. Before long, we were clothed in complete rain gear and had pulled out our pack covers and given in to the urge to continue moving. We tramped towards a vaguely visible lake shrouded in drizzle. The mood of the deluge shifted once more, and transformed it into sleet. Pellets ricocheted off my jacket before changing again, this time into tiny snowflakes.

The weather's fickle personality seemed to feed our sense of isolation. We all turned inward, lost in our own thoughts as our feet carried us farther. Hat off. Jacket off. Jacket back on when the wind picked up again. A cluster of blue sheep scampered along the rocks in

5. For more about our string of prayer flags, see Chapter Six: Bhutan—A Trickle of Change Enters the Secluded Capital of Thimphu.

the distance. They looked more grey than their namesake hue. We hiked on. The views started to open up. Spiky peaks of the Gangla Karchung range became visible. A rumble sounded in the distance. It reminded me of thunder, but it was a different type of crash. One of the fingers of drifting ice that grasped these peaks had lost a chunk of its icy tips. Fog rolled in. Its white puff slithered across the slate-coloured mountain range, and the fusion of light and dark merged into a haunting aura.

Huge black boulders lay around our campsite, daring me to climb atop them in search of the perfect post-hike resting spot. I succumbed. From the edge, I could look straight across to a giant glacier, dirty with grit and ever so slowly pushing its way across the rocky face. Nature's strength was clear here. It was impossible not to feel a sense of awe, of respect, and a little sadness that there are so few perfectly magical places like this left in the world. After a long day's hike, just standing there watching the snow, rock and fog swerve above me filled me with energy. The sheer silence, beyond the occasional rumbling when a glacier calved, felt intoxicating. My motivation for the days to come surged.

Our camp sat at an elevation of nearly five thousand metres. A breed of ravens that live above four thousand metres soared overhead. Plant life at this height was particularly striking. Stalks of wild rhubarb with leaves that had turned a creamy colour grew here and there, their white horns poking out from the mountainside and contrasting with the grey rock. Deep purple flowers nuzzled another plant's slender leaves that stretched low to the ground. Elsewhere a brilliant blue flower bloomed when the sun shone but clamped shut by early evening and stayed that way until dawn warmed it open again.

The next morning, clear skies exposed the great peak of Teri Gang, soaring to a height of 7,300 metres. Our guide said it was the first time in three years he had been able to see its peak from the pass that lay just beyond our campsite. The remainder of the day felt like an endless downhill traverse. We passed a pack of blue sheep grazing to our left. One youngster seemed to have overdosed on its morning caffeine. While its elders munched tufts of grass, it ran. This little guy raced circles around the flock and often hopped onto a massive boulder for added mountaineering practice. To our right, a glacier arm ended at an avocado-coloured lake. It looked innocent, but local alpine communities have been flooded in recent years as the glaciers have melted and receded. With the thawing ice, boulders loosen and create a hazard to the glacial lakes' fragile balance, causing them to overflow. We were told that a team of scientists from Japan were installing monitors in a nearby glacial lake. These devices were intended to send warnings to nearby residents and meteorologists if waters suddenly rose.

As we dragged our aching feet into camp about seven hours later, we were met by more than our horsemen. Four hairy yaks were lined up on the grass between the creek and the lush hill that enclosed our camping area. Each yak had a red tassel dangling from its ear, likely a marker to indicate who it belonged to. Their owner had tied them to a single rope but worked with each animal one by one. First, he tied the yak's legs. Then the yak herder gave a twist to the animal's tail. It was not an aggressive move, more of a suggestive manoeuvre that encouraged the beast to lie down. From there, it was given its allotted salt dosage. After heavy hauling and a long day's walk, this essential mineral was just what the animal needed. The yak herder then untied it, and it was free to wander for the remainder of the night.

We saw this same exercise later in our trek, except it took place in a family's front yard. Three daughters worked the rope while another person tried the tail-twisting trick. This group did a lot of sidestepping, circling and occasionally dipping down in an attempt to pull the animal to its knees. Their yak performed a similar dance in return. We watched for about ten minutes. They proceeded to prod and play with the animal until it finally laid on the ground, ready for its salt lick.

The four yaks at our camp were members of a group of eleven. As I crept out of our tent in the morning, they stood together. Their bodies steamed as the cool air touched their matted fur. The yaks were connected to a central rope. Shorter offshoots circled their forehead and horns before being knotted to the main line. The animals were fed from this position. I imagined they felt as groggy as I did. Then their gear was loaded, tightened and adjusted before they were ready to go. They stood resolute, sometimes scratching a leg with a turn and rub of their horn. They may not have known, but their lives were about to change. Families from this high mountain range had been yak herders for generations. However, as new technologies crept into their consciousness, children were losing interest in the trade. After all, it was a hard life living outdoors, camping continually, searching for clean water and hauling everything you own day after day. Those eleven yaks that we watched were being led to the nearest town. The father had decided to sell his herd. His health had deteriorated. His eldest son had died, and his daughter—at six years of age—was too young to manage the animals. So he was left with no choice but to sell and retire his family's tradition. Although the mountains felt idyllic to us as visitors, life here presented an entirely different reality.

Yaks grazing near Thoencha

I thought about the yak herder's situation and considered how life moves in unexpected ways. Is it all just a game? Do we reset the go button every morning when we wake and define the day's path by how we respond to events that are continually lobbed our way? That process of being served, assessing and reacting is really just a volatile game of endurance that is repeated every morning. It does not matter where we live, what job we toil at or what type of family we were born into. We all have to face what is thrown at us, kick it back and play on.

That day we walked past a milky river named Pho Chhu. Delicate mauve flowers grew behind moss-covered rocks, and rows of bleached white scree alternated with red-tinged rock. At one point, two red sections framed a white strip of scree and reminded me of the Canadian flag in abstract art form. We had reached the Lunana region. This is one of the most remote areas of Bhutan. Most people survive in these tough mountain conditions by herding yaks, harvesting caterpillars or both. We passed the small settlement of Woche on a plateau. Below, valleys intersected with near-vertical slopes shrouded with juniper trees and shrubs. Vegetable gardens, fields of buckwheat and red potatoes grew between the houses. White-crusted peaks reminded us we were deep in the Himalaya.

One lady carried an armful of buckwheat in her arms while her baby's wide eyes focused on us. He was bundled in thick layers of warm clothing and strapped onto her back with a band of handwoven material. We watched as a family harvested their field of buckwheat; some sliced, some piled and some tied the bundles into neat bunches. Another lady sat in her garden filling a white sack with red potatoes. She wore a long skirt made from woven wool. Everyone was completely relaxed when we arrived. They smiled and carried on as we walked past their homes. I could not help but notice a sense of health and contentment here. They were a beautiful people, with clear skin and perceptive eyes. Although the area was remote, houses were built in Bhutan's distinctive style. Wooden slats bisected whitewashed walls. The wood was painted with an intricate design of flowers, animals and other small patterns. Background colours alternated between dark grey and a soft orange.

During our trek, this idyllic geography was not always inclined to such perfection. Blue skies turned grey. I unzipped all the ventilation slats on my rain jacket. Although we were high up in the mountains, it still felt muggy. I thought of stopping to remove my boots and pull on waterproof pants, but they kept out not only the wet, but also any airflow. The trekking pants I wore dried quickly and would be much cooler, so my waterproof pants remained folded at the bottom of my pack. Instead, my bottoms started to turn a motley pattern of blue, darker where the raindrops accumulated. Twenty minutes later they were an even shade of dark blue.

I had never worn gaiters much prior to this trek, but they kept the slop off my pants. Imagine sliding into a tent with sticky pant legs—and not just from water and dirt. These trails were used by animals. With animals come plops that quickly get mixed into the mud. We did not need that extra scent seeping into our dreams.

Although we were trekking in the middle of the Himalaya, we passed through a valley filled with sand. Low knolls and wide expanses made the scene look more like a desert than a mountain range. A few buildings came into view in the distance. Was it a mirage? No, this was the town of Thoencha. It would be our home for our ninth and tenth nights, which marked the longest continual trek my husband and I had done. We were halfway through. As we settled into camp, most people from town came out to take a look. We were the circus who had come to their town, or so it seemed. Kids giggled, curious about these funny strangers. They loved to pose for photos and then look at themselves in our camera screens.

Local lady and her child near Thoencha

For our rest day, we walked a couple of hours up the valley along a ridge. I noticed a hut in the distance. It was made mostly from stone, with a blue tarp across part of the roof. Two children played outside. Later I noticed they had moved closer to me. When they were within earshot, I called out *"Kuzuzangbola."* They stopped in silence. The older sister slowly walked nearer but continued to play with her younger brother, pretending not to see me. I sat down. They edged closer. And closer. Soon they were standing a metre behind me. I tried my greeting once more. They stared back. The little boy's nose ran. Their clothing was somewhat tattered, but there were enough layers to keep them warm. I made an attempt to find out their names by pointing to myself while saying my name. When I opened my hands in their direction, they stared at me blankly. I continued with my mimes but did not get a word out of them. Twenty-five minutes later, I decided to move along.

Although education in Bhutan is free, parents must buy a national uniform for their children to attend school. This expense is too much for most yak herders, so I doubted either child had or would get any education. This is the reason that many kids are sent to monasteries or nunneries. There, they can get an education and ease the financial burden on their parents.

By day twelve, we faced our second-highest pass, Jaze La, which reaches 5,150 metres. It was initially hidden from view, around a few curves at the end of the valley we were hiking through. The air seemed different on this day. There was not a sound to be heard besides the crunching of stones beneath our shoes. Grey glacier arms poked around spiky mountain peaks. Rocky banks lined the valley. White lichen splashed across grey rocks as if Mother Nature had tried to reflect the glaciers of the massive landscape above us. Bushes with vibrant red leaves lit up the slopes and poked out from behind boulders. Their colour contrasted with the greyness everywhere else, as if they were sending a warning: "Don't mess with us. We may be small, but we are mighty."

In some sections, the trail nearly disappeared, so my husband and I followed the assistant cook. He had diligently carried our lunch every day, a countdown until noon when his load would be lightened. He was a quiet young man, more focused on clicking photos and gathering medicinal plants than on becoming a professional camp chef. He did not say much as we climbed the valley. We covered five tiers before we finally reached the ultimate pass. At the end of each level, a flat, sandy section made it easier to gulp down a few extra swigs of the thin oxygen. The ambience felt off. I listened and heard nothing. This was the meaning of pure silence. Not even the call of a raven pierced its calm, and the normally eccentric breeze had disappeared. The pass itself was a vacant plateau. Prayer flags, most of them faded and worn thin, settled across rocks. I knew the sun would quickly dull our new string of flags.

As we crossed into the next valley, a new shot of colour entered the scene. The grey facade cracked. Cobalt moraine lakes speckled the lower levels beyond the pass. Birds flitted overhead, and flowers in blue and red sprouted from sparse soil. The landscape seemed to have found its breath.

On our thirteenth day, we hiked through mist, rain and sleet. On this twenty-third day of September, Bhutan celebrated the auspicious Blessed Rainy Day, which was supposed to mark the end of the rainy season. We should have enjoyed sunny days and dry paths ahead. But climates change, and the rain clouds seemed out of sync with this festive turning point. Even the wee blue flowers had decided to clamp their coloured petals shut, with no sun to warm them open. The scenery varied over the day. A fuzzy fungus spread across a hillside, as if some rogue 1970s carpet salesman had unrolled a multi-toned orange shag to cover the rubble. Nineteen kilometres later we arrived at camp, and the sun finally decided to make an appearance. Our moods lightened, and that night we fell asleep to the sound of the crew singing from the cooking tent.

Our crew was an interesting mix. One chef used to be a monk, and the horseman had previously been the regional representative for his municipality. Our assistant cooked planned to become a professional truck driver, and our guide originally trained as a nurse.

By day fourteen, we had yet to tackle the highest pass. This would be the day. Rinchen Zoe La reaches 5,320 metres. Beyond the mere physical challenge, this day's walk dished out an array of delightful sights. My husband had been trying to get the perfect sunrise photo over the past few days, easing himself out of our tent by five o'clock in the morning, day after day. Today was different. Frost had crusted our tent, making it one of the coolest nights we had spent, and squirming out of a toasty sleeping bag was distinctly less inviting. But on this particular morning, his nemesis, the mist, had conveniently decided to slip away. In its place, blazing beams tickled the peaks all along the valley down from our camp, like a jagged smile filled with a mouthful of golden teeth. This was an exciting start to what turned out to be a memorable day.

The trail may have been pebbly and grey, but it was far from dull. A glint to the right caught my eye. We climbed a little higher and found a turquoise lake poised utterly still. Farther up, a second lake showed a different expression. This water was less intense. Instead, it had absorbed a pile of sediment, so it looked more like a green milkshake than a mountain lake. The atmosphere was hushed as we climbed. The ravens had disappeared once again. Only the rustling of prayer flags could be heard once we turned the final bend and came within a few metres of the pass itself. Reams of prayer flags had been placed here. Their bright colours fanned out from the trailhead like a spider's web, reaching for the higher rocks and boulders that surround Rinchen Zoe La.

After saying our thanks for reaching this height, we trooped onwards. An occasional yak herder's hut had been built near the trail. Sometimes all that remained was a lone rock wall, waiting for its next use. Other times, a large blue tent had been set up as the modern version of a yak herder's home.

This brings me to the main disappointment along this trek, the garbage. In 2010, my husband and I hiked the nine-day Jomolhari trek. There had been no stray refuse on that route. Random medicinal plant pickers kept to themselves and left no trace. There was nothing but rough ground and wooden fences around the vacant yak herders' huts. So I was taken aback to find sections of the Snowman trek strewn with chip bags and beer cans. I had expected it to be surrounded by even more pristine wilderness than the Jomolhari trail. To be fair, this mess was not everywhere. Few tourists attempt this trek, and most reputable companies carry out any garbage that cannot be burned. That said, there are always exceptions. We were told that the tourism council coordinates annual garbage-picking campaigns; however, I could not help but think it created a self-perpetuating job for those who discarded the rubbish and were later paid to go back and collect the very junk they had tossed. There must be a better way to reallocate the funds and incentivize cleanliness.

During our final trekking days, our daily climb switched to a daily decline. We would soon leave the dramatic peaks and glaciers that had become our neighbourhood. It was as if the landscape had come together to throw us a send-off party. Steep rocky ravines came alive with shrubbery in tones of yellow and green. We passed the sacred lake of Om Tsho. A crown of prayer flags fluttered around the rivulet where its sacred waters flowed. Waterfalls jumped out of crevices and danced in eccentric leaps across black rock. I turned back the way we had come to look at a crag on our route. It was cut so narrowly into the scree along a natural snake-like crease that it was barely visible. Ahead, a small lake of blue essence embraced the morning sun. A bleached yak skull balanced on a boulder, still clutching the long horns of a beast no longer in this world. Although the blessed Om Tsho sat well above us, this little pond felt more spiritual. I could only imagine the pilgrims who would camp on the grassy bank and the ceremonies that would transpire.

We tramped lower and lower. Mist often diluted the air, and vapour clouded the valley. The Nikka Chhu, a gentle river, guided us. Silver fir and pine trees covered the hillsides, and fuchsia flowers sprouted from low bushes. Near midday, the trees gave way to a small clearing. The ground had turned into a sludge of muck and yak dung, an indistinguishable gooey mess. This meadow surrounded an enterprising business, the only one we had seen for days. The wooden store was protected from yaks by a rail fence. I peered into the dark shop through the window. It had no glass and doubled as the sales counter. My eyes gradually adjusted to the shadowy room. One wall was dedicated to the local Druk beer and whiskey bottles. The remainder of the shelves were piled with instant noodle packs, soft drinks and bags of chips—not exactly the healthiest essentials. Everything would have been carried in on the back of a yak or some hard-working horse. A lone caretaker managed the shop. He spoke no English, and our three words of Dzongkha took us only so far. A few grey curls sprouted from his head to frame the widest grin I had seen in the Nikka Chhu valley. Actually, he was the *only* person we had seen in the valley. His smile was unique nonetheless. Most of his front teeth were missing, but that smile never faded. Perhaps he was relieved to have some company for an hour on this otherwise lonely afternoon.

Soon after we arrived at our campsite, a warm mug of spicy ja was ready. I think this might have been the favourite part of the day for the horsemen, who had finished unloading everything and could chill out for the rest of the afternoon. Our guide was nursing a sprained ankle and headed towards our final destination, the town of Sephu, to try to catch a cellphone signal. We later learned that he camped in an empty hut before reaching Sephu. Soon after he settled in, a troop of wild boars scurried past, and he managed to catch a video of them with his phone. Later, a bear tried to enter his hut, but our guide scared it off. Once again, our tent seemed preferable.

The Snowman trek is one of those experiences where the journey is far more rewarding than the destination. Our final few steps carried us up a knoll. There stood a wooden sign, marking that we had arrived at the town of Sephu. I scanned the meadow. One farmhouse sat at the end of a gravel road. A few horses munched grass. We camped our last night in the field. That afternoon, we lounged in the folding chairs that we had grown accustomed to sitting in for every meal over the past seventeen days. Our driver had arrived with a case of Druk 11000. I must admit, I am not a fan of lager, but that lukewarm bottle tasted good.

The Basics

Most useful item to pack: Scarpa Kailash GTX, Zanskar GTX or your favourite waterproof hiking boots, with the added protection of a layer of Zamberlan's Hydrobloc waterproof treatment applied in advance

Useful words in Dzongkha: *kuzuzangbola* ("hello");

kaadinchheyla ("thank you"); *la* ("mountain pass"); *mani* ("carved with prayers, such as on a small wall or pillar"); and *momos* ("dumplings").[6]

For more, refer to visitbhutan.com/useful_words_phrases.html.

For further travel information: Bhutan requires most foreigners to travel with a government-approved tour company and pay a regulated day rate. The government's intent is to promote high-quality, low-impact tourism. Whether you prefer to travel independently or on a group tour, it should cost about the same because of the standardized pricing system. The Tourism Council of Bhutan provides loads of information at tourism.gov.bt/plan/minimum-daily-package.

We first used Rainbow Tours & Treks in 2010, and the founder, Sonam Wangmo, has grown the company into one of the larger operators in Bhutan. Sonam continues to take an active role in running the business. You may even meet her while staying at the company's own Naksel Boutique Hotel & Spa, located just outside of Paro—home of Bhutan's international airport. Further information is available on their website: rainbowbhutan.com.

Rainbow does an excellent job at organizing high-quality, personalized trips. For our trek, they provided all essential equipment including warm and clean sleeping bags, sleeping mattresses, pillows, hand towels and two-person tents. They also coordinated virtually everything related to the trek including guides, permits, meals, cooks, horsemen, horses, first aid amenities and all camping equipment.

6. Based on Lonely Planet's *Bhutan Travel Guide* (see Bibliography).

Route: My husband and I had wanted to tackle the Snowman trek ever since we first visited Bhutan in 2010. It was then that we heard of this infamous twenty-five-day trek, purportedly the hardest hike in the world. We would need to train. We would need to save, for Bhutan is not a cheap country to visit given the mandated day rate. Seven years later, we were ready. There are two variations to the Snowman trek. The first ends in Sephu, while the second ends in the village of Duer and includes a stop at a hot spring.

We opted for a modified version. Since we had previously hiked the initial route as part of the Jomolhari trek, we cut this out and started from Gasa. This reduced the duration to seventeen days. The longest hike we had done up until this point was nine days, and at the time we had sworn never to do such a long trek again. So seventeen days was daunting enough.

This trek is arduous. You need to train in advance, both physically and mentally, to get through so many days of continuous hiking at high altitudes in changing weather conditions. The weather window is brief and uncertain. If you leave too early, you risk getting caught in the monsoon rains and extremely muddy conditions. If you depart much later, the snows can cause havoc. Weather patterns fluctuate from year to year, so even within these parameters, the decision is not completely clear. We started our trek on September 11 and completed it on September 28. Our guide later told us that a group who attempted a couple of weeks after us were caught in snow and had to be airlifted out of the valley. This predicament is not uncommon. Estimates indicate that only fifty percent of trekkers complete the Snowman trek. The biggest risks are getting snowed in on one of the passes or having to turn back because of altitude sickness.

We followed the guidance in Lonely Planet's *Bhutan Travel Guide* coupled with Rainbow's local advice. Acclimatization days were hugely beneficial for getting accustomed to the elevation gain and easing into day-after-day hiking. These days were called "rest days" on our itinerary; however, we still hiked for a few hours. On most days we covered sixteen kilometres and approximately one thousand metres of elevation gain or loss. That correlated into six to eight hours of hiking each day.

~~~
~~~

BHUTAN—TREADING MYSTICAL LANDS ALONG THE MERAK TO SAKTENG CULTURAL TREK

Hike through one of the last untouched zones in Bhutan alongside semi-nomadic highlanders and alpine biodiversity

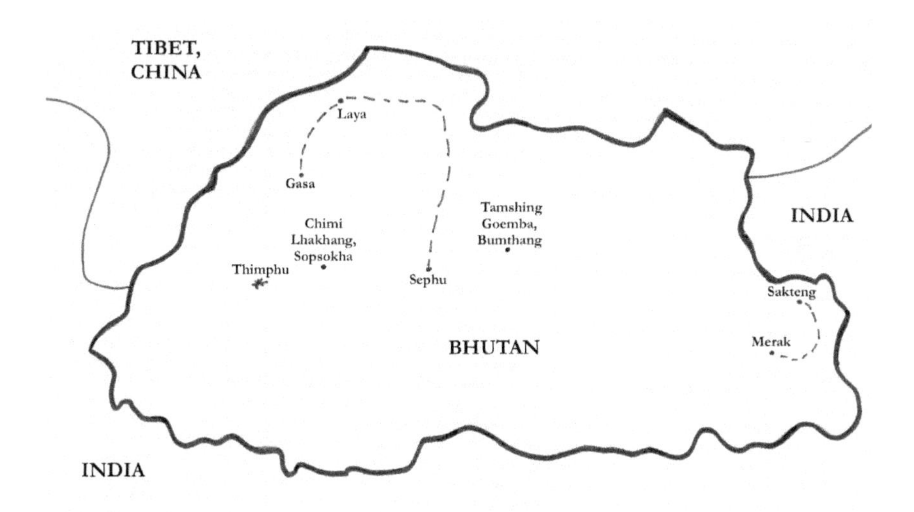

The Experience

It was the wispy tail of smoke that first caught my eye. The silent, ashen haze spiralled upwards from the hilltop above and to the right of where I was walking. Rectangular white prayer flags hung from hand-cut poles that stood near a small group of people sitting around a fire. Flags in yellow and red also hung nearby. They rippled in the wind like a flight of doves rushing ancestral prayers to the cosmos. My eyes darted back to the trail. It was strewn with rocks and splattered with animal dung, making it impossible to look away for long.

We had started hiking less than half an hour earlier from eastern Bhutan's isolated village of Merak. The route headed farther east to reach even more remote communities accessible only by foot. It would take us two days to hike from Merak to Sakteng and another full day to hike from Sakteng to the nearest road.

The pathway I followed veered left, and a cluster of juniper trees blocked the gathering from view. My eyes soon gravitated higher where another stream of smoke swivelled towards the sky. Once again, a small band of people huddled around smouldering branches. They sat in an open area, likely where animals often grazed. A spindly tree trunk, barren of most of its branches, stuck out of the ground at an unnatural angle. Instead of a prayer flag, this pole held a clump of scrawny twigs at its tip. I instinctively knew that the people were not cuddling together for warmth, nor were they preparing a meal over a fire. Their stone houses stood nearby, freshly whitewashed, indicating a certain level of prosperity.

The Brokpas, a semi-nomadic community, live in this region. These highlanders have their own distinctive language, dress and customs. These families were Buddhist, yet they were practising an ancient pagan ritual, a practice kept alive for centuries. An undercurrent of Bon beliefs flows throughout these remote hill villages of Bhutan. When Guru Rinpoche, the "precious master," originally brought Buddhism to Bhutan, he allowed people to integrate their existing belief system into Buddhism. In effect, residents adopted a hybrid faith with layers of their old Bon beliefs filtering through their new ideology. To this day, local Bon deities continue to be honoured. Deities are believed to protect a particular area, such as a valley or a mountain. It was for just such a local deity that smoke danced into the sky on the day we were hiking.

Bon practices are conducted by each family, not by a communal priest or spiritual leader. I looked across the hill and could see slight movement among the group. The eldest father would be leading the ritual. On this occasion, a sacrifice was made, which could have been anything from a rooster to a sheep or local cow, depending on what the family could afford. The carefully prepared liver and head were believed to remove obstacles, bring wealth and heal the sick if offered in the prescribed format. Pieces would be added to the coals, eventually rising as elements of the smoke and carried across the valley. This community handed down such pagan practices across generations but kept them private compared to the more widely accepted Buddhist traditions.

Is this not the epitome of tolerance, where one person can believe in two faiths? As an outsider, I found it confusing how one could sacrifice an animal as a gift for a local deity while believing in Buddha's premise of nonviolence. Likewise, Buddhism does not condone killing another creature of any kind, yet most Bhutanese ate meat. The clearest explanation I received was a practical one. People need to eat. They need protein. If an animal has been killed by someone else or by accident, or apparent accident, then the Bhutanese found it acceptable to eat it while giving due respect. In the process, they gave thanks for the animal through prayers. The slaughterhouses were based in India, and the meat was imported to Bhutan. In essence, a practice had been built to fit the people's perspective. As far as the Bon sacrifice, I presume their prayers of respect for the animal and the purpose of its offering satisfied a higher spirit and superseded the act of killing. Essentially, pragmatism beat definitive rules.

The sacrificial ceremony I was seeing continued unabated. They were too far away and too engrossed to be distracted by a few strangers walking by. I wondered if they had enjoyed a prosperous year or were trying to atone so that a better year would come. Was their deity satisfied or did it need placating?

The people of Merak are gradually emerging into the modern world. A couple of years before our visit, electricity had been introduced to the town. Slight shifts were visible. Mobile phones could connect to the national network, and portable solar panels hung from windows. The road—if you can call the two rutted tracks that needed a four-wheel-drive vehicle to manoeuvre a formal road—had been completed a few months before. Prior to this, the town of Merak had been accessible only by foot—be it on your own feet, by horse, by *dzo* or by *zhom*. A dzo is the male and a zhom the female cross between a yak and a local cow, resulting in a strong yet more docile animal than a purebred yak. Both the males and females had smooth black horns that curved across their heads and long-haired tails that nearly dragged on the ground.

I looked back across the town where shiny new roofs reflected in the sunshine. Rows of rocks had been placed on top of the metal sheets to ensure the roofing did not blow away. The stones also acted as pseudo-shelves for assorted items placed on the rooftops. Most homes splayed their favourite vegetable, the chili, across the top to dry. Baskets of wild mushrooms also shared the space, shrivelling in the open air. Dirt streets merged into front yards, consistently swept clear of clutter, leaving only the ridges from broom bristles as evidence. This was one of the tidiest towns I had come across in Bhutan. The pathway leading out of town was not speckled with empty chip bags, Druk 11000 beer cans or discarded plastic containers, as I had noticed along sections of the Snowman trek. This place had a different feel, one of order and pride.

We were hiking alongside a few men from the town. They had put our gear and food into handwoven baskets and strapped them onto the backs of their dzos and zhoms. A handwoven extension was fitted around the leather pack strap and beneath the animal's tail, adding cushion so as not to rub its skin raw. This piece was typically bright in colour with pink and beige triangular designs. Nine dzos and zhoms hauled our gear, supplies, food and anything else needed for our trek. Such trade was one way that tourism was helping the local economy, but on a small, sustainable basis as it went directly to the individual families who owned the animals. The heart of the locals' lifestyle remained entrenched in herding and farming, using the same methods their grandparents had been taught.

We had entered a protected environment, the Sakteng Wildlife Sanctuary. Its boundary encompasses a 650-kilometre valley including the villages of Merak and Sakteng. Eighty-three percent of the people living in this remote region rely on livestock to make a living.[7] Although these hills are covered in forest, patches have been cleared to grow crops. Some areas open into alpine meadows. This secluded area is also home to the endangered red panda and vulnerable snow leopard.

I could not help but consider whether the delicate balance of tradition had been ruffled as modern changes edged closer. We were told that some locals resisted the government's decision to open the region to tourists. His Majesty King Jigme Khesar Namgyel Wangchuck, the King of Bhutan, had visited the town of Sakteng to discuss the transition. He and the queen would have hiked along the same path we now followed. The king supported an approach to progress that would prioritize the protection of Sakteng's traditional practices.

7. whc.unesco.org/en/tentativelists/5701

Harvesting buckwheat in Sakteng Valley

When we passed through, there were no other travellers in any of the villages we passed or along the trails. So far, this region has remained the remote oasis of past generations. We savoured our glimpse into this isolated area. The path was not arduous. The first and highest *la* ("pass") reached 3,900 metres and seemed more a high ridge compared to the lofty passes we had crossed on the Snowman trek. Coloured prayer flags, worn translucent from the constant beating of wind, fluttered as we neared the pass. Piles of stones marked its highest point. Farther down the other side of the ridge stood a yak herder's stone hut. Pitchfork-like poles rose near the building. They were actually bare tree trunks wedged into the ground with twigs that stretched skyward tied to the poles' tips. Although ominous from a distance, they were placed out of respect and as a local custom. Farther along the path, rhododendron and juniper forests filled our view. Shrubs grew in most of the space beneath the trees. Moss took over where the brush stopped. We came across an occasional grass paddock, thick with mud and tufts of grass for grazing dzos and zhoms.

Midway through the first day, a light mist started to fall. In our earlier Snowman trek, the transport sacks had been lined with plastic to ensure everything remained dry. We had a new crew for this trek, and I had not seen them line the bags with plastic sheets when the animals were initially loaded. When I asked our guide, he shrugged and replied indifferently. We were nearing five weeks together, and I sensed his anticipation to return to his family. Within a few minutes, however, our entourage of dzos and zhoms stopped, and the head herder tethered one of the larger beasts. From beneath some bulky sacks on a neighbouring dzo, he yanked out a double-layered canvas sheet with blue on one side and bright orange on the other. As the dzo stood relatively still, occasionally ducking his head or shifting his weight from one leg to another, the man pulled, tucked and tied the plastic sheet around the exposed baskets. The mist strengthened into a steady rain. I noticed the dzo owner's blue rubber boots, which had endured many similar days.

The dzo and zhoms were a relaxed bunch; in fact, they often seemed a little too relaxed. Following our cook's lead, we all shouted "*choo choo*" to the animals in the rear of the group to help keep them moving. My husband jumped out to the side of the path on more than one occasion to block a wandering beast or nudge another along. Eventually the forested path opened into a broad pasture. Resident zhoms glanced up at our oncoming party, and a few even trotted over to offer a sniff of a greeting. The local herder's hut looked inviting, as the rain had saturated virtually everything else. I attempted to sidestep the deepest puddles and mucky sections, a futile effort. A few front-runners picked up their pace. This was a good sign.

Each step brought a clearer view of our camp up ahead beyond the field we were crossing. This location was referred to as Miksateng and had an elevation of 3,080 metres. As we got closer, we could see a few structures. Each had a roof, held up by a few wooden pillars. At one point, these open-aired roofed constructs had been a brilliant concept by the tourism council. They would offer cover from the rain and a reasonably dry site to pitch a tent. Unfortunately, one key aspect had been overlooked: maintenance.

At least three of the structures had collapsed. The others remained upright, tested by itchy dzos who used the posts to scratch their necks and do a full-body rub. So our tents were set up well away from the wobbly roofs, safe in the middle of the mucky field. The cooks took over one of two stone structures. The other solid building contained a row of toilets that had overflowed into a stagnant mess. Our toilet tent's freshly dug hole became unexpectedly appealing.

The herders had unloaded their animals and let them roam for the evening. Baskets, sacks, bags and piles had been sorted and doled out to their appropriate owners. However, something was missing. The green duffle bag my husband and I had packed with warm clothing, camera gear and a few toiletries had not arrived. I had handed it over to be loaded but failed to double-check that it was actually transferred when we switched into the four-wheel drive vehicle at the junction to Merak. By nine o'clock, our driver had confirmed it was resting safely back inside his van. I suspect there was confusion since it was the same bag we had purposely left behind for the Snowman trek, whereas we wanted it on this trek instead of our larger packs. Luckily these trails are well travelled. The dzo herders had connections in the valley and knew someone travelling to Sakteng the next day, the same day we were due to arrive in the village. Sure enough, at around three the next afternoon a young man walked up to our guesthouse—the only guesthouse in town. He had the straps of our green duffle bag slung around his shoulders and a wry smile on his face.

The Basics

Most useful item to pack: A small duffle bag for toiletries and spare clothing—double-check it actually gets packed on the dzos and zhoms

Useful words in Dzongkha: *kuzuzangbola* ("hello"); *kaadinchheyla* ("thank you"); *lam* ("trail"); *Jogey-la* ("Let's go"); and *chhu* ("river").[8]

For more, refer to visitbhutan.com/useful_words_phrases.html.

For further travel information: Bhutan requires most

8. Based on Lonely Planet's *Bhutan Travel Guide* (see Bibliography).

foreigners to travel with a government-approved tour company and pay a regulated day rate. The government's intent is to promote high-quality, low-impact tourism. Whether you prefer to travel independently or on a group tour, it should cost about the same because of the standardized pricing system. The Tourism Council of Bhutan provides loads of information at tourism.gov.bt/plan/minimum-daily-package.

We used Rainbow Tours & Treks in 2010 and on this trip in 2017. Rainbow does an excellent job at organizing high-quality, personalized trips. For our trek, they provided all essential equipment including warm and clean sleeping bags, sleeping mattresses, pillows, hand towels and two-person tents. They also coordinated virtually everything related to the trek including guides, permits, meals, cooks, first aid kit and camping equipment. All transportation except international flights is part of the tour package, including private vehicle, four-wheel-drive vehicle as needed and herders for the dzos and zhoms used during the trek. Rainbow is a full-service tour company and can arrange your entire trip around Bhutan, not only the trekking piece. Further information is available on their website: rainbowbhutan.com.

New treks across Bhutan are emerging to help reduce the impact on the environment by spreading travellers across the country. Ask your tour company about new routes. You can also check the Tourism Council of Bhutan website; however, their route information is fairly generic: tourism.gov.bt/activities/trek.

Route: We spent four days and three nights on this cultural trek, including a rest day to explore the extraordinary town of Sakteng. For more information on the trek, refer to bhutan.travel/activities/treks/merak-sakteng-trek.

We started early on the first day to drive from the city of Trashigang to Merak. The final two hours of the journey required a four-wheel-drive vehicle to navigate the newly constructed yet rough dirt road. Merak lies literally at the end of the road. Here, dzos and zhoms were loaded and we started the trek. Based on Rainbow's trip notes, we climbed 633 metres and descended 1,073 metres over sixteen kilometres of trekking on the first day. This took about six hours.

Day two was a shorter walk with less altitude gain and loss compared to our first day. We hiked for about four hours over four kilometres. There were gradual ups and downs along the trail, but nothing overly arduous besides sidestepping slick muddy sections.

Day three was spent in the village of Sakteng. We hiked to the Borongshi Goempa ("monastery") high on a hill overlooking the valley, watched a yak dance, cheered a weekend darts match and participated in a traditional women's welcome song. More of our time in Sakteng can be found in Chapter Four: Rare Festivals.

Day four started with a four-hour walk to the barely-there village of Taktu, where our trusty driver met us with his van. From Taktu, we drove to the city of Mongar.

~~~
~~~

ICELAND—FINDING SOLITUDE IN EASTERN ICELAND

Escape the crowds to experience a wasteland, a near empty expanse where, during the last ice age, volcanic heat mingled with glacial freeze

The Experience

Why would you visit a wasteland? The word conjures visions of emptiness—vast, boring nothingness. Well, a group of ten of us plus our guide did exactly that. Our small group came from France, Belgium and Canada. We all wanted to see Iceland, but not the Iceland that most visitors experience. Iceland offers a myriad of attractions along its tourist-friendly ring road. We chose to go deeper. Where would locals want to go?

During the first four days of hiking from Eyjabakkar to the Jökulsá river valley, we were alone. We did not meet a single human being except for the caretaker at our last night's hut, the Múlaskáli hut. Imagine walking for hours and seeing nothing but nature's expanse—no buildings, no infrastructure, no roads and not even a trail for much of the walk.

Rocky rubble covered a rolling landscape. We walked for twelve kilometres on the first day. Our packs were filled with everything we would need for four days along with a share of the group's food. Sausages, salami, apples and loaves of bread were carefully stuffed into every vacant space of my thirty-five-litre pack. It was large enough for this excursion but small enough to fit inside the overhead storage bin on the flight to Iceland's capital city of Reykjavik. Rain pants, gloves, a toque and a Gore-Tex jacket were essential for this fickle environment, even during the height of summer.

Our trekking guide, Dieter Van Holder, at a glacier stream

Remnants from previous rains speckled the ground. Lime-green moss softened the rocks and grew like a shawl caressing every stream.

Glassy droplets of water balanced on tender shoots. When you looked closely, the beads looked more like glass marbles encasing tiny diamonds than like any sort of liquid. Throughout our four days of hiking, we did not once have to boil water or use water purification tablets. Few animals roamed these regions, and humans were even less frequent. Glacier streams remained pure, unlike streams anywhere else I have been in the world.

Leaving Egilssel hut near Lake Kollumúlavatn

Although the first day's walk crossed gravelly terrain, the second day looked as if a lazy tiler had tossed shard after shard of rock fragments across the ground. Flat slabs were left wherever they had landed. Thicker and rougher stones occasionally distorted the image. A smattering of orange, white and black lichen camouflaged rocks, as if a bad case of acne had exploded across the landscape. Our vista changed dramatically on the third day. We entered Arctic tundra and then passed through an Arctic forest. Craggy cliffs lunged down deep river valleys that sliced through the landscape.

Our guide directed us up a nondescript hillside that appeared to be no more than a gravelly knoll. But he knew of a secret viewing spot. I scanned the horizon. It looked much as it had for the past hour, a barren expanse split in half by a jagged canyon. We neared the cliff edge and peered into a valley. Mountains of rhyolite spread before us. These were not bland rocks. Silica within igneous rock flashed shades of light blue, green and ochre. The sheen of these rhyolite deposits awakened with a life of its own. It reflected the sunlight in bands of varied colours that spread across the canyon's banks. Basaltic rock stretched upwards into tall pillars that looked like alien ghosts. Chunks of the same deposit curved into a partial bridge, promising to cross the valley yet falling short on its delivery. These geological formations date back five to seven million years, from the last ice age. This was a place where history began—not the human story, but where land was reshaped at the dawn of our world. This view was the most impressive part of the entire trek.

Overnighting among such panoramas was perhaps the second-best part. We did not have to squeeze into tents but slept inside huts. They were basic but well maintained and stocked with three essentials: cookware, a wood stove and mattress-topped bunk beds. Our second night's refuge sat above Lake Kollumúlavatn. For the bold, the lake provided an icy bath, but other than two gutsy French ladies, we remained cozy in our woolly layers. It was worth waiting, as we found an unexpected touch of luxury at our third night's shelter. For 500 *króna*, equivalent to approximately US$5, we could melt away any stiffness with a hot shower. This final hut even had flush toilets, a distinct advantage over the previous hut's nearly brimming outhouse. However, the presence of an on-site ranger suggested we were approaching civilization. The closing memory of this remote oasis came late in the night as my husband snapped photos of green northern lights flashing overhead.

The next morning, we all tramped off with the ranger. He joined us for the first twenty minutes until we reached a section of new wooden steps. He had built the stairs and wanted a photo of their inauguration. Before the steps, nine rocky outcrops stood like fingers along a ridge above us. As strange icons often do, these spires had earned their own local folk tale, which the ranger told us. Once upon a time, an ogress lived in these mountains. Unfortunately, her lover lived far away, and he never visited his sweetheart. So the ogress had to walk across the hills to see him. Luckily, she was a quick-paced walker, for ogres turn to stone if touched by sunlight. So she always visited at night, cloaked in darkness. Time passed, and life ensued. It came to be that the ogress had eight baby boys. When they were old enough to make the journey, she wanted them to know their father. On their return home, the young boys could not walk as quickly as their mother. They raced as fast as they could but could not beat the dawn's rays. Ever since, the ogress and her eight sons have stood as rock pillars on the mountaintop that would have led them home. The rangers had added their own epilogue to the story. If a ranger starts to think about inviting the ogress for an evening soirée, it is a sure sign to flee the remote hills and get back to society. The ranger we met limits his time at the hut to two months a year. Then he returns home to do "a little bit of this and a little bit of that."

Although we felt far from humanity, our guide ensured that we did not get lost in the wild remoteness of East Iceland. Except for the random trail markers we saw on our last two days, most of the hike followed no discernible track. Our guide relied on GPS, downloaded trail guides and advice from fellow guides gleaned before we departed. His information was perfectly attuned to the rugged reality, until the last day. We had been walking for a number of hours towards our final destination in a river valley just inland from the coastal highway. We were to meet a man in a van, somewhere at some time in the morning. The GPS trail appeared to drop down a cliff below which surged a river. The crucial section that we would be walking along was blocked from view.

With changing water levels and erosion, the route marked on the GPS tracker was not necessarily the present moment's preferred line. The group convened. Our guide scoped out the surrounding area, and a few of us walked in smaller groups to investigate potential alternatives. I was impressed with our guide's approach. He explained the situation and why he hesitated to follow the trail recommended on his GPS. He summarized our options. Ultimately, he recommended another route as the safest path down. We all agreed and followed his lead. Considering we were a group of people with different backgrounds and languages in unknown territory, the situation could have turned volatile. I found it interesting how the guide chose to be open about his uncertainty but brought us along during his decision making. Transparency and clarity prevailed. Later, after we had climbed down into the river valley, I looked back. We had chosen wisely. The alternatives would have landed us either deep in the river or stranded on a cliff.

Far too soon, our escape from the crowds ended. As we walked along the riverbed, a lone white van approached us. Sure enough, the someone, somewhere had materialized. We climbed into the van, lost in our own thoughts as we headed towards the town of Höfn. Over two million tourists visited the small island country of Iceland in 2017, and we had managed to escape them during our four-day trek. But our serenity was soon shattered. We pulled into Skaftafell

National Park—within the greater Vatnajökull National Park—where busload after busload of visitors swarmed the parking lot. Is there such a thing as tourist shock? People wandered everywhere to catch their own glimpse of the Skaftafellsjökull glacier and its surrounding lagoon. The nearby Svartifoss waterfall was another popular attraction.

My husband and I walked along a paved walkway that led right up to Skaftafellsjökull, "a glacier tongue spurting off from Iceland's largest ice cap, Vatnajökull."[9] The icy blue tones that you might imagine in a glacier were hard to see up close. Instead, its dirty truth became visible. Most of the ice was smothered in black pebbles and ash-coloured gravel. This beast had been slowly rolling into the valley, absorbing soil and forcing boulders aside. Skaftafellsjökull is receding, as are most glaciers in Iceland. It melted into a lagoon where its spirit drifted and memories transformed into icebergs. The remains of the glacier's powerful arm either thawed or broke off and floated slowly along a channel towards the sea. A few icebergs were stranded, partially stuck on shore or wedged together in an unmoving mass. Yet, as the minutes passed, fragments shifted. Blocks melted into lumps. Some tipped over. They would all eventually reach the sea, either by drifting or simply melting away.

Another way to escape the crowds lay directly above us. Mount Kristínartindar towered 1,126 metres above Skaftafellsjökull. The majority of visitors went no farther than the Svartifoss waterfall, which looked like a giant water faucet. Columns of basalt hung all around like litmus paper testing the water. We hiked past Svartifoss and kept climbing. Gravel and grass tufts pocked by mossy patches and mountain flowers covered the hillside. Kristínartindar's peak looked far off. Eventually, we came to a creek of fresh gurgling water,

9. guidetoiceland.is/travel-iceland/drive/skaftafellsjokull

perfectly placed to refill water bottles before the final slog. A series of stony switchbacks led to the top. At the summit, I found a logbook and pen tucked inside a metal box, inviting climbers to leave a record of their ascent. A handful of other folks arrived during the thirty minutes we spent lounging on what felt like the top of the world. Our group had found our sliver of serenity once more.

Our moment was interrupted by a loud rumble that sounded like a plane passing overhead. A second outburst followed. I looked down and across the vast Vatnajökull ice cap. Glacier arms spread from its centre cap through every valley that I could see. I counted four in total. The icy arm of Skaftafellsjökull—the same glacier we had walked to on the previous day—stretched around Kristínartindar's eastern side. A similar shaft wrapped the western side of the mountain and ended in a massive ice cliff. Giant waterfalls of ice occasionally appeared like a poof of dust as they crashed to the base of the glacier. This great plunge of snow and ice resounded across the valley, causing the rumble we had heard. Ice, snow, rock and empty skies filled the space around us. This was Iceland—pure, powerful and dazzling.

The Basics

Most useful items to pack: Full rain gear—remember, it takes a lot of water to create a country named after ice

Useful words and phrases in Icelandic: *halló* ("hello"); *góðan daginn* ("good morning"); *takk* ("thank you"); *já* ("yes"); *nei* ("no"); and *Geturðu sýnt mér á kortinu?* ("Can you show me on the map?").[10]

10. Based on Lonely Planet's *Iceland Travel Guide* (see Bibliography).

For further travel information: Icelandic Mountain Guides offers a wide range of tour packages, from day hikes to multi-day backpacking trips across Iceland, Greenland and even Antarctica. They also include some not so physically active tours for those interested in a more relaxed visit. Our guide had excellent experience, and the equipment provided was of high quality. Our seven-day tour was called The Wilderness of Glaciers, East Iceland Trekking parts 2 and 3. The four-day trek in the Lónsöræfi region from Eyjabakkar to Höfn was part 2, whereas the day hike up Kristínartindar was within part 3. For more information, see mountainguides.is.

All accommodation except in Reykjavik was provided as part of the Icelandic Mountain Guides package. In the capital city, we stayed at two places. Both are good options, but be aware that hotels in Iceland are intrinsically expensive.

Rey Apartments are smack in the centre of town. The kitchenette allowed for a nice break from eating in restaurants, and our room was spacious. The owner offered helpful local recommendations and advice. For more information, visit rey.is.

Slightly farther from the centre, but perhaps more homey, is Guesthouse Galtafell. You can pick your preferred style of room. The main house has a classic style, whereas the newer building beside the house offers a more modern, clean-line aesthetic. For more information, see galtafell.com.

Domestically, we flew with Air Iceland Connect. Each seat pocket held a travel journal. Passengers were free to write their own thoughts, memories or whatever they were inspired to add. I flipped through the pages of the journal in my seat pocket.

About a third of its pages were filled with handwritten stories from previous travellers. The notebook in my husband's seat was filled with an entirely different set of memories from those who had sat in his seat before him. One child's handwritten story stood out for me. They wrote about losing a grandparent shortly before visiting Iceland and how their travels through Iceland helped them deal with the loss. They wrote about the beautiful things they saw in Iceland and how it made them feel better. It was a simple yet poignant story, not something I expected to find in the seat pocket during our morning flight. For booking details, refer to Air Iceland Connect's website: airicelandconnect.com.

If travelling to Iceland via Copenhagen, Denmark, keep an eye out for Lagkagehuset in the airport transit hall. It is hard to miss the aromas of their freshly baked goods and the tempting takeaways displayed on their counters. Their yogurt and muesli with rhubarb and fruit was my particular favourite.

Route: We trekked for four days in Iceland's remote Lónsöræfi region. To reach the beginning of the hike, we flew from Reykjavik to Egilsstaðir, drove a short distance and then began trekking in the Eyjabakkar area. We hiked past Geldingafell mountain, then on to Lake Kollumúlavatn and down the valley of the glacial river Jökulsá. Each night we stayed at a different mountain hut. On our fourth day, a van from Icelandic Mountain Guides met us along the riverbed and shuttled us to the nearby town of Höfn.

For the remaining three nights, we camped in Vatnajökull National Park. The highlight was a nineteen-kilometre day hike up the Skaftafellsheiði trail to the summit of Kristínartindar. We returned along the Sjónarnípa path.

~~~
~~~

2

Little-Known Hikes

When skies are clear and daily demands shift aside, one of my favourite activities is to go hiking. Fresh air, beautiful scenery and a dose of exercise are the ingredients for a perfect day. The walks covered in this chapter have the added appeal of unspoiled and isolated scenery. Most locations are easily accessed, cover a variety of terrain and attract few other people. The trails are scattered across Latin America and Europe and give you a taste of natural beauty in four countries: Colombia, Cuba, the Faroe Islands and Portugal.

Colombia might be renowned for its beaches and exotic rainforest, but its mountain ranges and national parks at higher elevations promise cool respite and incredible hiking trails. We walked through one such place, the Páramo de Ocetá, an unusual alpine highland that echoes an ancient culture now nearly disappeared. The nearest settlement of Monguí lies a few hours' drive from Colombia's capital city of Bogotá. Although Colombia is often assumed to be a dangerous place teeming with drug cartels and weapons, the country has improved its safety record over recent years. We felt secure and comfortable throughout our travels across the country in early

2018, although we did avoid certain border areas. Check your home country's security guidance before travelling anywhere to have a better understanding of current risk zones. Lonely Planet offers a helpful article with links to various governmental travel advice websites.[1]

For an island escape, Cuba's western region around the town of Viñales was a great base for exploring the surrounding national park, tobacco fields and limestone karsts or *mogotes*. Even UNESCO recognizes this region's "outstanding karst landscape" and "rich vernacular tradition."[2] During our visit in early 2016, most tourists stuck to the beach resorts of Varadero or to Havana's lively city streets. Few foreigners joined us on Viazul's modern bus service, which travels directly from Havana to Viñales, a colourful town packed with reasonably priced *casas particulares* ("bed and breakfasts"). Fewer still left the main streets of town to wander the charming Valle de Viñales. There we met old-timer *guarijos* ("agricultural workers") and came to understand the soul behind Cuba's cigar industry. We followed red dirt pathways winding through a way of life once hidden behind the opaque bubble of international embargoes and travel restrictions.

We were later inspired in Europe's Faroe Islands, an archipelago of eighteen islands only recently starting to appear on independent travellers' wish lists. The Faroes lie in the North Atlantic Ocean equidistance from Scotland, Iceland and Norway. They reminded me of what Iceland might have been like before mass tourism overtook its shores, minus the icebergs. Mossy grass, craggy cliffs and waterfalls that blew vertically on windy days gave the Faroe Islands a courageous vitality. On the islands of Eysturoy and Vágar, we shared

1. lonelyplanet.com/colombia/safety
2. whc.unesco.org/en/list/840

walking trails with shaggy sheep, protective geese and a couple of daunting bulls grazing in the distance.

The final section in this chapter captures treks on the Portuguese island of Madeira, which lies closer to Morocco than to its mother country of Portugal, explaining its divergence in geography, with bold sierra instead of mainland Portugal's pastoral countryside. This small island grabbed my breath and tossed it over dramatically sharp cliffs before wooing me into its volcanic oasis. Madeira reminded me of scenes from the movie *Jurassic Park*, but with European comforts baked into its rocky ridges. The local bus system was efficient and reliable, trails were well marked and quality car rentals made remote destinations accessible. We covered three routes that hit rugged coastlines, dizzyingly spectacular volcanic mountains and forested tracks between remote villages. Madeira has leapt to be my top pick for the best place in the world for day-hiking enthusiasts. This is definitely a place I want to return to.

~~~
~~~

COLOMBIA—ENTERING THE HOME OF THE SUN GOD IN THE PÁRAMO DE OCETÁ

Stroll through rolling hills where whispers of an ancient people's sacred places echo in the wind and pointy frailejón *plants, once believed to guard the sun god, speckle the grasslands*

The Experience

I drained my steaming cup of coffee far too quickly. The beans were either grown on our hotel owner's family *finca* ("small farm") or packaged under the hotel's name—unfortunately my Spanish-language skills had worn too thin to differentiate between the two. It did not matter. The coffee was thick, rich, warm and exactly what I needed before stepping outside into the cool air. Sitting at 2,900 metres, the traditional town of Monguí was far cooler than most of Colombia's lower lands.

Our guide, Paolo, arrived slightly before eight o'clock. Although slight in stature, his mind proved thick with stories from this remote area. We later realized they poured out at the same consistent rate as his wiry legs carried him, both fed by an endless internal rhythm. Outside our hotel, the streets were notably hushed. Monguí's famous handmade football *fábricas* ("factories") remained silent behind locked wooden doors. Approximately three hundred thousand of these spheres are hand-stitched every year in this wee town and shipped across Central and South America.[3] During opening hours, shop after shop displayed an array of multi-coloured footballs hung across their walls and piled in metal bins for interested shoppers.

We had come to Monguí, however, for a different reason. Our purpose was to hike the surrounding Páramo de Ocetá. The rocky road we followed with our guide curved up and out of town. Most of the two-storey brick houses were painted white and topped with tile shingles. As we left Monguí's centre, smooth bitumen replaced the traditional cobblestone. Houses became more sporadic. Eventually, the path switched to gravel, the tiny stones rolling underfoot as the trail steepened. Occasional strips of cement curled around bends to add traction on sharp sections. The alternative would have been a slick mess on rainy days. As if to emphasize this unwelcome possibility, grey clouds huddled in the distance.

Eventually Monguí fell out of sight. We had entered the Páramo

3. http://www.mincit.gov.co/englishmin/publicaciones/7035/mincit_helps_mongui_footballs_access_new_markets

de Ocetá, a unique ecosystem found in only six countries. Páramos are situated at an elevation of three to five thousand metres and sustain vast levels of biodiversity. In Colombia, it is thought that seventy percent of the nation's water is supplied by páramos. As a result, in 2016 the Colombian courts ruled that any extraction of natural resources from páramo regions was unconstitutional. Oil, gas and mining activities were banned outright in these high-altitude regions.[4]

We walked alongside Paolo, listening as he retold mountain stories and tales of a lost civilization that used to roam these hills. Paolo had lived his entire life in Monguí. His steps conveyed a comfort gained after years of wandering this wilderness that was his second home. Despite my imperfect Spanish, his stories rekindled ancient realities that transcended the present moment. As if to match our newfound knowledge, fresh vistas surfaced across every ridge, whether they be layers of rocky sheets or a blanket of wild shrubs.

The Muiscas, also referred to as Chibchas, thrived in this region until around the sixteenth century. Their downfall coincided with the arrival of the Spanish conquistadors as their bows and arrows could not defeat the newcomers' rifle power. The balance of power shifted, and the Muiscas, once the regional leaders, had to succumb to their new rulers, who suppressed much of the indigenous language and culture. Animosity rose, and conflicting accounts of the past brewed.

Paolo helps to restore the Muiscas' culture by recounting stories passed down over generations. One quirky tale related to the potato, which was introduced to Colombia by the Spanish. The Muiscas noticed a striking resemblance between the foreign vegetable and

4. theguardian.com/environment/andes-to-the-amazon/2016/feb/21/colombia-bans-oil-gas-mining-paramos

the male anatomy. As subtle revenge and with a hint of humour, the Muiscas referred to the Spaniards' potatoes using the Chibcha word for bull testicles. As we walked, legends began to unfold, and the humanity of the people who once lived in these hills started to emerge, erupting before us far more vividly than the pretty landscape.

A sacred ridge to our right revealed another example of secrets hidden in the páramo. Traditionally, only women would have climbed its innocent-looking sierra. Our guide pointed to the pathway they would have followed down the valley and up its ridgeline. Most of the mountains were covered in green grass, but the serpent-like ridge to our right displayed layers of rock that jutted out in slivery jags. My eyes followed his finger to the highest point where trees failed to grow. It was like the rocky ground had spit out roots to peel open the earth and expose a stony crevasse. The Muiscas believed that this opening connected the home of the sun god, which lay beneath the Páramo de Ocetá, with their world. Throughout the day we learned of many more sacred sites, all linked to life, death and the sun god. Paolo pointed out similar crevasses across the páramo and explained that these fissures were thought to be locations where the ground had ruptured and the first people of earth had climbed out. Muisca women came to these places when they were pregnant, an example of the relationship people felt between themselves, the land and the origin of life.

The trails across the Páramo de Ocetá have been used for hundreds of years to access burial grounds, sacred sites and neighbouring communities. We followed a twenty-kilometre loop and learned of the region's history as we walked amid its unusual terrain. The path was said to follow a bog; however, when we hiked, the trail was just cushy enough to absorb any impact our tender knees might have otherwise felt. We encountered multiple varieties of the *frailejón* plant, a spiky-leafed shrub that dominated the grasslands. These plants stood like an army of mint-coloured starbursts, on duty to protect their dear sun god. Their sturdy frames typically grow only one centimetre per year. I felt rather young pausing beside frailejón plants that stood taller than me. Elsewhere, riverbeds scoured the grassy hillside, marked by a swirl of arnica plants that grew so thick you could not walk through without damaging their leaves. Nearly every narrow leaf was lined with water droplets like a row of peas bundled inside their pod.

As we climbed, the grasslands gave way to an occasional swatch of rocky teeth that seemed to spar with the sky. As we reached the highest rim of the hill, the air cooled and the wind picked up. We had climbed 1,050 metres in elevation to reach our highest point along a ridgeline at 3,950 metres. On one side, the mountain had fallen away. I could barely hear the delicate gurgle of the stream far below without leaning close to the edge, where the ground almost tipped over. Looking up, I searched the sky for a glimpse of Colombia's national bird, the rare Andean condor. Its wing span can reach three metres and would have appeared like a bolt of obsidian lightning overhead. Sadly, their numbers are declining. The vacant skies stared down on grassy slopes, and rocky bluffs stretched until they blurred into the horizon.

Dark clouds swirled in the distance. By this time, we had passed the midway point and were circling back towards the valley we had first crossed. I pulled out my rain jacket to help block the cool breeze. As the trail escorted us farther down the slope, the blasts of wind slowly eased and eventually left us alone. Initially, this section looked similar to where we had started. Scruffy bushes grew alongside plains of grass. We neared an area known as the Centre of the Earth, a grassy meadow filled with a battalion of frailejones. Dead leaves clung to their stalks for insulation, much like a set of army fatigues.

Before long, our path jutted to the right. After four hours of hiking through rolling hillsides, the scenery promptly changed as we ducked beneath a cluster of trees. The dry grasslands transformed into a slick, muddy chute that seized my boots in an attempt to drag me down. The twisted, narrow, yet resilient arms of the trees beckoned to me like a buoy bobbing in a rainstorm. I grasped one branch and then another to climb deeper into the narrow ravine. Ridges in the rock layers offered grips to use as handholds. The channel was about one metre wide, and the light grew more muted with each step. My right hand instinctively shoved my sunglasses onto my forehead, as they were useless here in the dappled shadows. Sunlight was further blocked by the miscellany of leaves and vines loitering overhead among the confined rock walls.

We had entered a sacred place, virtually invisible from the upper Páramo de Ocetá grasslands that surrounded this snake-like slice of earth. This was an ancient cemetery used by the Muiscas. The rock surface rose ten to fifteen metres on either side. After we had slid between moss-covered trunks and loose-hanging vines for about twenty metres, a bare patch came into view. I looked up at an elevated cavern that had been carved into the wall. Blackened lichen cloaked its rocky interior. Hundreds of years ago, the Muiscas had buried their dead in this and similar cavities. They mummified the bodies, which would have been curled into a fetal position before being placed inside the rock chamber. Rituals were performed to encourage the spirits to return to their earth-bound birthplace. Today, little remained beyond vacant holes. Various Muisca artifacts found across the páramo regions are, however, on display at Bogotá's Museo del Oro.

We continued to wind through the cavern until we pulled ourselves up one last mucky section where rocks acted as handles and tree stumps offered support. Outside of the narrow forest, the sun reappeared, and grass took over once again. I looked back. The deep chasm looked like nothing more than a few mangy trees. I would have assumed it to be a little gully of no consequence if Paolo had not exposed the depth that lay beneath. As we retraced our steps back to Monguí, images of another time floated across my mind. Many of the stories cannot be found by searching Google or reading history books. Only through people like Paolo, who has sought to share the legacy of his region's ancestors, can we learn the human side of a nearly forgotten culture.

The Basics

Most useful items to pack: A rain jacket with ventilation zippers and a hat

Useful words and phrases in Spanish: *hola* ("hello"); *gracias* ("thank you"); *sí* ("yes"); *no* ("no"); *mañana* ("morning *or* tomorrow"); *tarde* ("afternoon"); and *Estoy perdido/a* ("I am lost [male/female]").[5]

For further travel information: Monguí can be reached on a comfortable bus from Bogotá. The Libertadores bus line runs frequent buses to Sogamoso along a four-hour drive. Their large buses and smaller shuttle vans offer Wi-Fi service. At the Sogamoso bus station, we switched to a smaller regional bus for the final thirty-minute ride to reach Monguí.

We stayed at the simple but comfortable Hotel Otti Colonial.

5. Based on Lonely Planet's *Colombia Travel Guide* (see Bibliography).

The owner was exceptionally friendly and arranged the local guide for our hike. We awoke to a hearty breakfast served with rich coffee and a basket of locally grown high-altitude peaches and apples. The hotel does not have its own website at the time of writing, but rooms can be reserved through Booking.com.

A few buildings away, the Camina a Calicanto served consistently tasty meals, including a side salad and fried plantains for about 18,000 to 24,000 Colombian pesos (approximately US$6 to US$8).

The tiny Restaurante el Velero, located just off the plaza on Carrera 3, was noticeable more from all the locals filling its tables than from the tiny sign that hung above its door. They served up a huge lunch of soup, fried chicken, rice, beet salad and beans for 5,000 Colombian pesos (approximately US$1).

Route: The Páramo de Ocetá is a unique place. Our Lonely Planet *Colombia Travel Guide* described the páramo as a "glacier-formed tropical ecosystem" (see Bibliography). The páramo type of landscape lies in eastern Colombia where elevations range from three to five thousand metres. The Ocetá is one such páramo region. Our local guide referred to the twenty-kilometre loop we followed as La Ruta del Sol. It climbed to one of the highest points in the Páramo de Ocetá and crossed a sloping plateau originally believed to be the home of the sun god.

For more information, refer to visitsugamuxi.com/paramos.html.

~~~
~~~

CUBA—UNITING SIERRA, CIGARS AND SOLITUDE IN PARQUE NACIONAL VIÑALES

Navigate limestone mogotes *amid tranquil fields bursting with local charm full of the same inspiration that fed Cuba's tobacco roots*

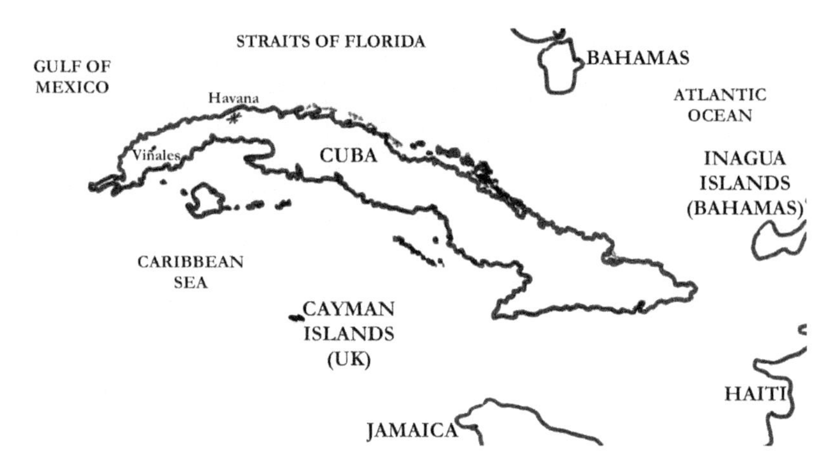

The Experience

Auburn clouds burst from the soles of my feet with each step, each dusty step. Invariably, the dried path transformed into bands of impassible muck at regular intervals. This is the curse and salvation of a tropical climate; it is wet and it is fertile. Trails of red earth spread across the landscape. The dirt was not the flaming red of a forest fire running rampant, but the carrot toned-soil of a region steeped in agriculture. It was as if the tips of a hundred thousand cigars lit the pathways that weaved through the Sierra de los Órganos mountain range with their golden glow. This unexpected vista runs through western Cuba's Valle de Viñales alongside the similarly named Parque Nacional Viñales. UNESCO recognizes the park for its limestone *mogotes* ("outcrops or karsts") and traditional farming practices, labelling it a "living landscape."[6] Country paths are wide enough for a horse cart but too narrow for the 1950s-era vehicles found elsewhere. Out here, we had the trails almost entirely to ourselves. The Valle de Viñales felt grounded, if not slightly sedate, compared to Havana's medley of activities.[7]

The nearest town was Viñales, a bizarre place where the cord of modernity had been severed and quaint *casas particulares* ("bed and breakfasts") were flung back in its place. Houses alternated from one pastel colour to another, engulfing the town in a rainbow of homestays. Although practically every house was a casa particular and the streets were filled with more tourists than locals, few visitors ventured beyond the edge of town. The trails were virtually empty when we walked around the flat plain of the Valle de Palmarito beneath towering limestone mogotes. These knobby outcrops reminded me of the karsts of Vietnam and northern Laos. Tracks of copper-coloured mud stretched across the valley like long stitches that appeared and then disappeared beneath the crops. Lush trees obscured sections, and leaves camouflaged what lay underneath. We passed no signs. No labels as to whose field or which lane we might be walking on. Our hiking trails were really just scattered farmers' tracks. Routes intersected and dirt roads veered away to unmarked destinations. Sometimes they led to a farmhouse or a tobacco field or both.

The people who walk these corridors know one another like family. We met some of the *guarijos* ("agricultural workers") during our hike. A couple of older men had convened at a junction of barbed-wire fences. By their relaxed slouch, I presumed this was a regular catch-up spot. Stories would likely get repeated and complaints reiterated from the previous morning's gab. We took

6. whc.unesco.org/en/list/840
7. For more about Havana, see Chapter Six: Cuba—Losing Yourself in Havana's Tangle of Art, History and Authority.

advantage of this opportunity to tap into local knowledge. The farmers seemed happy to see us exploring their farmland. We called out with the standard morning greeting, *Buenos dias* ("Good morning"). Cuban Spanish has its own lilt, a slightly different lingo than we had studied in Guatemala, but our "good morning" starting point remained unchanged. They grinned back, seemingly pleased for something fresh to add to their daily topics of conversation.

These old guarijos held tightly to their traditional way of life. By the look of the barren trails, few foreigners had glimpsed their world. We asked if it was all right for us to carry on, wanting to ensure we were not unwittingly intruding into someone's territory that should not be crossed. They were unconcerned. One of the gentlemen offered us a fresh coconut. It was a hot morning, despite the patches of shade from the scrubby trees that lined much of the trail. The men motioned us to carry on along the track ahead.

The trail continued to weave through a patchwork of fields, interrupted by the occasional clump of coconut palms or thatch-roofed huts. Houses here tended to be more colourful, and many had a veranda painted lime green or an outer wall of sky blue. In contrast, the thatched huts, constructed entirely out of palm leaves baked by the sun, assumed varying shades of beige and charcoal. Their colour hinted at their purpose: these were the tobacco drying sheds, for Parque Nacional Viñales is the main source of Cuba's most iconic creation—the cigar.

In the nearby town of Pinar del Río, the dried tobacco leaves would be rolled to just the right thickness. Most craftspeople created 100 to 150 cigars each day. We visited the Fábrica de Tabacos Francisco Donatien, a workshop with high ceilings and fans that ran all day. Latino tunes played from a central radio box, and the workers joked together, creating a light atmosphere. Horse-drawn wooden carts were used to haul the dried tobacco leaves from the fields to such factories. This was in 2016, but it appeared that the process had remained unchanged for decades—just like the 1950s vintage vehicles that plied roads between Viñales and Pinar del Río. There must be many expert mechanics to keep these classics running smoothly. Dedicated painters ensure the cars' finish is shiny and bright, often in tones of violet or cobalt. These old cars operate as *colectivos* ("shared taxis") to shuttle people between towns.

The goal of our second walk was to reach the Mural de la Prehistoria by hiking a loop from the town of Viñales. Most of the walk passed through the eastern tip of Parque Nacional Viñales; however, the park borders were unmarked, so we could not tell when we actually entered or left its boundaries. Without such formalities, it felt more like a country walk than a woodland expedition. After rounding a bend, I noticed a piece of the mountain ahead of us had transformed into the same colour as the sky. A few steps closer revealed a similar chunk but in yellow. Across the mountain face, patches of rock were painted with splotches of bold colours. The mural itself was not prehistoric, as the name might imply. Rather, eighteen people had painted archaic dinosaurs and human figures on the cliff face in the 1960s. We could have paid an entrance fee to enjoy a closer look; however, I feared if I got any closer I might choose to run in the opposite direction. In my view, the idyllic mogotes and lush countryside provided a far more interesting vista than the colossal creatures splattered across this escarpment.

Even out on these serene country lanes, we were reminded of Cuba's revolutionary past. A red billboard, faded by the sun but still clearly legible, stood along the roadside as we approached the town of Viñales. It was titled "*Monumento Km 18.*" The image depicted a man with a rifle poised beside words once said by Fidel Castro: "*Si ustedes triunfan, habrá milicias en Cuba,*" which means "If you succeed, there will be militias in Cuba," referring to the voluntary revolutionaries.

Monumento Km 18

Castro spoke these words of encouragement to a small group of local militants who had fought in support of his revolution in the 1950s. Their mission targeted a group of bandits believed to be backed by the United States Central Intelligence Agency. The fighting took place near Pinar del Río where we were now walking.[8] On the streets of Pinar del Río, two signs had also caught our attention. One commemorated the fifty-seventh anniversary of the revolution with the phrase "*La Patria está hecha del mérito de sus hijos,*" meaning "The homeland is made of the merit of their children." It clearly aimed to remind citizens of their ongoing duty. Another fresh-looking sign recalled the words of Cuban hero José Martí

8. http://www.granma.cu/granmad/2013/10/21/nacional/artic03.html

calling on Latin American states to stand up against the United States: "*¡Los árboles han de ponerse en fila, para que no pase el gigante de las siete leguas!*" ("The trees must form ranks to keep the giant with seven-league boots from passing!"). Considering that Barack Obama was due to visit Cuba in the coming month, it was apparent that emotions surrounding Cuban and US relations were simmering—at least, the government was making its point of view clear.

Once back in Viñales, we visited our favourite local café, J Rompiendo Rutina Cafeteria, an unassuming café located a block off the main street. Its espresso was robust, and each bite of the *ropa vieja* ("spicy shredded beef") melted with tender flavour. Compared to the touristic restaurants on main street, this little café's reasonable prices enticed us back for nearly every meal during our time in Viñales. We also learned another lesson in the tiny yet touristy town. Only one central place supported Wi-Fi access. It was across from the ETECSA office, the office of Cuba's public communication body, La Empresa de Telecomunicaciones de Cuba S.A. Its location was obvious from the congregation of people sitting or standing along the sidewalk madly tapping on their devices.

We learned the difficulty of printing anything without a network connection. Printing shops existed but were outside the Wi-Fi zone, as were most establishments. We were trying to print our onward Viazul bus tickets because another unexpected obstacle in Cuba is that pre-purchased bus tickets ordered outside the country are not visible on Viazul's internal ticketing system. We needed a printed copy in order to prove we had bought tickets. If we had waited and purchased our tickets once we arrived in Cuba from the Viazul ticket counters, we would not have had this problem. In the end, the owner of our casa particular saved the situation by transferring our file to her

USB stick, which we could then give to the printing shop. One more example of how friendly locals are often a traveller's best friend.

The Basics

Most useful item to pack: A Spanish-English dictionary or phrasebook to facilitate a chat with one of the local guarijos you will invariably meet along the paths

Useful words and phrases in Spanish: *hola* ("hello"); *gracias* ("thank you"); *¿Dónde está …?* ("Where is …?"); *¿Me lo puede indicar en el mapa?* ("Can you show me on the map?"); and *colectivo* ("shared taxi").[9]

For further travel information: In the town of Viñales, the Parque Nacional Viñales visitors centre offers a chance to pick up local tips and information about trails. From my experience, the centre had little in the way of maps or guidance, but it is worth asking when you get on the ground. We gained more helpful instructions from our Lonely Planet *Cuba Travel Guide* (see Bibliography). The trails were really just local access routes used by farmers to get on and around their fields. None of the paths we followed were clearly marked. Consider any walk as more of a meander through the valley rather than a formal, designated route.

Route: We hiked through the Valle de Palmarito, which can be done as a loop from the north end of the Adela Azcuy road in Viñales. The trail passes around the Mogote del Valle, past Mural de la Prehistoria and then back to Viñales on the main paved

9. Based on Lonely Planet's *Cuba Travel Guide* (see Bibliography).

road. On another day, we explored the Valle de Silencio, even less of a defined trail and more of a random wander, with a little help from Google Maps and a few locals we met along the way.

~~~
~~~

FAROE ISLANDS—DODGING WIND AND RAIN ACROSS VÁGAR AND GJÓGV

Like your moody aunt, the Faroe Islands display characteristics of cranky, wind-blown isolation in the most endearing manner, tempting visitors to chip away at her mysterious beauty

The Experience

When I looked back, the town of Gjógv (pronounced "j-egg-v") had completely disappeared. I had been climbing the surrounding hills for over an hour. The wind attacked in gusts, rushing against my face before backing off until its next cycle. I knew the rain would pay a visit too, a reminder to replace my rain jacket after its less-than-stellar performance during the last downpour. I looked towards the cloud of fog that had erased the far hill I was heading towards. My destination lay beyond its white mass. I wanted to see Búgvin, the tallest sea stack in the Faroe Islands. It reaches 188 metres in height and is home to wide-eyed puffins and a myriad of other sea birds. As I peered into the distance, all was obscured except a distant sheep hut that had managed to evade the mist's tentacles.

Then something caught my eye. Two boulder-like shapes emerged from the fog and stood close to the shack. I struggled to get a clear view of them. One moved ever so slightly. An image of a rhinoceros flitted across my mind, but I discarded this notion just as quickly. These creatures were much bigger than the sheep I had come to expect elsewhere on this remote island. I scanned the barren grasslands where I stood alone and confirmed that no one else had ventured into this valley today. As I glanced back towards the grazing beasts, I remembered excerpts from the map I had purchased at the guesthouse: "things to notice along the trail…in the past it was the best escape along the road from angry bulls…best retire from angry bulls." When I had read them, these comments seemed like a reference to old folk tales and legendary boulders. Yet now I recalled the barbed-wire fence, five hundred metres back, that I had had to climb over to continue along the trail, whereas every other crossing had a gate. A large boulder had sat nearby.

The lack of a typical Faroese wooden gate had seemed odd, yet between my local trail map and my Google Maps GPS tracker, I was convinced I was following the correct route. Thoughts swirled through my head. Here I was, inside a sturdy fenced pasture, alone with two bulls in springtime. I grew up on an acreage, and from what I recalled, bulls get particularly feisty during their springtime mating season. This did not bode well. My instincts buzzed and my legs sprang into action. Two litres of water weighing down my pack could not impede my pace. Only once did I slow to glance over my shoulder. The mysterious bulls remained frozen in the distance, oblivious to my frantic exit from their lush pasture. I continued to run. Finally, after reaching the fence and swinging my legs over, I became conscious of my pounding heart and wheezy breath.

The grey blobs lingered in the distance. Had I imagined the impending danger? It was now impossible to reach my targeted sea stack, and I was not gutsy enough to attempt a second approach, even if the animals looked innocent from this far-off vantage point.

Still, it seemed strange that the hotel would send guests walking straight into a field with cranky bulls. Or was it? Perhaps it was a not-so-subtle attempt to dispel the gradual influx of visitors who were cramping the tiny town's otherwise untouched ambience. Once back at the guesthouse, I asked the lady who had sold me the map whether the trail could have passed through bull territory. She glanced at the chef and their faces erupted into knowing grins. Looking back at me, she nodded and confirmed that there were only sheep, or "angry bulls," around these hills. This lady handled everything from reception to waitressing. Maybe our incessant tourist demands had pushed her just a little too hard; perhaps this was her bittersweet revenge.

For the remainder of my time in Gjógv, the most northerly village on the island of Eysturoy, the rain and wind gods danced a fidgety duet. I suppose it was not surprising; after all, the Faroe Islands lie in the middle of the North Atlantic Ocean between Iceland, Norway and Scotland. Mist blew in, only to be replaced by drizzle, which was followed by torrents of sideways rain. The little seaside town of Gjógv was home to fifty residents, but most had vacated during my visit in the spring of 2017. The odd rustic home still bore traditional sod roofing, although most were capped with a solid metal sheet of orange, black or green. Wooden siding was painted one of two colours, lemon yellow or white, which blended into the mustard-yellow grasses and patchy black soil that surrounded the town. More sheep roamed the streets than locals.

The town's name means "gorge" and refers to the rock-walled crevasse north of town. This blackened inlet has offered a haven to fishermen over the centuries and was nowadays lit up at night by a multi-coloured LED lightshow. This psychedelic spectacle seemed out of character with the town's otherwise sleepy facade, but then again, a somewhat offbeat island spirit flowed through this place. One of the few residents I did see was an old-timer throwing handfuls of hay onto a tiny chunk of grass beside his house. His flock of shaggy sheep darted around their fence-free pasture, eager to snatch a mouthful of hay. The only other indication of life, or former life, were fish hung by their tails from the eaves of homes. These tasty morsels dried in the sea-salted air and stayed out of reach of the insatiable sheep but would surely catch you by surprise if you brushed one when walking after dark.

My thoughts turned to my return bus trip. I had learned an important lesson about the Faroe Islands' bus system when I travelled to the remote little town of Gjógv—always have a backup plan. My journey had begun on the island of Vágar, the same island where the airport is located. It had started out so smoothly. From my hotel, I had walked two hundred metres along a slightly muddy track—inevitable with the regular mist and rain—to the airport bus stop. Friendly staff at the tourist information kiosk reconfirmed that my planned bus route and connections were indeed correct. As I waited for the bus, sheep clip-clopped by under the cover of the airport's overhang, walking from a field at one end of the airport to a nearly identical field on the other side. Later, another herd travelled back in the opposite direction, eyeing the grass across the way. The back-and-forth click of their hooves somehow sounded appropriate at the Faroe Islands' unassuming airport.

When the bus arrived, the woolly critters had disappeared. I boarded as the sole passenger on a modern full-sized coach. The driver sold me a ticket that covered my entire route, all three legs. He even accepted debit or credit card for payment. I was looking forward to an entire day cruising the Faroes' vast countryside dotted with blackened waterfalls and tiny sod-roofed villages, all from my cushy seat. The sheer number of waterfalls that covered the islands was astounding. Water gushed from one-hundred-metre bluffs and trickled around saturated farmlands. At times, the fierce Atlantic air caused steady streams to explode into mist or reverse their course completely and spray vertically as if in a backwards fall.

Gorge near the village of Saksun on the island of Streymoy

By my third connection, the seemingly perfectly constructed itinerary began to unravel.

I stood inside a small glass bus shelter along the roadside of the incredibly quiet town of Oyrarbakki. This was the location of my third and final connection. Three hours ticked by as winds picked up and then subsided, as rain blew in sideways before blue sky shuttled the clouds away and the cycle started again. Beyond a grocery store and an occasional vehicle passing by, there was little else to see. An older gentleman joined me for about thirty minutes before his connection came and went. He spoke perfect English. We chatted about the changing island culture, rising tourism and random facts, such as how sixty percent of the Faroe Islands' fishing catch, its primary resource, is sold to Russia. Eventually, what I thought was my bus pulled up.

With a smile, I showed the driver my ticket and repeated the name of my final destination. Her response jolted me out of my relaxed state. In low season, riders were supposed to call and request the Gjógv leg at least two hours in advance. Otherwise, her route finished at Eiði. Thirteen kilometres and a high pass separated the two villages. The driver had received no call to request this extension. No one at the tourist information desk had mentioned this on either of the occasions that I checked my itinerary with them, nor did the bus driver when I originally bought my ticket to Gjógv.

This final bus driver invited me to sit inside, since, once again, there were no other passengers on the bus. She kindly agreed to call on my behalf, spurred by my shocked expression and mention that I had no phone. I could not understand the Faroese language or her conversation with the bus office. So I waited. We were still over twenty kilometres from my destination and it was getting late in the afternoon.

I recalled seeing one or two taxis during my three-hour wait—a backup option. After nearly five minutes of discussion, the driver hung up. She looked at me through her rear-view mirror and said without much explanation that she would drive me to Gjógv. I am sure she could see my shoulders relax as I exhaled with relief and then slipped her a well-deserved tip. I soon learned why the road between Eiði and Gjógv was avoided. Even in the early spring, ice clung to the narrow road as it twisted back and forth over the highest section.

When it came time to leave Gjógv, I expected a smoother journey. This time my husband and I would travel together, as his photography workshop was finished. The hotel agreed to call and confirm that the bus would pick us up in Gjógv. Sadly, I was foiled again. On the eve of our journey, the receptionist informed me that our first bus would not run due to a public holiday. Somehow, the holiday did not stop the buses on our second or third legs. I had a feeling that the village's isolation often affected transport. But there surely would be a solution—there always was. The owner of the guesthouse made some calls and within twenty minutes had arranged a taxi to cover the missing leg. The friendly taxi driver normally worked at the Ministry of Education but had taken up the hobby of driving stranded folks like us on his days off.

Back on the island of Vágar, one final site beckoned us. Our destination was Lake Sørvágsvatn, or as it is sometimes called Lake Leitisvatn, the largest lake on the Faroe Islands. Its tantalizing charm was a mirage—the water appeared to hover above the ocean. This photographer's dream can be seen only by walking up a steep bank between the lake's edge and a coastal cliff. Luckily, Lake Sørvágsvatn was located just beyond the airport, a short bus ride from our hotel. The same bus driver who had just dropped us off now pulled in to start his loop once more. As we were his only customers, he insisted that we hop on board using our previous ticket for the short ride. Five minutes later, we disembarked at what appeared to be an abandoned sod-hut community on the shores of Leitisvatn. It was easy to imagine Vikings skinning reindeer and repairing their longboats along this stretch.

A trail led from the sod huts towards the ocean, where our view would take shape. We kept the lake to our right and headed towards the water, which lay about three kilometres in the distance. Along the walk, the wind occasionally slowed, only to be replaced by tiny blackflies that floated above the pathway. Dark clouds swirled in the distance. By this point we were accustomed to the way of the Faroes. Full rain gear including pants, jacket and waterproofed hiking boots were essential daily wear.

The lake curved like a scythe. At its tip, a section of rocky bluff tipped upwards and separated the lake from the wild sea. We climbed up. As we looked back, the embankment seemed to shrink and level to resemble a thin band of land, making the lake appear to float overtop of the ocean. In reality, the lake sits thirty metres higher than the frothy waves. The porous, jagged cliffs had eroded into pockets, in which birds made themselves at home. The wind gusted, birds squawked and the ocean roared, but the lake looked serene. The view was like a family with all its differences on display. This perspective offered a final unforgettable image of the rough and endearing Faroe Islands.

The Basics

Most useful items to pack: Full rain gear including pants, jacket and waterproofed hiking boots and a rain cover for your pack

Useful local words and phrases: *halló* ("hello"); *góðan morgun* ("good morning"); *ja* ("yes"); *nei* ("no"); and *Um tær ikki dámar*

veðrið, bíða so bara í fimm minuttir ("If you don't like the weather, just wait five minutes").

For more translation help, check out faroeislandstranslate.com.

For further travel information: I visited the Faroe Islands in 2017 with my husband, who was on a photography workshop with the dynamic Offbeat group. Further information can be found at offbeatphoto.ca.

If you happen to see a one-storey black building settled alone between the airport and the town of Sørvágur, then you have spied Hotel Vágar. Despite its location right next to the airport, there were so few flights in and out that noise is surprisingly minimal. Instead, you can sit in the hotel's restaurant with a warm mug of coffee and partake in some daily entertainment from the windows. Watch as a distinctive yellow truck drives up and down the runway to chase away the many seabirds that have congregated on the tarmac. This process is done a few times a day, before each flight is due to arrive or depart. For further information on the hotel, refer to hotelvagar.fo.

Our second location was in Gjógv, on the island of Eysturoy. This quiet village had one guesthouse, which also cooked all our meals. The largest and nicest rooms were located in a separate building a few steps beyond the main reception area. For further information, refer to gjaargardur.fo.

A rented car would have provided the most flexibility to explore the endless hidden inlets around the islands. While I visited during the low season, I used the very comfortable public bus system. On the plus side, the buses were in excellent condition, ran on schedule and offered ample space among mostly vacant seats. However, my route from the Vágar Airport to Gjógv included three different buses and took over five hours, compared to just over an hour if by car. The trip cost less than US$20. Bus schedules can be found at ssl.fo/en.

Most flights arrive from Denmark, Scotland or Iceland. At the time of writing, only two airlines service the Faroe Islands: Atlantic Airways and Scandinavian Airlines. If you prefer a slower option, Smyril Line runs a ferry service from Iceland and Denmark during summer months: smyrilline.com.

For a helpful and clearly organized tourism website with a wide variety of travel planning information, refer to visitfaroeislands.com.

Route: On the island of Vágar, I tackled three hikes. Most were not clearly marked, so it helped to have GPS and/or a map. For more information on hiking in the Faroe Islands, refer to hiking.fo.

Our first route from Hotel Vágar followed the seaside road through Bøur and then partway along what is dubbed the Postman's Hike. Our walk was seventeen kilometres round trip, so a little too far to include the entire Postman's Hike in one day. For more information, refer to visitfaroeislands.com/place/boeur-gasadalur.

For my second walk, I once again started from Hotel Vágar. The return trip covered twenty-four kilometres, mostly along the main highway. Drivers were respectful of walkers, so it was quite pleasant. I passed the town of Sandavágur and walked to the end of the street named Úti á Trøð. From there, a walking trail led to a great view of spiky cliffs overlooking the ocean.

For the last walk on the island of Vágar, my husband and I caught the local bus from the airport to the Vatnavegur trailhead, a five-minute bus ride around part of Lake Leitisvatn. We disembarked before the highway cut away from the lake. The trail was three kilometres each way. If you skip the bus and walk from the hotel, the entire route is seventeen kilometres.

From Gjógv, you can choose from a number of walking routes. The guesthouse in Gjógv, the only place to stay in town, sells maps and their website lists walks that explore the surrounding sights: gjaargardur.fo/en-GB/Gjogv/The-village-walks-and-adventures.aspx.

~~~
~~~

PORTUGAL—CAPTURING THE MILKY WAY IN MADEIRA

Traverse spiny ridges along the lush island of Madeira before refuelling with a chunk of succulent honey cake or immersing yourself in oh-so-nice Portuguese hospitality

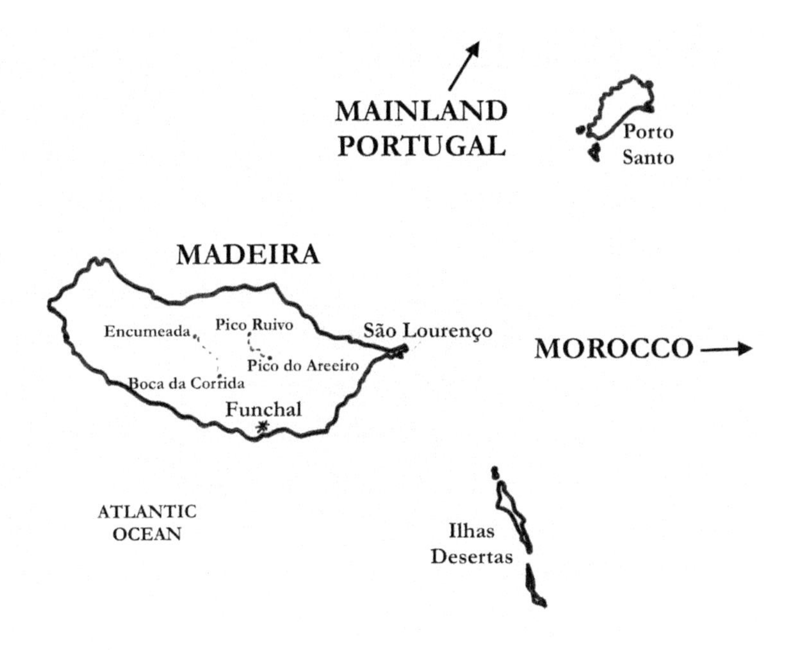

The Experience

Our bus looped around roads that bent back and forth as if we were riding the double-knotted laces of a tennis shoe. Clouds shifted into fingers of fog, and the Atlantic Ocean faded into a blue mat too distant to be of use for our dusty hiking boots. We were closing in on the first hike of three routes we had chosen, all within easy access of the island's capital city of Funchal. A web of trails formerly used by residents to reach remote villages are nowadays maintained for day hikers. Alternative routes follow an array of *levadas* ("carriageways") or water canals originating as far back as the sixteenth century. These chutes transfer water 2,500 kilometres around the island. Madeira proved an unexpected paradox, where European comfort and cuisine are paired with an untamed landscape. Had we found the elusive hikers' paradise?

Our introductory walk skirted the peaks of the island's central mountains. For three hours we hardly saw another person. Madeira is a volcanic island, and our footsteps weaved through ancient eruptions apparently frozen in time. As the lava was spewed skyward, crests had formed and held tight, leaving craggy points and sheer edges for future hikers to endure. Forested cliffs rose from Madeira's coastline at every imaginable angle, like distorted reptilian vertebrae. Occasionally, clusters of red-tiled roofs reflected the sunlight, revealing tiny villages neatly tucked into the mountainside far below us. How isolated these communities must feel in the middle of the winter storms that so frequently sweep across the Atlantic. Perhaps it was nature's demeanour that forced their handiwork in building roads, a never-ending quest to bolster access routes washed away by rains and fill pot-holed passages. On Madeira, accessibility took on the persona of a bratty child, continually seeking a weak point to sneak in and cause havoc. Luckily, we never met the kid and completed the hike in a shaded valley, and from there our return bus shuttled us back to the city, albeit after an hour-long wait on the side of the road.

I silently wondered how our second hike would compare. We planned to venture to the far eastern peninsula of São Lourenço not only for a day hike but also for reconnaissance. Our secondary goal, for a later date, was to photograph the smile of the Milky Way curving above Madeira's jagged shoreline. Success would depend on a number of factors, all playing into the essential condition of being in the right place at the right time. Each night these critical factors shifted. The intensity of the Milky Way's visibility; the time of the moonrise, whose reflective light could overpower the starlit sky; and the arch's position overhead: all of these followed their own rhythm. The cycles could be researched and prepared for in advance, but the final factor—weather—proved our most twitchy foe.

During daylight, cliffs donned stripes of coloured rock; some layers were horizontal while others ran on angles or vertically against the background of a deep copper-coloured base rock. Wind swirled or stopped, depending on which direction we turned on the meandering trail. Thistles bloomed with purple flowers alongside scruffy grass that somehow survived on this gravelly and dusty ground. A lone sailboat, anchored in a protected inlet, suggested we were not alone. This walk was stark, beautiful and best covered in the early morning. By mid-morning, the track reminded me of an ant superhighway. The parking lot was the nest, filled with tour buses and visitors' cars.

After finding a suitable location to return to for the photos, our next requirement was a way to get there in the middle of the night. Our chosen location was remote, an hour's drive from the city of Funchal and far from the lights of Caniçal, the nearest town. We needed a car. Finding one proved an easier task than expected. The owner of the studio apartment we had rented connected us with a local agency that offered fair rates and a nimble Citroën hatchback. Pick-up and drop-off service was included as a bonus. There was only one small setback. As we pulled away from the rental office, the petrol gauge hovered just above the red zone, in a city with an abundance of one-way, unfamiliar streets. Initially, we hoped to find a petrol station along the road heading out of the city.

Our little white buggy zigzagged up and out of Funchal, thankfully not meeting too many oncoming vehicles on the blind corners and narrow streets made narrower by tightly parked vehicles. However, we similarly did not meet any petrol stations. When the buildings faded, our chances of finding fuel waned. We decided to retrace our loops back towards the centre.

The road turned out to be popular with more than just vehicles. A group of runners overtook the lanes. As they darted past, we pulled over. While the runners kept trudging upwards and we sat waiting, a third group entered the scene. A handful of musicians dressed in satiny red capes and silver helmets walked solemnly downhill. It was an odd sight, panting runners and devout band members, both out to fill their soul with whatever energized them. After the whirlwind of activity eased, we revved the engine and carried on in search of our little car's life force: unleaded petrol. Soon enough, the car's navigation system flagged a refuelling station. As is possible only in Europe, this tiny gas station also served up tasty *bicas* ("espressos") of surprisingly good quality and sufficient strength to refuel us as well. Although we were only a few blocks from where we had picked up the car, life was good and we could start the day—again.

Weather became the next challenge. Different reports offered different forecasts. A clear night sky dangled uncertainly during our final days on the island. A couple of climate websites forecasted rain, while some offered varying percentages of cloud cover. Every few hours the reports updated, shifted and ultimately withheld any definitive assurances. We wondered if driving out to a remote part of this foreign island at midnight was rather mad, while at the same time it was that madness that taunted us with possibility. As the day progressed, our two favoured weather websites gave hopeful but still uncertain advice. We decided to go.

Roads were clear during the forty-five-minute drive to the peninsula. Only two other cars were in the parking area when we arrived, one of which was parked at the far end and looked as if it had been abandoned. Beyond the trailhead's car park, we had to walk for forty-five minutes along an unlit stone path, making headlamps mandatory. Luckily, we had scouted locations during our daytime walk. The blackness of a clouded night sky settled around us. Our headlamps' bobbing beams seemed out of place on this rugged peninsula, which was more accustomed to an evening of solitude than an exploring hobby photographer and his sidekick. I felt a slight prickle of exhilaration, knowing we had this isolated point to ourselves while nearly everyone else was far away amid the city's glow.

That said, few places allow you to be completely alone. Iridescent spiders and pairs of social beetles scattered beneath the flicker of our headlamps. Wind slithered through the air, brushing my cheeks and attempting to tickle my hand. I tightened my jacket's hood and pulled my fingers inside my sleeves. The garbled call of seabirds cut through the hush of night in spurts, as if they had rolled over in their sleep only to be abruptly reminded of the sheer drop just outside their nest. Then the night turned silent once more until the next bird's gurgling outburst.

At a tight bend in the path, we caught our first hint of something unnatural. A whiff of campfire smoke was the initial sign, followed by a French-accented and slightly surprised "Hello." The stranger was shrouded in darkness while we held our brief conversation. His first question was "Are you not scared?" It seemed strange to ask such a question, as he himself had also chosen to come to this desolate place late at night. Personally, we had little concern. We had asked a few locals earlier, who assured us that it bore no particular risk.

The lack of empty beer bottles or cigarette butts during our daytime walk further confirmed that it was an unlikely venue for late-night trouble. Our fellow night walker explained that he too was there for photography, and we bid each other well.

We carried along farther until the trail reached a higher point. We had plotted this vantage earlier as it offered appealing foreground imagery without blocking the very Milky Way we were there to capture. The best time would be between one and two o'clock in the morning, before the moon had risen but after the Milky Way revealed her core. After we had switched off our headlamps, shadowy bluffs and tarnished skies slowly solidified into the landscape before us. A lighthouse flashed on and off at the farthest tip of land. White foam burst against the cliff base sporadically, indicating that a fresh momentum of wind had caught the waves. One hour passed. Clouds shuffled and shaded the stars across much of the sky before splitting open to display a meagre bouquet of lights. Moments later, the sparkles faded behind another dark cloak. The grey blanket finally thinned, and pockets of pinpoint beads greeted us. A thicker band of stars and planets soon emerged from the arena above. This was the core of the Milky Way. It remained in sight for about half an hour.

Milky Way radiating over São Lourenço

I stood still with my headlamp switched on, trying not to move for a long exposure shot despite sporadic gusts of wind that blew with a moody tendency. A pair of lights farther along from where I stood flashed before my eyes. It was not a rogue duo of stars. They flickered near ground level but were far bigger than the tiny glints of iridescent spiders I had noticed earlier. They froze when caught in my headlamp's light but darted back and forth once out of the spotlight. In a glint of movement, I spotted the outline of a ferret-like animal. Our game continued. Light on. Light off. The animal slunk closer and then scuttled away. Only five types of land mammals reside on the island of Madeira: one mouse, two types of rat, a rabbit and—the only one resembling what I saw—a feral cat.[10]

As clouds thickened and the moon started to rise, we walked back along the dark, rocky path towards our car. It was two thirty when we pulled onto the highway and headed towards Funchal. The lanes were clear of cars. If only the sky could have been so vacant of clouds. We did not know it at the time, but some of our favourite photos from this trip came out of our night's roaming on the peninsula of São Lourenço.

The sweet melody of our alarm yanked us back to reality at seven the next morning, far too soon. One final hike awaited before we returned our vehicle to the rental agency later that day. It started in Pico do Areeiro (sometimes spelled as Pico do Arieiro) and finished at Pico Ruivo, the latter being the highest point on the island at 1,862 metres above the ocean waves. The hike there and back covered fourteen kilometres and crossed the rims of ridges that felt like we were meandering along a suspension bridge hung between the air and the earth's outer edges. A white astrological dome marked the trailhead. From there, the path swerved past stone tentacles that reached towards the sky. Vertical drops alternated from one side of the trail to the other. I am not sure if the crisp air or the stunning

10. madeira.seawatching.net/landanimals.html

vistas was more effective in acting as our morning caffeine, but I certainly felt alive walking along that track. At times, the pinnacles were too sheer to hike around, so tunnels veered through the centre of mountain peaks and dropped us at equally narrow paths to continue our walk on the other side.

This was a tough trail, often transforming into near-vertical steps carved directly into the mountain. We met a couple of men repairing a section of safety barriers that were placed in particularly precarious locations. Thin metal rods held equally thin railings and stood between us and the valley below. The views were too spectacular to be feared. Each bend in the trail brought new perspective. We watched as valleys filled with mist, cooled, and then became overcome with warmth, producing clear vistas around the next corner. Yellow-flowering shrubs coloured the trail's edge, and at a few of the less vertical sections, large trees with papery white bark grew in clusters. During the final few kilometres, the sun beat down, blue skies glistened and chipper birds sang their melody. Life was good. Sleep could take her turn later.

The Basics

Most useful item to pack: A headlamp for night excursions

Useful words and phrases in Portuguese: *olá* ("hello"); *sim* ("yes"); *não* ("no"); *Pode-me mostrar no mapa?* ("Can you show me on the map?"); *aberto* ("open"); *encerrado* or *fechado* ("closed"); and *saída* ("exit").[11]

For further travel information: Madeira Regional Tourism Board has a fantastic website to help plan your trip. The site

11. Based on Lonely Planet's *Pocket Madeira* travel guide (see Bibliography).

is arranged by activity, and the trekking section includes links to webcams and weather reports to check before heading out. For further information, see visitmadeira.pt/en-gb/what-to-do/activities.

Walking maps and trail information can be found at visitmadeira.pt/en-gb/what-to-do/activities/search/madeira/activities/walks.

Trail information and maps for the three hikes we covered are found at the following links:

Boca da Corrida to Encumeada: visitmadeira.pt/en-gb/what-to-do/activities/search/pr12-caminho-real-da-encumeada

Ponta de São Lourenço: visitmadeira.pt/en-gb/what-to-do/activities/search/pr8-vereda-da-ponta-de-sao-lourenco

Pico do Areeiro to Pico Ruivo: visitmadeira.pt/en-gb/what-to-do/activities/search/pr1-vereda-do-areeiro

We booked a studio apartment at the Den Apartments through Booking.com. They also rent larger apartment units, which would be preferable for a longer visit. Stay in the Den, its alias, can also be found on Airbnb. The apartment building was located in central Funchal, but along a reasonably quiet street. The owner, Steve, offered helpful local advice and was incredibly friendly and responsive. For more information, refer to his website: stayintheden.com.

Steve also arranged our car rental. The car was in great condition and included a useful navigation system. Atlantic Rent a Car is based in Funchal: atlanticrentacar.net.

Madeira's bus system is very modern and easy to use. From the airport, the Aerobus operates a direct service to central Funchal. During our visit in 2018, one-way rates were €5 per person, and return tickets cost €8. For more information on the airport and other buses around the island, refer to sam.pt/informacoes-aerobus.html.

A similar bus line covers central and western routes: horariosdofunchal.pt.

~~~
~~~

3

Ancient Temples

Religion—a word that stirs emotion and incites action. This section explores physical creations that have arisen out of such beliefs. Although most other chapters in this book cross continents, this chapter stays wholly in Asia. Further, all the temples in this chapter are connected by a common thread: they are all Buddhist. I had no intention to focus on one religion or region. But the structures and experiences in these select group of temples stood out with such resonance that it was worth sharing, from one curious traveller to another. The sites are old, but the activities performed to this day kept them vibrant. I find that by exploring such sanctuaries, aged by time and devotion, I gain a sense of clarity over my own thoughts. Petty irritants and the busy bustle that often takes over our days tend to fall away in these havens, allowing priorities to rise to the surface.

This chapter steps through sites located across three countries: Bhutan, Myanmar and Sri Lanka. The temples radiate a distinctive aura, and every temple in this section has its own story to tell.

Bhutan is a diamond-shaped country that lies along the Himalaya Mountains in the middle of Asia. China wraps across its northern border, while India hugs its southern edge. India is a close ally, providing military assistance to the Royal Bhutan Army. Bhutan has a few defining qualities, including being the only nation in the world to measure its people's gross national happiness. There are no traffic lights in Bhutan, not even in its capital city of Thimphu. Road signs participate in the country's quirky sense of humour; "If you are married, divorce speed" and "Be Mr Late not Late Mr" are a couple of examples. Another unusual quality is that Bhutan's king relinquished certain powers and pushed for a shift towards democracy in 2008. It is therefore unsurprising that this remarkable little country is home to an equally remarkable temple. This memorable site was built in the name of the Divine Madman, an unexpectedly virile saint from the sixteenth century who won people's hearts with his unconventional lessons, often linked to his fondness for women and alcohol.

Moving farther east in Asia, Myanmar is gaining momentum with travellers and is the setting for three amazing experiences covered in this chapter. The first took place during sunset in Bagan, central Myanmar. A young key man unlocked the door to a temple thousands of years old. From its heights we watched the sun fall against blackened silhouettes of hundreds of similar temples spread across the plains of Bagan. The second story took place in eastern Myanmar, where life revolves around the waters of Inle Lake. There we found a small teak monastery tucked into the marshland and a very special monk. We end in Myanmar's capital city of Yangon, at its most austere temple, the Shwedagon Paya. Beyond its monumental design and the hidden hairs of Buddha encased deep inside the temple centuries earlier, the people that visit this space day in and day out are as diverse as they are enchanting. These three completely different experiences in temples give a taste of Myanmar's hospitality and depth of culture.

The chapter closes with two sections from the teardrop-shaped island of Sri Lanka. It sits in the Bay of Bengal, south of India. After twenty-six years of suppression during the country's civil war, which ended in 2009, the people of Sri Lanka have leapt at the chance to showcase their country to the world. Hotels, private drivers and tourist-friendly sites are plentiful. Many still retain a personalized atmosphere that feels neighbourly rather than artificially adapted for tourists. Two temples carried us along on their present-day story, where a mix of old and new ways unfolded. At the first temple, where Buddhism was introduced to Sri Lanka, devoted locals performed traditional dances and rituals to enliven their faith. The second location was a temple set into a large boulder that overlooked the central plateau of the island. These sights have earned my respect, as have the people that revere these sacred grounds.

~~~
~~~

BHUTAN—CHASING DEMONS IN CHIMI LHAKHANG

Visit a five-hundred-year-old temple inspired by a phallic-swinging, liquor-loving Buddhist saint known across Bhutan as the Divine Madman

The Experience

Seven years before, on our first visit, there had been only one restaurant in the village of Sopsokha, and it had belonged to the brother of our guide. During our second visit in 2017, the main road of this small town in northwestern Bhutan looked much the same, except that four or five of the homes had become restaurants. Regardless of a building's purpose, Bhutanese architecture has an exceptionally distinctive style. Here, penises the size of ponies are painted on exterior walls, usually beside the main doorway. These are popular murals across Bhutan, but especially in this region. The image symbolizes the Divine Madman. Some say that he used a walking stick with the head of a penis to subdue demons, while others thought it was his own virile member that he wielded. Regardless of the precise source, his powerful shaft is referred to as the Flaming Thunderbolt of Wisdom.[1] To this day, people decorate their homes with massive phalluses as a sign of protection and, although not immediately intuitive, to show their devotion.

This wacky mystic's real name was Lama Drukpa Kunley, and he lived in the fifteenth and sixteenth centuries. He attained enlightenment, the highest spiritual level that a Buddhist can attain. That transformation led him to travel between Tibet and Bhutan, where he taught lessons of Buddhism in his own peculiar manner, weaving poems and jokes into his performance. Essentially, his unorthodox antics, songs and sexual exploits endeared him to many and played a major role in spreading Buddhism across Bhutan.

The Chimi Lhakhang, which roughly translated means "no dog temple," [2] was built by Lama Drukpa Kunley's cousin at the end of the sixteenth century. However, it is more commonly referred to simply as the Temple of the Divine Madman. It was built after the philandering saint subdued a demoness who had been terrorizing all who tried to cross a nearby mountain pass, the Dochu La. The demoness is said to have fled to the adjacent Lobesa valley, where she promptly turned herself into a dog. This is the valley we were visiting, where the current town of Sopsokha lies. Back when Lama Drukpa Kunley was battling the demoness, he was not fooled by her disguise, and with his magic appendage he subdued her malicious spirit. How he actually achieved this divine act is not clear, but this story has been passed down and believed unquestionably as part of Buddhist mythology. During the Divine Madman's dramatic conquest, he buried the demon dog's body and persuaded the

1. At the time of this writing, a biography entitled *The Divine Madman: The Sublime Life and Songs of Drukpa Kunley*, translated by Keith Dowman and Sonam Paljor, is freely available to download as a PDF document at promienie.net/images/dharma/books/drukpa-kunley_divine-madman.pdf
2. asiasenses.bt/category/places-of-interest

demoness to transform herself into a guardian deity to protect the valley. To this day, she continues to be considered the protector spirit of the valley.

This quirky little temple is tucked away from Sopsokha on a small knoll, the same mound where the demon dog was buried. It is now surrounded by rice fields. To reach it, we walked past whitewashed houses decorated with painted deer, spurting penises and magical lions. Wooden beams jutted out from the homes and were further bedecked with painted flowers and swirly designs. Beyond the town, we followed raised dirt pathways that separated fields of rice. A cluster of white prayer flags fluttered in the breeze about midway through our walk. As we neared, the rippling sound of the flags intermingled with a low chant. Three elderly folks sat at the base of a *chorten* ("Buddhist monument"). The stone pillar was not much taller than I am and was painted white, with prayer wheels hung inside niches on all four sides. As is customary, we walked around it in a clockwise direction. The prayer wheel handles gleamed from use. Gobs of grease soothed the wheels' axles, allowing an easy spin from just a light tug. The group of three seemed oblivious to us as we passed, clearly absorbed in their chant, which they repeated slowly, over and over.

A giant bodhi tree welcomed our arrival at the temple. This fig tree originated from a sapling taken from the great Bodhgaya bodhi tree in India—beneath which the first Buddha attained enlightenment—and was transplanted here in western Bhutan. We walked around the exterior of the temple, spinning the row of prayer wheels that lined its walls before entering its illustrious interior. A golden Buddha sat in the centre, and two slightly smaller statues sat on either side. Flowers had been left by previous devotees, and the fragrance of butter lamps hung in the air. They left a distinctive aroma, nothing like melting butter in a saucepan but a heavier scent that reminded me of the yak herders' huts of Tibet. After all, many of the Buddhist gurus in Bhutan had come from Tibet. The temple's walls were painted with scenes from the Divine Madman's life. His tales certainly lived on in this isolated Himalayan community.

The Chimi Lhakhang is often visited by local women keen to resolve fertility problems. The lama prescribed a special ceremony, and in return the women donated an offering for the Buddha, which in itself is not unusual. What is unique to this temple is that the women would spend the night inside. As dawn arrived, they would recount their dreams to the lama for his interpretation. The lama might reveal good news of a healthy baby on the way or warn them about an illness or other issues to be wary of for their expected little one. The practice is believed to be successful, proven by the piles of envelopes received by the temple full of photos of newborns and children born after their mothers' visits. During our stop, we were handed a photo album to flick through. Its pages were filled with pictures of smiling parents and chubby babies as evidence of the temple's potency.

I preferred to dash away before any fertility charms could take hold, but we had one final thing to do. The last time we were here, my husband had rolled the lama's dice to test our fate on our upcoming trek. He had rolled good numbers, and it was foretold we would have a good trek. On that first visit, a bird had also relieved itself—*splat*—on my husband's head, which we were told also signified good luck. I am not sure which had more effect, the dice or the bird's offering, but we certainly had a great trip. That was our Jomolhari trek in 2010; our adventure can be found in my first book, *Dust in My Pack*. It remains one of my favourite treks to this day. For our current visit, we had come to Bhutan for another multi-day excursion, the Snowman trek, and were curious what the dice would reveal.

The lama knelt over a stash of indistinguishable items tucked in the corner. He pulled out a tray with dice resting on top. After shifting the cubes to the centre, he held out the tray. My husband rolled. Fourteen. The meaning of this two-digit number was ambiguous. Fifteen would have been worse, but fourteen was inconclusive. My husband shook again. This time the dice spun and landed on seven. As the lama spoke, my husband looked into his eyes before turning to our guide, who translated. This roll had landed on a good number. Little explanation was given as to why seven was such a good number, yet we were assured it indicated a positive sign for our upcoming trek. After a little digging, we learned why the Lama Drukpa Kunley favoured the number seven. The Divine Madman was the youngest son of seven children. On one auspicious occasion, he met seven girls singing, and he drank seven servings of *chhang*, the local beer. So seven is deemed a very positive sign. Our upcoming trek, seventeen days long, would be the longest we had ever tackled, and it passed through Bhutan's northern Himalayan mountains. Refer to Chapter One: Tackling the Snowman Trek to find out how lucky we actually were.

Soon enough, the little temple filled with people seeking the Divine Madman's blessing. Parents entered with their young children and dipped down in prostration before the central Buddha statue. A prostration usually entails kneeling down on the floor and touching one's forehead to the floor, whereas a full prostration requires stretching out from head to toe, lying flat on the ground. In Bhutanese temples, one sometimes sees monks shuffling along the wooden floors wearing yak-haired socks to buff the floorboards, ready for any devoted visitors to pay their respects. As families entered the temple, I sensed the lama would soon move on to fertility blessings. This was my signal to slip out the door.

Back in the sunlight, the mood felt different. Curious yelps and muffled hollers pulsed through the air. We noticed a small group of people gathered between the grassy area surrounding the temple and a neighbouring cornfield. A cluster of white prayer flags fluttered in the breeze. Although white flags typically signify prayers for the deceased, this gathering was not a sombre one. People milled about or lounged on the ground as if gathered for a family picnic at the park. Two sticks had been wedged into the ground about twenty metres apart. *Whoosh.* A dart whizzed past. It flew towards one of the posts to my right. A couple of people cheered softly. Another monk stepped forward. Another steel dart flew by. Spectators weighed in and players critiqued the play while we stood a couple of metres back. Within a few minutes, one man eyed us and looked rather uncomfortable. A moment later, one of the monks stepped forward, gesturing with his arms to indicate that we should not take pictures. We had not taken any photos but readily agreed to tuck our cameras away. Our guide later explained that the attendees were anxious only because monks were participating. Monks are not supposed to play games and would certainly not want any evidence of such a match.

Leaving them to their game, we returned across the rice fields along a different trail. This route passed a mud-brick house. Its interior was dark, lit only by sunlight falling through the open door and scattered beams that pierced the window. A middle-aged lady in the corner sat on the floor. She had devised a one-person assembly line to make crispy rice crackers. The rice dough sat to one side. She rolled it into a ball, then plopped it onto a press. From there, she dropped the flattened patty into a large frying pan filled with bubbling oil. A few browned spheres floated beside the newly arrived white disk. While it cooked, she started her process over again. Periodically, she would swipe the crispy chips out of the oil and plop them into a basket to cool. In her final stage, she would bag these edible delights and then take them to the market to sell. I recalled seeing large clear bags of what had looked like Chinese shrimp crackers sold at market stalls, but they were actually these fried rice puffs. I wondered how many ladies did the same thing day after day. Rolling, flattening and frying. The lady we watched did not even flinch as we walked past. I am sure she was used to the intrusion by other passersby and was more interested in keeping her flow to earn an income.

As we neared the village of Sopsokha, we came across a housing construction site in progress. Handmade mud bricks lay next to our walkway to dry in the sun. A few defective blocks had been piled to one side. The good thing about manual labour is its simplicity; the downside is its precision or lack thereof. This meant the formed blocks could easily dry in a slightly irregular shape or get knocked over by a rogue puppy, leaving the pieces useless. Around town, a few new buildings stood at various stages of construction, perhaps awaiting the next load of freshly baked bricks.

Stray dogs hovered nearby, which was normal, but there seemed a greater concentration here than in other villages in Bhutan. They certainly endured a tough life on the street; one limped with a broken leg, and another was missing half of his hair. Sopsokha had no public veterinarians or services to manage stray animals. The wild dogs were left to fend for themselves, a common predicament in many places around the world. This is part of what made this place such an eclectic spot, a gorgeous fertile valley with a timeless temple trapped between the realities of hardship, hope and a drive to build a better future.

The Basics

Most useful item to pack: Small change to donate in return for a roll of the dice or fertility blessing, depending on what you seek

Useful words and phrases in Dzongkha: *kuzuzangbola* ("hello"); *kaadinchheyla* ("thank you"); *chhang* ("beer"); and *Gâti mo lhakhang* ("Where is a temple?").[3]

For more, refer to visitbhutan.com/useful_words_phrases.html.

For further travel information: Bhutan requires most foreigners to travel with a government-approved tour company and pay a regulated day rate. The government's intent is to promote high-quality, low-impact tourism. Whether you prefer to travel independently or on a group tour, it should cost about the same because of the standardized pricing system. The Tourism Council of Bhutan provides loads of information at tourism.gov.bt/plan/minimum-daily-package.

The Chimi Lhakhang, or Temple of the Divine Madman, does not have a website, but your tour company will be able to organize a visit. Refer to Chapter One: Tackling the Snowman Trek for further information on our highly recommended tour company, Rainbow Tours & Treks, and visit their site at rainbowbhutan.com.

The Chimi Lhakhang is located near Punakha, approximately eighty-five kilometres west of Thimphu. It can be visited on the same day as the Punakha Dzong, which is located at the

3. Based on Lonely Planet's *Bhutan Travel Guide* (see Bibliography).

confluence of the Pho Chu and Mo Chu rivers. Punakha Dzong is the site where Bhutan's first king, Ugyen Wangchuck, was crowned in 1907. It still functions as both a monastery and a regional administration office and is worth a visit. For more information, refer to bhutan.travel/destinations/punakha.

~~~
~~~

MYANMAR—BIKING THROUGH BAGAN'S FOUR THOUSAND TEMPLES

Roll along dusty tracks and discover ancient Buddhist temples tucked behind bushes or clustered in fields tilled by water buffalos and plows

The Experience

Across the Ayeyarwady River, low mountains offered a dramatic landscape to explore for remote temples or, at the very least, a rambling photographer's backdrop to the thousands of temples spread in front of us. This is formally known as the Bagan Archaeological Zone, a thirteen-by-eight-square-kilometre area that looks like a normal agricultural plane scattered with villages, except for one striking difference. It is the site where kings launched a temple-building spree that lasted from the tenth to the fourteenth centuries. Over four thousand temples were originally constructed, but between age and earthquakes, just over half remain. Yet the image of two and a half thousand spires peeking up over grasslands and between palm trees in a space not much bigger than downtown Manhattan leaves quite the impression. A handful of the larger temples drew crowds, leaving us a host of others to explore on our own.

Three main villages mark the temple zone: Nyaung-U, Old Bagan and New Bagan. Nyaung-U is closest to the airport and feels like a bustling centre, with markets, restaurants and hotels. Old Bagan sits a few kilometres downriver and is closer to the more popular and larger temples. New Bagan rests south of Old Bagan, and to us it felt less enticing, perhaps because it was established only in 1990. We were far south, off the main road that connects the town of Nyaung-U with Old Bagan, when we rolled through the lowlands on silent electric bikes, or ebikes. The mountain ridges added texture to the distant sky's otherwise hazy demeanour, with their outline only subtly discernible from the southern plain where we rode. Within these silhouettes of mountains and palm trees, spindles and square edges hinted at the more than two thousand temples that covered the land as they had for a thousand years.

My husband and I were keen to find our own space, our own distinct views and experiences away from the tour groups. We found the Dhamma-ya-zi-ka Zedi, a particularly pretty structure tucked along a back road in the southern part of Bagan. It was built by a local king in the twelfth century to house relics given to him by the king of Sri Lanka. I found the terms *zedi*, *pagoda*, *paya*, *pahto* and *stupa* were all used almost interchangeably to describe temples, shrines and other holy monuments in Myanmar. The rock or brick structures are often shaped like teardrops with the upper tip gilded in gold. This tip is referred to as a *hti.*

Dhamma-ya-zi-ka's exterior alone made coming this extra

distance worthwhile. Curving rainspouts dotted the levels of red brick, which were then topped with a golden *hti*. This umbrella-like ornament adorns most Buddhist temples in Myanmar. The entire structure reminded me of a gold-plated rosebud covered in thorns. Statues of lions guarded the zedi—a Buddhist monument usually in the shape of a bell. The air was still muggy, even at four o'clock. I hopped back on my ebike, eager to feel the cool breeze once again as we rode northeast towards our next target, the Wi-ni-do group of temples.

Our ebikes rolled along the dirt trail, a shortcut to our destination that bypassed the busier paved road. The sun would set within the hour, but it seemed to be working overtime as the blazing heat triggered another trickle of sweat down my back. My bike and I sailed over small ruts and around muddy sections like a smooth wave too sluggish to stir the air. We pulled into Wi-ni-do's empty parking area and left our ebikes balanced on their kickstands beneath the wispy shade of a tree. Various structures filled our view, more than the three marked on our map. This clutch of temples was constructed around 1243. As we walked beside such antiquity, the air fell silent. We were snuggled underneath a blanket of pure tranquility. We had the place to ourselves—or so we thought.

A voice emerged from somewhere nearby. "Sunset?" I could not see anyone at first in the long shadows that had started to form as the sun drifted down. We followed the voice to the edge of the main temple's terrace, below which a twenty-something-year-old man stood, puffing on a cigarette. Another had been tucked behind his ear. He wore stonewashed jeans, and his hair was styled like that of most young Myanmar men—a long, floppy top flipped over to expose short, neatly shaved sides. This one innocent word, *sunset*, opened the gateway to an unforgettable evening.

Temples of Bagan at sunset

We learned the man's name was Zaw Zaw, pronounced "Zō Zō." He was a painter by trade, while his parents both worked for the Department of Archaeology. Zaw Zaw was also the key man for the Wi-ni-do temples, just as his father had been before him and his grandfather before that. He led us over to a smaller temple in the cluster and opened a metal-grate door. Interior stairs lay just inside the entrance, which was marked by a low stone archway. He offered a flashlight before warning us to duck our heads. Beyond, it was pitch black. We pulled out our headlamps and took the narrow stairwell up to the next floor. From there, we climbed up a wooden ladder onto a narrow platform where three steps took us to the uppermost walkway. It was uncovered, and the landscape opened around us as we followed a brick ledge about half a metre wide. It wrapped around the entire exterior of the temple. The sun was quite low by this point. I gazed into the distance, where peaks of temples pierced the terrain wherever I looked. A short stretch to my left, shockingly white lights lit up a large temple called the Leimyethna Pahto. Its evening spotlights eclipsed any visible details on this ancient shrine, originally built in 1222. Elsewhere, most temples were left in darkness. Intricate pinnacles stood out as black silhouettes against the setting sun. Palm trees swayed, and starlings whizzed through the air. The sun turned the sky into flaming layers of red and orange while the misty lowlands transformed into a blueish hue before our eyes.

Three women eventually clambered up for a look. They did not stay long and soon went back down. A couple of other people arrived and set up their cameras for a short time; otherwise, we had the views from this obscure temple to ourselves. As the photographers captured the setting sun, Zaw Zaw explained the history of Wi-ni-do to me. The main temple was built in the mid-1200s by monks who lived in the area. Their labours had inspired the mother of the head monk, for she too wanted to take part in such pious efforts. So he taught her the basic methods of construction. Other local women joined the mother's undertaking because they wanted to build a temple as well. The temple standing right beside the one we stood upon was the result of their work. Zaw Zaw referred to it as the *women's temple*. Sadly, it had been badly damaged during an earthquake measuring 6.8 on the Richter scale that struck Bagan on August 24, 2016. As happened at many temples across the Bagan Archaeological Zone, the quake had knocked the decorative hti off the top of the women's temple. Pieces of the roof fell, and chunks of walls crumbled loose. However, this ill-fated temple seemed to have found its counterbalance. A man from New Zealand learned of the damage and funded its reconstruction.

Some temples around Bagan have since been repaired. Others are still undergoing reconstruction, and many wait for their turn on a long list of temples awaiting funding. Because of the damage the earthquake inflicted across the vast site, many temples were closed off entirely or access to their upper levels was barred when we visited in 2017. For example, North Guni was closed, but the adjacent South Guni was open.

One morning we were the first to arrive at the South Guni temple, long before the sun peeked over the horizon. We balanced our ebikes on their kickstands and walked through a stone archway into the temple's grounds. We still needed our headlamps at this early hour, and we tentatively climbed the narrow stairwell towards the second floor. We emerged onto an open-air platform and followed a few more steps up to our left where another raised level offered the highest point to watch the sunrise. The balcony circled South Guni's small upper chamber, inside of which a Buddha statue rested, also waiting for the morning sun. We sat down near the Buddha, and the three of us stared eastwards.

Before long, a few more early risers crept up to our vantage point and spread around the balcony to find their own space. Sunlight started to spread across the field below and shone across two dark lumps on the lower platform. Earlier, we had walked across this terrace and had seen nothing. One lump moved. Then a mop of hair emerged from the other. The person rolled over and glanced up at the eight or so people who had by now gathered on the upper level. She seemed indifferent but sluggishly nudged her friend awake. They had certainly picked a perfect view to wake up to.

Temples of Bagan at sunrise

Soon enough a local souvenir seller arrived. He looked young and was irritatingly chipper at that early hour. The rest of us seemed content to ease into the day and slowly watch as light reflected off golden pinnacles dangling on the tops of pagodas across the farmland. However, this young vendor was immune to the calm vibe and instead hopped around the group, offering postcards and kitschy ornaments, trying desperately to tempt us away from the sun's radiant reality. My husband and I soon returned down the dim stairwell and discovered South Guni's previously shadowed interior also had something to offer. Moderately preserved paintings and niches holding cement statues peppered its walls. The ground and ledges had a layer of dust from fragments broken by the earthquake but not yet swept away. Although not pristine, this perspective provided context to those temples that had been repaired. Its gritty setting seemed pure, an untouched testament to the strength that radiates across Myanmar.

One of the more remote temples that had been restored was the Tayok-Pye Pagoda. With a fresh facade, the temple was given a new name: Nara Thihapatae Hpaya. When we entered, a lone man sat on the floor near the entrance. His paintings were spread in a grid of artwork against the hard stone floor. I try to travel light and have lost interest in buying souvenirs, so I strove to avoid his eye contact. It can seem cold while so many struggle to earn a small share of the tourist market, but reality forces you to prioritize. Some moments are harder than others. This painter was one of many unassuming people we met in Myanmar. He spoke clear English and greeted us without slipping into the standard sales pitch I had grown to expect. As I inspected a mural on the wall, he stood up, walked closer and pulled out a flashlight. He shone it towards a section of the wall no bigger than a football, his paintings forgotten. Delicate brushstrokes came to life with colour where archaeologists had cleaned a small section of the wall. Just a hand's width away, dust crept over the surface, only vague hints of what lay beneath glinting through. It was easy to imagine what this temple would look like if the entire wall were restored to reveal its delicate designs.

The man explained the temple's new name when I mentioned that the sign outside did not correspond to the label on our map. Purportedly, the former name was not proper, whereas the new name honoured the king who had built the structure. My husband and I carried on farther into the interior corridor that circled the inner core of the temple. Our headlamps slit through the darkness, exposing paintings of people that held extraordinary detail for such old pieces of work. As we went to leave, the painter had returned to his designs and tore a piece of linen-like paper from his pad. His hands moved in smooth arcs, a curve here and a couple of dashed lines there. Soon, a recognizable shape began to form. Within sixty seconds, a dancing elephant holding a decorative wand in its trunk balanced on the page. He handed the drawing to me but shook off any offer of payment. By this point, his knowledge of the temple and relaxed demeanour had won me over, so I broke my rule and handed over some bills of Burmese *kyat*.

Sketch from Nara Thihapatae Hpaya

There are a lot of painters around Bagan. With such an emotive past and inspirational views, I can understand the source of their passion. At each of the more popular temples, painters place their creations on the ground in front of the entrances in hopes of catching the eye of some visitor. Their artistic work is usually quite impressive, established from training passed down through generations or from neighbour to neighbour. It offers a way to make a living in a place where few other means exist. Those who choose not to farm, or have no land to cultivate, see opportunity in tourism. Painters, sketch artists and craft makers are among the many who sit in front of their chosen temple, every day, vying to sell one more of their creations.

Between touring temples, we pedalled through the small village of Pwa-Saw. It felt like a tiny bubble of the industrial revolution, separated from the fields and dirt pathways we had passed on our way. As the dirt track we were following approached the town, palm thickets and grassy fields were replaced by thatch huts and palm-reed fences. We passed the occasional person walking, each of us sharing a comfortable smile and a wave. In the centre of town, a large hut sheltered what looked like most of the townsfolk. It was more a roof with a few pillars for support than a fully enclosed building. Residents gathered here, but each worked independently on their own projects, usually carving or lacquering gifts for tourists. These were the creators of many of the souvenirs sold around Bagan. They hardly glanced our way as we rode past. Farther along, a couple of cows were tethered at the side of the road. They looked bored, unneeded while nearly everyone was busily working at the central hut. These residents were linked to the tourist trade by their craftsmanship, yet the town seemed a world away from the busier streets of nearby Nyaung-U.

Despite such divine density of temples, the seemingly plain

farmland plays an equally influential role in Bagan's mystique. Perhaps the contrast between ancient artistry and simple necessity drives both aspects together in a balancing act that perfects the scene. Plots are small and tilled by hand. They are usually enclosed by a row of palm or tangled bushes. Earlier in the day, we had gone around a bend in the narrow red dirt track and come across a farmer with two water buffalos. The beasts were connected by a wooden post, positioned across their silvery-white shoulders and kept in place by a knobby lump high on each animal's back. They looked strong and healthy, used to pulling the plow to till the fields and sow seeds year after year. We greeted the farmer with "*Ming guh la ba*," which simply means hello. A smile spread across his weathered face. We each held up a hand, gave a nod and carried on with our activity, he to his field and we to our temples.

I found it hard to imagine the scale of Bagan's temples before I saw the site for myself. The area covers a massive expanse, encompassing multiple towns and rural communities. Of the thousands of temples, each shrine contains similar elements yet stands unique. From virtually any vantage point, hundreds of small temples poke between palm trees or stand beside a cluster of houses. It must feel strange for local residents to experience the recent influx of foreigners wandering their backyard to get a glimpse of the very sight that has laid outside their kitchen window for generations. Tourism in Bagan and Myanmar in general has picked up since the military government released its grip and democratic elections were held in 2010. International sanctions have eased, and global businesses have flourished in the capital city of Yangon. The transition has not been without challenges, such as the devastating earthquake in 2016 and severe clashes between Muslims and Buddhists in the western state of Rakhine. The country's stability remains uncertain. Yet most locals we encountered in Bagan lived simply, smiled endearingly and generally seemed unfussed by our presence.

The Basics

Most useful items to pack: A sun hat for outside the temples and a quick-dry, long-sleeved shirt to wear in the temples

Useful words and phrases in Burmese: *ming guh la ba* ("hello"); *jày zù ding ba de* ("thank you"); *hoh'gé* ("yes"); *híng ìn* ("no"); *Be hma lè...* ("Where is..."); and *zedi* ("temple").[4]

For more, refer to worldnomads.com/explore/southeast-asia/myanmar/useful-burmese-phrases-for-travelers-to-myanmar.

For further travel information: A kiosk at the Nyaung-U airport sells tickets for the Bagan Archaeological Zone. In 2017, tickets cost 25,000 kyat (approximately US$20) per person and allowed a week's access to all temples. We were asked to show our tickets at a few temples, so keep them handy when touring. Tickets are also sold at the boat jetty for those who arrive by boat along the Ayeyarwady River.

For a solid midrange hotel, I recommend Motel Zein. Rooms were spacious and clean, if slightly dated in decor. It was the staff who set this place apart. An endearing family ran the hotel and recommended two restaurants that turned out to be our favourites across all of Myanmar. For more information, refer to their website at motelzein.com.

Free maps of the temple area are available from most hotels. We

4. Based on Lonely Planet's *Myanmar (Burma) Travel Guide* (see Bibliography).

also purchased a larger map that provided slightly more detail of secondary pathways that connected various temples, which was quite useful. We purchased it at a market stall immediately before the front entrance to Shwe-zi-gon Pagoda, located on the outskirts of Nyaung-U. The map cost about US$2.

Initially, we attempted to walk to the temples, as we craved some exercise after the cramped seats of multiple flights to get to Asia and then to Bagan itself. After we had spent a couple of hours wandering in the heat and consuming a few litres of water, it was clear that foot travel was not the optimal approach. The site is massive. The sun was oppressive. A convenient alternative is to hire an ebike, which can be rented from most hotels and many stand-alone shops. We paid 6,000 kyat (approximately US$5) per bike for a full day, which included recharging if needed. The bikes ran whisper soft and were easy to manoeuvre. Our hotel also offered to come rescue us if we found ourselves stranded with a low battery. One of ours did run low just after sunset one evening, but it was near town, and we pushed it the final stretch.

~~~
~~~

MYANMAR—MEETING MONKS IN NYAUNGSHWE

Explore rural roads tucked among rice fields and discover monasteries unchanged for decades and gentle souls cloaked in serenity

The Experience

It took only one thin silver ring to jam and incapacitate my bike. We were three kilometres from our hotel, where we had borrowed the bicycle. I looked down at the simple contraption that transformed the bike from my most treasured transportation to utterly useless. A release knob was supposed to open the metal loop that was slipped around the bicycle tire to bar the spokes from rotating. It was an effective security device. I tried to turn the key, but it only slid forward slightly with minimal effect. A curse slipped through my lips, which I immediately regretted since I was kneeling beside an old, auspicious temple and a monastery.

Off the same parking area there was a new multipurpose temple that could be used as a classroom or, as it was currently, a football court. Three young monks kicked a ball around the temple-turned-arena. My husband grabbed my bike and carried it to the building's side door. He called out, "*Ming guh la ba*" ("hello"). The boys looked over hesitantly, uncertain about these strangers standing in their temple grounds. One brave boy walked forward. My husband motioned towards the bike and spoke a few slow words of English, hoping he would understand our predicament. The boy sauntered over, looked down, inserted the key and then nudged it *sideways*. Clink! The locked ring disengaged and snapped open. The secret was to slide the key sideways like a release lever after inserting it fully, not turning it as I had done. It was such a simple manoeuvre. The boy monk grinned, turned around and returned to his game. Crisis averted.

Our day had started early to coincide with the daily activities in the area. Soon after we pulled out of our hotel's driveway, around five thirty in the morning, we had met six young monks walking along the road towards us. They were headed away from town, presumably visiting the country folks who would want to give alms in the hopes of earning good karma, a common early morning ritual in Buddhist countries. The black pottery bowls carried by the young monk boys would be used to collect such charity. Like most boys anywhere in the world, they laughed at some inside joke as they walked. The two at the front of the line looked at us shyly but warmed as we greeted them with "*Ming guh la ba*." They carried on and we rode past. As we neared Nyaungshwe's main street, women on pedal bikes started to file onto the road. We stuck to side streets, away from the busier and main Yone Gyi Road.

A row of about thirty monks filed past us near Yadana Man Aung Paya, a gilded stupa, or Buddhist monument, near the centre of town.

They walked barefoot, unfussed by the rivulets of rain from the night before that now trickled along the road. The monks' maroon robes flowed loosely around their legs but were wrapped tightly around their necks for warmth in the cool morning air. Other residents wore hoodies and jackets, but we were unaccustomed to Myanmar's heat and already felt warm in our thin shirts. The monks walked in single file or in pairs, looking more solemn than the younger group we had seen outside of town. The men near the front of the line each carried a silver pot covered with a lid that doubled as a plate. They padded past us to collect their alms for the day while we rolled forward, unsure what we would find on this day.

We carried on across the town of Nyaungshwe to the teak monastery of Shwe Yaunghwe Kyaung. It was exquisite, but the adjacent stupa and temple were even more alluring. A circuit of tunnels surrounded the central stupa. The tunnel walls were covered in a network of niches, each about the size of a man's hand. Donations from people all over the world had funded the renovation of this temple. Hundreds of donors' names had been inscribed on plaques and affixed below the niches. Some displayed the donor's full name, address and country of origin, while others were more vague. One particularly cryptic label contained one word, "werehere"—a brilliant way to protect one's privacy and an indication that submission guidelines were loose. Each niche contained a Buddha statue cloaked in shiny red material. Eight thousand of these statuettes filled the tunnels. Translucent silhouettes painted on turquoise glass danced across the walls to create an ethereal ambience. In between the glass figurines, the cement walls were painted a rusty red or golden yellow.

In the middle of the temple, four shrines faced outward to align with the four cardinal directions. Each shrine was essentially a collage of shelves, statues, donations and incense, doused in sunlight that shone through the open ceiling. Purple parasols covered protective deities that stood beside golden Buddha statues. A vase of fresh flowers sat beneath the central statue alongside plastic water bottles and burning candles, all offered to the Enlightened One. We were certainly not the first visitors of the day to this vibrant sanctuary. Its calm enclosure burst with energy.

It did not take long for the sun to warm the air. We had explored everything of interest from our guidebook and were not leaving Nyaungshwe for another day. With no particular destination, we trundled along the gravel road towards the opposite end of town. As we neared the main bridge, people began to take interest. “Boat?” one man called from his motorbike as he drove slowly past us. Another fellow sat down on the bank near the bridge and motioned towards the water as we pedalled by. Each of these men would have had their own boat or, at the very least, a connection with someone who did. A string of long boats lined the water’s edge, bumping into one another with passing wakes like a symphony of ripples. This channel connected with the greater Inle Lake, the main reason most visitors came to Nyaungshwe. At this time of year, there were far more boat drivers than visitors. The men were just trying to make a living, but we were not interested in a lake tour today. With a wave, we continued along the curvy road before taking a sharp right onto a lane lined by tall, lush trees. Between the breeze from our bikes’ speed and the shade, I felt pleasantly comfortable.

To our left, houses stood on stilts a few metres off the road. They had window openings but no glass panes. Doors were left open to let breezes swirl through the living quarters. A channel of water ran underneath. Snails the size of my palm clung to river grass before slithering a few inches and disappearing into the murky water. It was unclear whether this was an offshoot from the main Inle Lake or some manmade diversion to feed the rice fields that filled any space not taken up by road or house. The area reminded me of a delta with veins of waterways feeding the land.

We turned left onto a narrow gravel route. I nudged the kickstand back into place with my foot as, once again, a dip in the pebbly road had shaken it loose. The track curved between rice paddies still drenched from the monsoon rains that had only begun to subside. At the turnoff onto this smaller track, four women sat on the ground, peeling bamboo stalks into smooth chunks. We stopped and one lady giggled shyly when I walked over to watch her work. The bright white flesh was sure to attract potential customers heading to or from town, as it proved the stalks had been freshly peeled. These women remained along the main paved route. They did not venture onto our quiet road.

A tiered tin roof that almost floated above an intricately carved teak building had caught our attention and beckoned us down this unnamed track. Other than a rice farmer's thatch lunch hut and a few shady trees, there was little else here. We rolled to a stop atop a small bridge and listened to the sounds of hammering that came from the monastery grounds. Gravel crunched as a man pedalled up behind us and stopped. We exchanged the customary greeting, "*Ming guh la ba.*" The man then switched to English and asked, "Where are you from?" Before long he invited us not only to see the Ywa Thit Monastery but also to meet his teacher.

Two large wooden doors of the teak building swung open. The interior was dark, brought to life by a wiry old monk who stepped into view after he had opened the door for us to enter. He was wrapped in the monks' customary maroon robe, which left his right arm and shoulder exposed. His thin physique was deceptive as he stealthily padded barefoot up a set of side stairs and swung open a further set of heavy-looking teak doors. The gentleman who brought us here had discreetly disappeared. Through the heavy doors lay a spacious room taking up the entire upper level of the monastery, intersected only by the occasional supportive pillar.

This little nondescript sanctuary caught me by surprise. At its far end, an arch of gold spanned the width of the room. Sunbeams from the windows that ran along both sides of the room cut through the darkness. Rays reflected across the arch's polished and ornately carved expanse. The sun's harsh light somehow seemed gentler here. Beneath its brilliance sat a row of shrines, each roughly the size of a dressing bureau. In contrast to the bright gold overhead, these pieces were made from a darkened wood and carved with extraordinary detail. A statue of Buddha sat in the centre of each one. The monk encouraged us to look around. Behind the first collection of shrines another similar lineup stood, but it faced out towards the rear windows. By their dark and almost weathered appearance, the collection looked quite old. I noticed a neatly arranged pile of shallots and another of garlic nestled on the floorboards beneath a corner window—this room was more than just a place of worship.

We were later told that the monastery had been built 127 years before, and it had been the elderly monk's home for thirty years. A life full of experience curved along his face, his eyes imparting both gentleness and liveliness when he spoke. He explained that he had become a monk at age twenty, and during the fifty-eight years since, he had lived in only two monasteries. He lived in this monastery with one other monk, but they were an industrious duo. In front of the shrines, sacks of rice and bags of packaged crackers were stacked beside cardboard boxes filled with more donated goods. These supplies were intended for an upcoming ceremony either lasting for or occurring in twenty-two days, or perhaps it was on the twenty-second day of the month—the exact description was lost to our language differences.

The old monk scurried off and returned a few minutes later carrying a plate of bananas. He insisted that we sit and eat, referring to us as his brother and sister. He explained in clearly annunciated English that the bananas were "different" varieties, even asking us to spell it out—D-I-F-F-E-R-E-N-T—implying he had only recently added it to his vocabulary. He repeated the word carefully a couple of times, seemingly to lock it in his mind. Both types of bananas were grown on the monastery grounds.

As we soon learned, the monk's not-so-secret passion lay in photography. After he had happily posed for a few shots, he motioned us towards a table sitting off to the side. Envelopes, books and an assortment of stuff were stacked underneath. Within moments, he located an envelope from Blacks Photography, a Canadian chain, and handed it to me. I delicately slid the flap open. The photos inside had been taken by another Canadian couple, who had visited this monastery three years earlier. The images were beautiful.

The monk then said something that we could not quite understand. He repeated. We were puzzled. He then slowly spelled it out for us, at times squinting his eyes in deep concentration: "S-E-L-F-I-E." I could not help but grin after hearing such a modern term coming from an elderly monk in this little, isolated monastery. So the three of us sat down on the floor as new friends and captured an unforgettable selfie.

Monk from Ywa Thit Monastery

The Basics

Most useful item to pack: Airy, three-quarter length pants, comfortable in the heat but not baggy enough to get caught in a bicycle's chain

Useful words and phrases in Burmese: *ming guh la ba* ("hello"); *jày zù ding ba de* ("thank you"); *be be' hma* ("left"); *nya be' hma* ("right"); *sháy dé dé hma* ("straight ahead"); and *Se' bàyng hngá jing ba de* ("I would like to hire a bicycle").[5]

For more, refer to worldnomads.com/explore/southeast-asia/myanmar/useful-burmese-phrases-for-travelers-to-myanmar.

For further travel information: Nyaungshwe is the town that most visitors use as a base to visit Inle Lake. The town has embraced tourism and offers a wide selection of hotels, restaurants and excursions. I expected that this influx might have tainted the town's authenticity, but it was not so difficult to peel back a few layers and uncover a more authentic side to the area.

Our favourite restaurant, the Lin Htet, is in a corner building off Yone Gyi Road, the town's main street. We were the only foreigners at its tables during our many visits, but the restaurant was consistently busy with locals, a good sign. The woman who runs the business with her sisters also offers cooking classes. Another decent option is the Golden Kite restaurant, also along Yone Gyi Road. It was the only place with functioning Wi-Fi during our visit, regardless of the many signs that were posted on the front of most cafés claiming internet service.

5. Based on Lonely Planet's *Myanmar (Burma) Travel Guide* (see Bibliography).

A Little Eco Lodge offered comfortable and spacious accommodation on a quiet country lane near town. The hotel was built on stilts, with the rooms and an eating area above ground. Weavers sat beneath one end of the building, cooled by breezes flowing through their workplace. Their looms were made from wood and stood taller than me. The ladies adeptly wove coloured threads through the warps to create intricate designs. During the day, we heard a soft purr pulsing through the air in tune with their feet as they pressed the pedals. A Little Eco Lodge also offered complimentary bicycles to help us explore the region on our own. For more information, refer to their Facebook page, @alittleecolodge, or search on Booking.com.

For another idyllic taste of the Inle region, I highly recommend staying a few nights at Inle Sanctuary. Six eco-friendly bungalows sit on stilts above Sakar Lake—often called Samkar Lake—a three-hour boat ride or two-hour drive south of Nyaungshwe. The owner and his wife prepare all the meals and focus on high-quality, sustainable tourism. They can help arrange transport there and a variety of local excursions such as visiting a nearby monastery-cum-orphanage, fishing with a local fisherman and exploring village life. For more, refer to inlesanctuary.com.

~~~
~~~

MYANMAR—BEHOLD GOLD AND TREASURE AT YANGON'S SHWEDAGON PAYA

Tread barefoot on cool tiled floors as the mayhem of the city fades into a choir of nuns in flowing pink robes and teenage boys with ruffled hair offering flowers to golden shrines and sacred spaces

The Experience

In a city where more than five million people rush about, religion still weaves a timeless rug beneath the footsteps of its residents. Yangon is Myanmar's capital and a hectic city trying to balance growing international businesses and honoured tradition. We passed shopfronts for Mercedes, BMW, Toyota, Nivea and Gloria Jean's Coffees and ducked through narrow streets crammed with street-food market stalls. We knew which stalls were best by the proportion of plastic stools that were full. If no stools were available, it was the sign of a winning grill. Nearby streets were lined with buckets brimming with fresh flowers for sale or tables piled with bananas and limes. Pedestrians had smeared a yellow paste across their cheeks as a traditional sunscreen, the Burmese favourite despite the arrival of more modern skin-care options. The residents of Yangon went to work, connected through their mobile phones, and tried to find time to pick up groceries, just like people living in big cities around the world. How did one of the oldest temples in Yangon cope with modern city life?

The towering golden spire of Shwedagon Paya was hardly visible from the labyrinth of city streets and ornate architecture until our taxi made one final turn and pulled beside its gate. We stepped through Shwedagon Paya's eastern golden gates and watched as an array of scenes unfolded in front of us. This is a place where modern pace meets traditional practice. Golden spires stretched into the air. Ravens balanced on bobbles and flitted onto electrical wires. Bands of neon lights arched around Buddha statues. A blanket of gold seemed to cascade over everything in sight. Some people sat in front of the statues; others slowly walked around. It looked like some, dressed for office jobs, had stopped by the temple to pray before starting their day. A teenage boy and his mother walked side by side, each holding a string of threaded flowers. The boy's hair splayed in various angles with bits still pressed flat from his pillow, and it looked like he had not changed from his pajama pants. His mom was not letting him off easily. She held his arm and walked with purpose in a long skirt and matching shirt, ready for their morning devotions.

A dozen girl nuns sat cross-legged on the tiled floor in front of a pair of shrines, their knees touching. Their tilted shaven heads reminded me of a cluster of rosebuds nestled among pink petals. Their pale top offset a long burgundy skirt and a burnt-orange shawl that draped from their left shoulder across their right arm. A soft melody arose from the group. Each young nun clasped a little book filled with hymns written in the exotic swirly letters of the Burmese alphabet. The graceful language seemed to fit the nuns' peaceful gathering. Just as their singing melted unobtrusively into the ambience, they dissipated like water sprinkled across the dry earth.

A pair of nuns approached a low wall in front of a row of stupas, or Buddhist monuments. Golden engraved images from Buddha's life decorated the wall's outer ledge, and an array of offerings—long white wax candles, plates of fruit and metal tubes to hold sticks of incense—had been placed along its top by visitors earlier in the morning. The little nuns lit a handful of sand-coloured incense and then touched their embers to the candles' nibs. Each movement was subtle, but its meaning was great. These offerings built merit and added positive karma, which is believed to help people move towards enlightenment and earn a better next life.

Not far away another group of nuns gathered on the floor. These girls were older. They sat behind the main walkway on a low step beneath one of the rear temples, like most teenagers who prefer to edge away from an adult's watchful eye. Turquoise booklets guided them through their mantras, or prayers, captivating them with the words. Small groups of people walked past, lost in their own thoughts and hardly taking notice of the nuns.

The physical structure of Shwedagon Paya is big and bold, but its atmosphere is soft and subtle. One man sat recounting his prayers while the lines on his skin told another story. His clothing was thin, not a bad thing in Yangon where the sun reigns during the day. The man's eyes looked beyond any person around him. Did he see the golden roofs, the spun leaves made from gold that hung from poles or the iconic pinnacles encircling the temple? I think instead he was deep inside his head, leaving any longing and suffering on the cement step he sat upon while his mind drifted high above.

Nun at Shwedagon Paya

Farther along, three people stood in front of the Monday planetary post. Eight such shrines are staggered around the temple, one for each day of the week with two for Wednesday. People usually visit the day that corresponds to the day on which they were born. This practice relates to astrology, an integral part of Buddhism. Myanmar astrology recognizes eight ruling planets, each linked to a distinctive animal and day of the week, adapting to the seven-day week by splitting Wednesday across two planets. For example, Sunday is associated with the mythical *garuda* ("legendary bird-like creature") while a tiger represents Monday.

I watched as one lady poured water over the Monday post. She poured three ladles, which could have meant she was born on the third day of the month or her lama had advised her to pour this auspicious number of cups on this particular planetary post to appease an ill-fortuned spirit or pestering planet that was causing her harm. Another person held a small bunch of flowers, awaiting her turn to tuck the bouquet into a vacant space at the base of the shrine before dousing it with her water offering. People tend to send wishes along with their prayers when they visit these planetary posts. It is all part of a process believed to attract good karma and bring them a better future.

There was a lot to take in at the Shwedagon Paya. It was not a single temple sitting by its lonesome on a hilltop, but a lavish central site surrounded by a network of sacred shrines. The main stupa itself curves to a point reaching 110 metres in height. Its exterior is sheathed in gold plates and encrusted in over four thousand diamonds. Deep inside the temple, eight strands of Buddha's hair are believed to be held. They are protected by not only gold but also layer upon layer of silver, copper, bronze, iron, marble and brick, all encasing the saintly relic. Stories swirl about this site. Centuries earlier, Queen Shinsawbu donated her weight in gold only to be outdone by her son-in-law, who gave four times his weight. Most shrines across Myanmar are topped by a parasol made of gold—called a *hti*—while Shwedagon Paya has added tiny golden insignias that fluttered as an ensemble across its temple peaks. Crows seem particularly fascinated by these dangly pieces. One bird was determined to disconnect a too-tempting sparkly object as the perfect nest ornament or possibly a gift for his raveness-to-be.

Shwedagon Paya at sunset

Around the central stupa stand an assortment of temples, pagodas, giant bells, a bodhi tree and other sacred sites. The occasional sanctuary painted bright white stands out like a snowflake in a storm of gold. A pair of *chinthe* statues, mythical guardians that look part lion and part dragon, protect many of the structures. As we walked around, there was continual movement through the passageways on the outskirts of the temple, often as much as along the main walkway. As some people entered, others left. Beneath one shrine, a middle-aged nun sat cross-legged with her arms held up and her palms pressed flat together. The sun burst across her delicate pink robe and lit the golden wall behind her. Her forehead was creased in concentration, and she was oblivious to the activity around her. She was another patron lost in her own thoughts, sitting alone but integral to the overall mood. A few steps away, an older gentleman walked past, also engrossed in his musings while twirling a string of *malas* ("prayer beads") between his fingers.

Temples have occupied the Shwedagon Paya site for 2,500 years. Over that period, structures have crumbled, and shrines have fallen. Earthquakes have rumbled beneath the earth, and wars have ravaged the lands. With every wound, the paya has been rebuilt, cracks filled and gold leaves reapplied. Maintenance continues to this day. While I sat beside one stupa, I heard clunking sounds behind me. Curious, I went to investigate. Gnarled bamboo stalks had been bound together to form scaffolding around a small temple. About five workmen hammered, held and lifted boards onto the wobbly-looking platform. A Burmese woman and her son, only a couple of years old, stood watching. The boy was intrigued and attempted to drag a four-metre piece of bamboo that was lying on the ground. Eventually, a workman came over and took the piece from the wee boy. There were no hard hats or safety straps, but a reliance on a shared responsibility to look after oneself and each other. Such resiliency was a common trait I noticed across Myanmar. People had learned how to cope, to accept and support one another in an unpredictable life.

The Basics

Most useful item to pack: Slip-on sandals

Useful words and phrases in Burmese: *ming guh la ba* ("hello"); *jày zù ding ba de* ("thank you"); *hoh'gé* ("yes"); *híng ìn* ("no"); and *Da poun yai lo ya mala?* ("May I take a photograph").[6]

For more, refer to worldnomads.com/explore/southeast-asia/myanmar/useful-burmese-phrases-for-travelers-to-myanmar.

For further travel information: Sunrise and sunset are the coolest times to visit Shwedagon Paya. Watching the evening rituals as a line of floor sweepers congregated and pushed off in unison to circle the entire temple was entertaining in itself. Alternatively, visit in the early morning and listen to young nuns sing their mantras. Become absorbed in the charms of the temple as the sun's rays light up each hti and mini-shrine that together form a village-like collage around the main temple.

The temple opens at 4:00 a.m. and closes at 10:00 p.m. Entrance fees for nonresidents were 8,000 kyat (approximately US$6) per person in 2017. Visitors' clothing should cover the knees and elbows. Be prepared to walk barefoot as is customary at all temples in Myanmar. Some countries in Asia allow socks in Buddhist temples, but they are not appropriate in Myanmar. For more information, refer to the temple's website at shwedagonpagoda.com.

~~~

6. Based on Lonely Planet's *Myanmar (Burma) Travel Guide* (see Bibliography).
~~~

SRI LANKA—WALKING WITH PILGRIMS AT MIHINTALE

Wander a sacred hill's jumble of cherished sites and watch it transform as the sun rises and hundreds of white-clad devotees ascend its peak

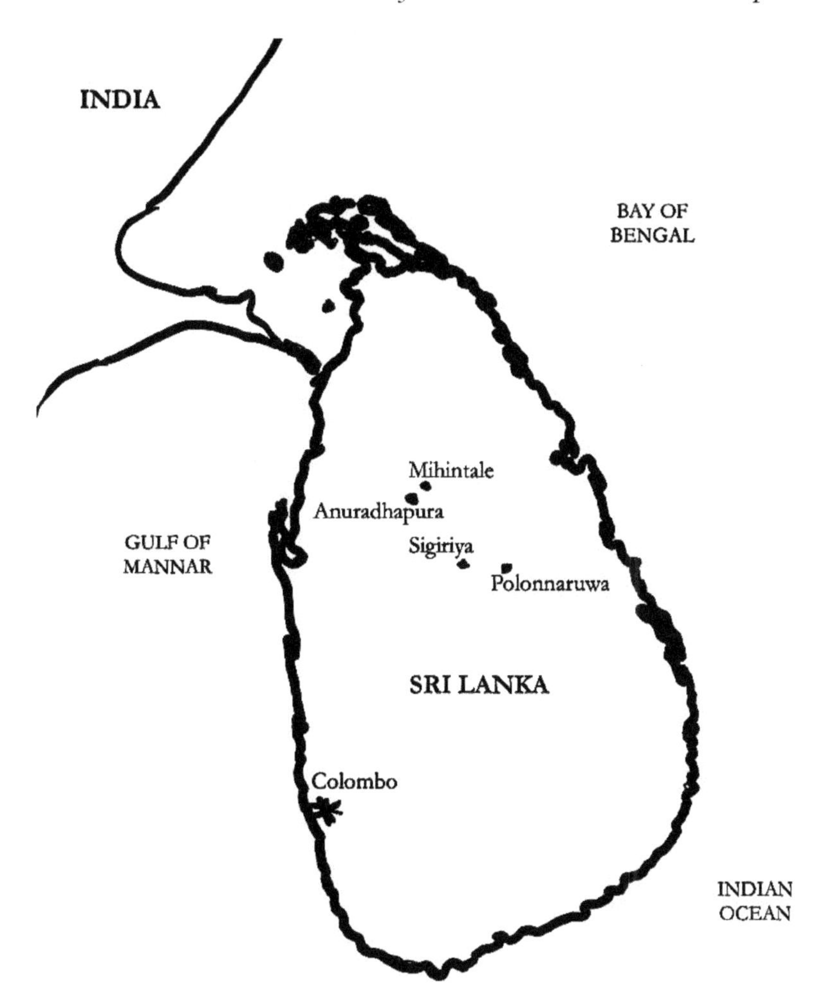

The Experience

I peeled the curtains aside and looked out onto the dark yard and quiet roadway that lay just beyond our hotel window. It was hard to pull myself out of bed and shake the sleep away, but I knew we would return in a few hours to a sumptuous breakfast and savoury cup of coffee. The clock read four thirty. My husband and I tiptoed down the outdoor stairwell, aware that the sound of our footsteps carried and there was another guest sleeping in the room at the top of the stairs. The hotel's tuk-tuk driver rolled his three-wheeled vehicle to meet us at the front entrance. I ducked through its open door and slid across the seat. Once inside, he handed us a big bottle of water and a spare umbrella, as the rainy season was ready to pounce on central Sri Lanka. During the previous afternoon, rain had scoured the streets of Anuradhapura for nearly three hours. This morning, the road was dry when our driver pushed the tuk-tuk backwards onto the barren lane and then switched on its ignition.

By five o'clock, the otherwise quiet road had transformed. Vehicles condensed and traffic slowed to a crawl. Our tuk-tuk edged forward. Automobiles squeezed into the right lane because the left lane had been taken over by a throng of people. The walkers seemed to glow in the darkness, but it was only the effect of the headlights reflecting off their white clothing while everything else was shrouded in darkness. Their dress varied between T-shirts, long-sleeved button-down shirts, flowing skirts and cotton pants. Some had fancy lace while others wore plain cotton, but the colour was consistently white for purity. Midway through the crowd, a gold-rimmed glass box balanced across the shoulders of a small group of men. Neon lights lit up the chest, which protected a mysterious yet sparkly bodhi tree inside.

The road had become thick with vehicles heading in the same direction as the pilgrims. Our driver proceeded patiently as his engine burst with a cadence reminding me of corn kernels softly popping. He then saw an opening and revved the motor, and our little carriage sailed between the slow-moving cars to our right and even slower pedestrians to our left. At the front of the procession, we passed a band leading the people. The musicians also wore white but had added red and black explosions of colour. Some pounded on drums hung around their necks while others blew into flutes. The melody sounded both turbulent and exotic to my ear. We had merely come to watch the sunrise over the ancient temple of Mihintale but had arrived during a *poya* ("full moon") celebration.

We had the advantage, for our tiny tuk-tuk could slip through narrow gaps in the traffic impassable by most cars. The worshippers walked at a slow pace, which was fine since our goal was to arrive at the temple before them to get a taste of its solitude. Only a couple of people were at the base of the stairs when we arrived. The ticket collector opened his kiosk and charged a relatively minor fee, less than US$5 per person. From there, we began our ascent up 1,843 steps that led visitors to the peak of Mihintale's rock temple. Sacred spaces, carved caverns and palm trees were scattered on the walk. Mist rolled over the mountain temple and greeted the sun with a hazy glow, hardly the dazzling dawn we had expected to awaken these stone pillars and ritualistic rocks.

There is no obvious main temple at Mihintale. Ambasthale Dagoba is the most central shrine, with its domed stupa lit up by a thousand bulbs of blue, red, yellow and white strung in rows. Ancient pillars topped with flowery carvings surround the dagoba. Nearby, a statue of the first king to accept Buddhism into Sri Lanka watches over his kingdom with stony eyes. From his initial awareness of the Buddhism ideology, the temple of Mihintale was born. Pathways and steps lead in various directions from the Ambasthale Dagoba to higher temples or side sanctuaries that have been cut from stone boulders. One set of grooves travels up a section of exposed rock to a lookout. On this morning, fog swirled around us at the highest ledge and hid what lay below. Soon, the thumping of drums and piercing horns lured us back to the lower levels for an entirely different sight. The mass of pilgrims had arrived, emerging from the haze.

Ambasthale Dagoba at dawn

The musicians emanated emotion while the dancers radiated motion. In baggy white pants, dancers leapt from foot to foot, gyrating as if under some mystical incantation. A silver pendant covered each of their chests. It was strapped on with silver bands that wrapped around their shoulders and waist, secured by a pair of matching silver shoulder pads. Lustrous earrings dangled down to their shoulders. Each metallic piece shimmered as it fluttered. The group paused at the plateau beside the Ambasthale Dagoba. Band members stepped to the side to create an open space into which younger dancers jumped to lead the show. Their moves were a little like a breakdance contest as, one by one, each entertainer took the centre stage. The dancers flipped and twisted in mid-air. Each manoeuvre would have taken hours of practice. The crowd circled, and the locals were as dazzled as we were.

One performer lunged in and then began to stomp his foot. He spun faster and faster, all while stamping to propel himself around and around with one leg while balancing on the other foot. Charm bracelets tied around his ankles jangled with his movement. Just before the point of losing control, he halted and nonchalantly skipped out of the ring. Another man bounded across the sandy space, flinging his body upside down in a string of back springs. He was replaced by a third acrobat who performed an even longer sequence of flips across the dirt ground. Their individual displays continued for about five minutes before they converged once more and performed a choreographed set. It reminded me of Bollywood, but Sri Lankan style. Arms shook, legs kicked, bodies flailed and the men kept in sync with one another. Our cloud-covered sunrise was soon forgotten.

Dancing continued intermittently over the next twenty minutes. During each break, the congregation of white-clad pilgrims walked a little farther. Eventually, the dancers passed the lead role back to the band as smoothly as stretching soft buttery toffee. Band members stepped forward and the people followed. Some percussionists looked like they had been playing for decades, while others might have been performing for only a few years. I imagined it was a skill passed down through generations, with each drummer immersed in his role. It must have carried an element of respect, elevated with impressive costumes that stood out against the simple white clothing of everyone around them.

Drummers during poya ("full moon") celebration

Red, black and white satin was stitched into a decorative sash that the members wore slung around their neck and shoulders. A flowing white sarong hung to their knees or ankles and was cinched with bright red swaths of material wrapped tightly around their torso.

Brass rings encircled their bare forearms. A drum hung from their neck on a string of white beads. The instruments were decorated to match the players' attire, and white and black turbans completed their masterful look. The players were proud of their craft, poised with perfect posture for their essential role in the ceremony. Then, just as smoothly, they slid into silence, and the monks took over.

Eventually, the mass of people shifted to an alcove behind the Ambasthale Dagoba. From here, Mihintale's monastery, the monks' refectory, a relic house and a couple of windy pathways extended from a small courtyard that was now full of people sitting cross-legged wherever they could find space. We joined the crowd and found a vacant slice of concrete on the terrace. From there, we were only metres from a row of monks who appeared ready to start the next phase of today's pilgrimage. The golden box that had been carried up to the hilltop temple on the pilgrims' shoulders rested on a table in front of the monks. The glistening bodhi tree had been removed and sat beside the chest. First, the head monk spoke. After his prayer and message, a lady in the audience addressed the monks and then held the bodhi tree on top of her head. The audience replied in unison before the older monk addressed the crowd once more. Although I could not understand the Sinhalese, it seemed the woman had asked for guidance and received advice and a blessing from the monks, along with confirmation from her peers. The ceremony was brought to a close when the monk shared a few additional words of wisdom and the crowd slowly scattered. This was the most sombre part of the celebration.

Soon after, the band resumed. Drummers led the crowd to various sites around the temple rock, and a short ritual was performed at each location. The golden box with the silver bodhi tree played a key role. Bystanders put their palms together and touched the golden platter whenever it passed by. The drummers rapped. The flutists played a tune, and the audience recited a short verse in unison before moving on to the next site to start the process over again. A few members ventured away from the group to explore the area on their own, giving us the feeling that we were nearing the end of the formal proceedings. The fog had mostly burned away, revealing walkways that led in nearly every direction. We wandered up over boulders chipped with small footholds and along pathways to remnants of ancient shrines overlooking the tangled jungle of the lowlands.

Ruins, caves and temple grounds were sprinkled all over Mihintale's hillside complex. Renovations had taken over one section, implying more temples lay beneath its construction tarp. Nearby, a couple of older ladies scrambled up a rocky outcrop. Their toes gripped notches carved into the slippery slope while a metal railing offered additional support. Although the fog had cleared, its damp residue clung to the rounded surface, which was still worth the climb to reach a higher sanctuary. I chatted with one of the ladies, who cheerfully told me she was seventy-three years old. Age is revered in Sri Lankan society, something to be proud of and respected.

Back at the main plateau, many of the pilgrims had dispersed, and the mood had shifted. Tension curdled. Families clustered and groups of three or four people huddled together. I heard soft whimpering. A young boy, perhaps aged seven, hung his head while his mother and father hovered around him. He wore a distinctive white robe, and a cotton head scarf was tied tightly and knotted into a fan shape that stood straight up from the boy's head. Something was clearly going on around us, but exactly what it was mystified me. I spotted another boy dressed in a similar white outfit, looking similarly pensive.

Eventually five boys in these peculiar white robes emerged from the gathering and lined up together. They stood in the open area in front of the monks' relic building. Two monks led them towards the Ambasthale Dagoba, and their families followed. The monks sat on the floor, and the boys copied their movements. Everyone else gathered around closely. White mats had been placed on the ground, along with five rolled-up monks' robes. Mantras were spoken, and the boys tentatively repeated the sacred verbiage. Their hands fluttered with uncertainty, and the senior monks helped the young novices. A lady standing beside me pressed me forward to ensure I could see. Then an older lady nudged me farther still in front of the crowd for a clear view of the entire event. She kept her hand on my back, ensuring I felt part of the process.

The boys' expressions alternated between uncertainty, reflective bewilderment and nervous shyness. As the ceremony on the floor of the temple progressed, their confidence grew little by little. The older monks sitting across from the boys acted as mentors, correcting a movement or repeating the mantra. The boys' families stood in the front rows and looked down on their soon-to-be-monk sons, resisting tears that were determined to overflow before being swiped across their cheeks. One woman pressed her palms together as her brows furrowed, and she leaned against one of the ancient stone pillars as if her legs were not quite willing to support her. I could almost read the words running through her head: "What will become of my baby?" Grandfathers held onto grandmothers. Sisters clutched aunts.

Novice monks at Ambasthale Dagoba

A final ceremony was conducted, and the boys held up their hands in prayer. They struggled to follow a new, strange protocol that in time would become natural. But at this moment, in front of everyone dear to them, it felt awkward. The monks handed the orange robes to them, and their white hats were removed to expose freshly shaven heads. Young eyes shone wide. Eventually, the monks, new and experienced, stood up and walked single file back to their quarters. It must have been such an emotional turmoil for the families, happy for a son or grandchild to become the holiest of persons yet sad for them to leave at such a fragile age. What inspired each boy—a personal decision or the harsh reality of economics when families cannot afford to feed and school their children?

The Basics

Most useful item to pack: A notebook to capture the miscellany of details and contrasts that unfold, often unexpectedly

Useful words and phrases in Sinhalese: *aayu-bowan* ("hello"); *owu* ("yes"); *naha* ("no"); *istuh-tee* ("thank you"); and *karuna kara* ("please").[7]

For further travel information: Mihintale can be visited as an easy day trip from the ancient city of Anuradhapura. The site is considered the birthplace of Buddhism in Sri Lanka. On this hill in 247 BC, King Devanampiya Tissa of Anuradhapura met Mahinda, the son of India's emperor Ashoka. Their discussions led to the king's conversion to Buddhism and its subsequent introduction to the people of Sri Lanka. Ever since, Mihintale has been considered sacred. Temples, monasteries, caves and even an ancient hospital were built on this hill. For more information, refer to lanka.com/about/attractions/mihintale-mountain.

We took advantage of our hotel's reliable in-house tuk-tuk

7. Based on Lonely Planet's *Sri Lanka Travel Guide* (see Bibliography).

service to travel in the wee hours of the morning to the hilltop temple of Mihintale. Viewing the ancient ruins at sunrise was our goal, and returning to our hotel for a full breakfast instilled motivation to get up so early. Our driver pointed out and explained a few of the ruins scattered around the parking area and along narrow pathways that we would not have otherwise noticed.

The friendly Kutumbaya Resort is a solid choice for accommodation. Its rooms were recently built in a modern, cement-deco style with a partially open-air ensuite. Staff are incredibly friendly and helpful in arranging transport, either long distance between cities or within the Anuradhapura area. They also prepare evening meals upon request. The owner was in the process of building a café and planned to add soundproofed windows and doors to the rooms after we left. For more information, refer to their Facebook page, @kutumbayaresort, or search on Booking.com.

~~~
~~~

SRI LANKA—SCRAMBLING UP THE BOULDER TEMPLE OF PIDURANGALA

Meet a reclining Buddha carved into the rock face before your final scramble up Pidurangala Rock for views of a tropical valley and Sri Lanka's iconic Lion Rock

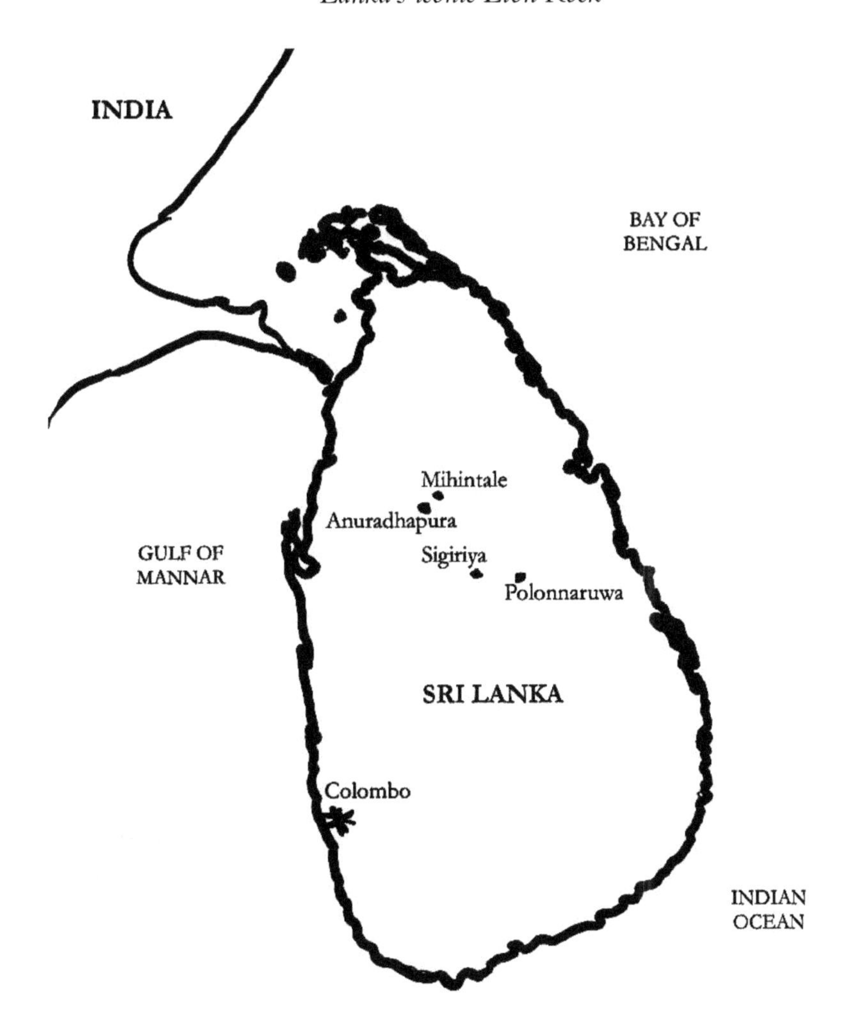

The Experience

We had come to Sigiriya to climb what Sri Lankans call the eighth wonder of the world, the town's namesake, Sigiriya ("Lion Rock").[8] The ancient fortress, built on top of a rock outcrop that dominates the lush flatlands of central Sri Lanka, beckoned us to climb its smooth expanse. It was not the rock alone that we found appealing. Frescoes and caves carved into its walls centuries ago led to ruins of a disappeared kingdom. This pinnacle lies on the massive boulder's upper plateau. Getting to this place, however, would prove tricky due to a combination of a rickety staircase along exposed sections of the boulder's edge and monsoon rains that not only made the path slick but also dampened the views.

As we pulled into our guesthouse's driveway, Mother Nature decided to highlight our conundrum. Big raindrops began to splatter across our taxi's windshield. The monsoon season had arrived with a vengeance, and within a few minutes, the rain obliterated our visibility to a few metres. While we sat on our guesthouse's veranda, the walkway turned from carefully placed stepping stones into soggy puddles and finally rushing rivulets that spread across the yard with muddy tentacles, all within the first thirty minutes of our arrival.

The guesthouse owner, a young energetic man, joined us on the roof-covered patio. He had grown up in the town of Sigiriya and had watched as tourism exploded after Sri Lanka's civil war ended. New hotels had opened, and entrance fees had risen. In 2017, it cost US$25 per person to climb the esteemed Lion Rock. Gates did not open until 8:30 a.m., removing any chance to climb in the cooler hours before sunrise. As we talked, he told us about some less commercialized activities in the region such as wild-elephant viewing and little-

8. sigiriyatourism.com

known temples. There was a smaller yet similar rock temple that overlooked Lion Rock. Its name was Pidurangala Rock, but it was usually referred to simply as Little Rock. Entrance fees were 500 rupees (equivalent to US$3), and the ticket office opened at 5:00 a.m., definitely preferable as it would allow us to avoid the daily rains and muggy afternoons. As the three of us drank tea, rain splattered on the edge of the terrace, and pellets ricocheted off the tin roof like a steel drummer spellbound in his rhythm. An early morning start seemed considerably better than a soggy afternoon spent climbing Lion Rock.

By four forty-five the next morning, the driveway had drained. The owner's friend and tuk-tuk driver waited for us. His headlights illuminated a patch in front of his vehicle, providing just enough visibility to see the road ahead or any elephants that might be lurking in the ditch. As we drove, I peered into the matte black curtain that embraced us but did not spot any glinting elephant eyes staring back. The gravel road widened marginally, and our driver slowed to a stop. Initially, the area seemed deserted. Then as our eyes adjusted, we saw the ticket shack on one side of the road and a small sign pointing towards the trail on the other side.

The light from our headlamps exposed stone steps that led around a smooth rock wall. We passed a caretaker's home and a small temple before the wide stairs gradually turned into footholds carved directly into the rocky ground. In some sections, tree roots acted as both our step and our handrail. A light mist began to spread through the air as the walkway narrowed. Large boulders stood on either side of us. Around one bend, the boulders gave way to jungle. Then the hillside opened like a gaping mouth to reveal a giant reclining Buddha carved directly into the rock face.

The path continued upwards. Sunlight flickered between leaves, exposing what lay beneath the shadows. The last section threw in a mild scramble with a couple of narrow squeezes that hugged our daypacks as we slid through. After emerging from this grasp, we met a large boulder that blocked our path. Pidurangala's top lay just above where we stood. Scrapes from previous, more daring visitors revealed a steep route above a shallow crevasse, a thoroughly unenticing option. Instead we decided to follow what we expected to be a dead end, if only to get an alternative view.

As we stepped around a ledge circling the boulder, a gently sloping path emerged. This hidden route led directly to the top of Pidurangala Rock. As we climbed, the lowlands spread below us, and Lion Rock stood resolute in the distance. As on Lion Rock, a large stone plateau marked Pidurangala's apex, but without any archaeological ruins. Clouds obscured the sun's golden salute, yet the valley below revealed misty farmlands and a vast palm forest. One other couple sat at the far end of the rock. Shortly, two more women reached the top. I was not convinced we would gain much better views from the larger Lion Rock, especially later in the day when the clouds would most likely converge and thousands of raindrops would be the sight most visible. We could see rickety scaffolding wrapping the distant rock to support the many visitors that hike Lion Rock daily.

By the time we started down, it had started to drizzle. Soon after we were tucked back inside our tuk-tuk, the sprinkle turned to drops that echoed against the tuk-tuk's canvas cover. Once we were back at our guesthouse for breakfast, the skies erupted. I slipped off my sandals and walked ankle deep in the newly formed stream that covered the walkway back to our room. Any desire to climb Lion Rock faded as we settled down to enjoy steaming roti and caramelized coconut.

Sigiriya ("Lion Rock")

The Basics

Most useful items to pack: A rain jacket and walking sandals

Useful words and phrases in Sinhalese: *aayu-bowan* ("hello"); *istuh-tee* ("thank you"); *Ehika kiyatada arinneh?* ("What time does it open?"); and *koh pi* ("coffee").[9]

For further travel information: The Otunna Guest House is a standout for its friendly owner and home-cooked meals. A private veranda welcomed us to a spacious and clean room. The owner's mother prepared a delicious dinner of vegetable curry, rice, potatoes and fruit. The flavours had depth and surpassed any other meal we had in Sri Lanka. Breakfast was similarly outstanding, with steaming roti served alongside a chunky spread of fresh coconut with onion and chili and additional plates of caramelized-coconut-filled roti, eggs and a massive

9. Based on Lonely Planet's *Sri Lanka Travel Guide* (see Bibliography).

platter of fresh fruit. Just thinking of it triggers a craving for another helping. The owner is passionate about supporting local, sustainable tourism. He can help arrange wild-elephant tours, hikes to lesser-known temples and visits to other sites in the area. At the time of writing, Otunna Guest House did not have its own website, but details can be found on their Facebook page, The Otunna Guest House Sigiriya, or by searching TripAdvisor and Booking.com.

For more on Sigiriya, refer to sigiriyatourism.com.

~~~
~~~

4

Rare Festivals

One of the quickest means to gain a sense of a place is to step inside a local festival. Some of my best memories have come from stumbling upon a quirky festival and letting myself become immersed in the unexpected. It can feel like you have been handed a looking glass through which the elements of a place explode with clarity. All these fragments carry people's stories, strung together by a cohesiveness that gives residents the strength of tradition to launch forward in an uncertain future. For an outsider, festivities of an unfamiliar culture magnify deeper layers within these communities. They yield a grain of understanding that would otherwise lie dormant as you wander ancient sites or remote spaces vacant of activity. And from my experience, locals enjoy the shows as much as I do.

From Asia's Bhutan to a tiny island in Africa, each festival in this chapter tells a unique story.

The tiny country of Bhutan is awash with festivals. Dates change annually. Delays are common. But Bhutan's truly unparalleled festivals are worth the effort and flexibility in your itinerary. Regional festivals weave music and local folklore across days of masked dancing, Buddhist chants and symbolic practices into an intimate extravaganza unlike anything I have seen before.

The first section of this chapter captures the most unforgettable moments from the Sakteng Valley in the far east of Bhutan, a region opened to foreign tourism only in 2010. It took two days of trekking to reach the village of Sakteng; for more on the trek refer to Chapter One. In reverence of the great yak, herders performed a dance representing the taming of the beast. The entire town came out to watch and cower in mock fear of the life-sized dancing yak, surrounded by forest-clad mountains, buckwheat fields and prayer flags. It was also the time of year when families perform their annual cleansing ritual, or *Jalashi* ceremony. The second section of this chapter reveals our personal encounters when we were invited into their homes to watch as lamas chanted mantras, monks boomed *ngas* ("hand-held drums") and everyone shared in homemade *arra*, a fiery homemade liquor.

The third section shifts to central Bhutan, where we trod through mud in a dark mountain valley to join monks and locals alike beneath a burning arch of branches. Shadows leapt across people's faces as the fire purified the area of evil spirits. Performers had tied wooden masks around their faces, carved decades earlier and used for generations. A measured tempo reverberated from hand-held drums, and horns howled a slow, rhythmic refrain. This evening launched a multi-day festival of dances and religious mantras.

The fourth section captures Bhutan's capital city of Thimphu in the western end of the country. We attended a special ceremony that takes place every nine to ten years. Inside a relatively new gigantic Buddha statue, ancient scripts of Buddhism were reviewed and restored by a small team of monks. While they worked diligently inside, an entourage of monks from surrounding communities sat outside and chanted mantras in unison with a head lama's throaty call. The entire process took three months to complete.

Just north of Bhutan, in China's Tibet Autonomous Region, we encountered another festival that seemed lost in another time. Monks unrolled a giant hand-knotted *thangka*, a carpet the size of a mansion, down the cliffs overlooking the ancient city of Gyantse. Leading up to this grand event, the town held fire puja ceremonies and masked dancing while locals conducted their personal *koras*, a religious walk intended to release their spirits of past wrongdoings. The wholehearted dedication that seemed to envelope the town led to a captivating experience that shed new perspective on the Buddhist practices in Tibet.

The final festival covered in this chapter was purely for entertainment purposes. On Likoma Island, a parody of observations about Malawi's former colonial military from the perspective of local recruits had morphed into a dance competition. Music screeched from hollowed gourds, and uniforms were topped with hats made from strips of newspaper and feather plumes. This performance was a completely unexpected event and one of the most memorable from our time on the island.

These festivities are just a taste of the dynamic scenes we have encountered around the world. Tradition wrapped in unique local customs revealed themselves and in effect allowed us to delve one layer deeper into the essence of the places we were so lucky to see.

~~~
~~~

BHUTAN—UNMASKING THE YAK CHAM

Watch yak herders return from the hills to perform a truly enigmatic yak cham *in the fields of the Sakteng Valley*

The Experience

I sat at the edge of town, beside a low stone wall. Its rough edges circled the village of Sakteng, separating the houses from the fields. Pastures extended towards the horizon before being intercepted by rugged mountains. The farmland was not idyllic meadow but the kind with misshapen rocks and irregular ridges. Grass was barely visible after alpine sheep had grazed its tantalizing sprouts from the lumpy ground. A couple of children stretched out along a knoll and waited for something to occur. I waited too. Clouds churned across the sky, threatening rain but restraining themselves for the moment. Pockets of mist hovered and swirled farther down the valley. I could have been looking at the foothills of the Canadian

Rocky Mountains—except for the clusters of prayer flags dotting the landscape and Buddhist temples poised atop ridges.

Flagpoles were planted in seemingly random—but most certainly auspicious—positions around the village. They speckled the hillside, tickled by a steady breeze. I could just see the outline of Borongshi Goemba ("monastery") from where I sat. Its dark silhouette revealed an ancient temple above the terraced buckwheat fields bordering Sakteng. The monks living in the goemba had moved on to a more accessible monastery in recent months, leaving only an elderly caretaker. On the following day, we visited the monastery and met its caretaker. She showed us centuries-old paintings and handed us a butter lamp to light as an offering to Buddha before we returned to Sakteng.

No roads lead to this village, although that may change in coming years. For now, locals travel by foot and carry in everything with the help of yaks or horses. My husband, two friends and I had hiked for two days to reach this valley's distinctive culture, hidden from much of the outside world. When we arrived in the village of Sakteng, children scampered past, shy and nervous of our strange faces and odd clothing. Electricity was introduced only a few years ago. Houses are constructed of stone and timber beams, as they have been for centuries. The wood is stained a dark brown, sometimes painted with intricate flower designs and embellished with carvings, a look unique to Bhutan. Stone walls line the walkways meandering through town. As I sat, smoke twirled into the air, rising above intermittent homes. Families here burn juniper branches inside shrines carved into the rock fences surrounding their homes to awaken and send their respects to the local mountain deity. I felt as if I had stepped through a time warp, into a mystical land where Buddhism runs deep and tribal tradition permeates even deeper.

We spent two days in the village. They were full days packed with emotive moments and unexpected insights. This gem of a destination completed the final days of our five-week trek across some of the most remote regions of the Himalaya (see Chapter One). Yet this little community left more of an impact than I expected. Perhaps it was the people's sincerity, their unassuming openness to share a culture so different from my own. The Brokpas, a semi-nomadic people, settled in Sakteng and Merak. These two villages are nestled in the highlands of eastern Bhutan, which opened to tourists only in 2010. The people seemed to balance a subtle sense of humour with a gritty resiliency, imperative to life in such remote territory.

My thoughts returned to the present moment as I sat in my plastic chair out in the field. Four men had gathered beside a furry mound, its charcoal-coloured hair shimmering in the sunlight. I silently watched as the blackened face, nearly as long as my arm, dipped and charged. White scarves dangled from its black polished horns, fluttering in the wind as the creature galloped towards me. The drumbeat quickened like a rumbling heartbeat that echoed across the valley. The animal did not have such a smooth gait; it was more of a lopsided trot. Two men beneath the yak costume stepped slightly out of sync. Yet the brute's towering stance and penetrating eyes created the illusion of an overbearing beast.

The yak's wooden mask leaned in towards me. The head bobbed and then wobbled. Its forehead was marked by a white ring of paint around a blob of red ink. Above this circle, a silver medallion had been stuck. The creature kneeled and lowered its head. Its mask swayed once more. I patted the rough wood, and it wobbled in response. I rubbed behind its ears, which only encouraged the costumed duo to nuzzle the yak's face against my leg. After I had pressed some small bills of *ngultrum* into the hands of one of the dancers, the team seem appeased, and the yak backed away. I was witnessing a special dance in honour of the Brokpas' most revered animal, the yak. The *yak cham* ("yak dance") is said to represent the taming of the wild beast. It is performed out of reverence for the great animal. The people of Sakteng rely on yaks as a source of income, transport, clothing and, on occasion, sustenance. In this Buddhist society, killing is forbidden, but in practice, eating the meat of an animal already dead is accepted.

The lead performer held a *nga* ("hand-held drum"), thumping it with a thin S-shaped wand made from wood. A simple yet resonate melody flowed across the field. Three other men wore carved wooden masks strapped to their faces, with each facade painted a different colour: ochre, brown and black. Wide carved smiles and plump cheeks defined these images. The dancers wore identical brown felt jackets, adorned with embroidered panels that hung from their necks down to their knees. Multi-coloured ribbons were wrapped around their torsos, both for decoration and to prevent the colourful panels from swinging in the men's way as they bounded around. Some strips trailed at their waists, flinging as they kicked their feet and spun. Two more dancers hid beneath the massive yak costume, about the size of the real animal. All six men wore rubber boots, which now functioned as essential dancing shoes for this unusual performance.

The drummer stood to the side. His tempo signalled slight changes to the dance, moving to a new scene or a different song. The trio of dancers often approached the hairy yak. They hopped forward and then skipped back to avert the lunging brute. A goddess, her neck adorned with beaded necklaces and amulets, sat on the yak's back. Although only the size of a small child, the effigy exuded opulence. Her face mask was painted white with rosy cheeks and crimson lips.

Her hands were held up as if to convey her power—she needed no reins. Flowers painted orange and green decorated an elaborate headdress from which red, yellow and blue fans stuck out in place of her ears. Like the yak's face mask, the figurine swayed from side to side as the animal danced.

Villagers performing the Yak Cham

Aunty

About thirty people from the village joined us in the field. Children clustered together and watched as if in a trance. An elderly lady lay on the grass, instinctively rolling a set of orange prayer beads between her fingers. Her hair was cut short in a pixie hairstyle beneath a rose-coloured wool toque that stood nearly vertical except for a slight kink on one side. Her face glowed with an ever-present smile. We later got to know her as Aunty. She lived with the family who operated the only guesthouse in town, and she chattered continually to whoever would listen.

Another man stood nearby wearing a yak-fur coat wrapped with an embroidered ribbon around his waist. Other locals clustered together on the grass. They had taken a break from daily chores to watch the show. The animal mascot mock charged them as well as us foreigners. One man rolled backwards, head over heels in feigned fright. He then chuckled and handed over a few bills. White scarves were passed around before being returned to the dancers while slipping some money into their hands. After all, the dancers were yak herders themselves. They had taken time away from work, normally conducted in the hills, to dance for us.

Typically, yak herders perform the yak cham annually or on special request. In 2015, the king and queen of Bhutan hiked the same trail we did. They too came to Sakteng and watched the indigenous yak cham, among other festivities. They undertook this visit to connect with the residents and listen to their concerns. Young people were leaving the small town for opportunities elsewhere. Locals were worried about losing their heritage. The king discussed the importance of maintaining tradition and sovereignty while also building prosperity for the people. These issues are not so foreign. Parents want a future for their children without neglecting their own values. Is this so different from what happens in the remote communities and rural towns of your home country? Sometimes foreign practices might seem strange, yet when you unravel conventional habits, common threads clearly exist across cultures.

The Basics

Most useful item to pack: Local currency in small bills for a donation to the dancers

Useful words and phrases in Dzongkha: *kuzuzangbola* ("hello"); *tashidelek* ("good wishes"); *Jogey-la* ("Let's go"); *Chögi pâ ci tapge mä?* ("Can I take your photo?"); and *yâ* ("yak").[1]

For more, refer to visitbhutan.com/useful_words_phrases.html.

For further travel information: Bhutan requires most foreigners to travel with a government-approved tour company and pay a regulated day rate. The government's intent is to promote high-quality, low-impact tourism. Whether you prefer to travel independently or on a group tour, it should cost about the same because of the standardized pricing system. The Tourism Council of Bhutan provides loads of information at tourism.gov.bt/plan/minimum-daily-package.

We first used Rainbow Tours & Treks in 2010 and were so impressed that we travelled with them again in 2017. Their guides are well trained, and the company can customize your trip based on your interests. If you want to experience some of Bhutan's amazing festivals, ask for their recommendations when planning your trip. Further information is available on their website: rainbowbhutan.com.

1. Based on Lonely Planet's *Bhutan Travel Guide* (see Bibliography).

The yak cham is specific to the Sakteng region of eastern Bhutan. We first learned of the dance from Sonam Wangmo, the energetic owner of Rainbow, who is originally from the Sakteng Valley. Her local insight ignited our interest to see this enigmatic performance. We visited Sakteng as part of the Merak to Sakteng cultural trek (see Chapter One for the trekking experience).

~~~
~~~

BHUTAN—GLIMPSING SAKTENG'S SECLUDED CEREMONIES

Immerse yourself in a sheltered society where the sounds of time-honoured ceremonies curl through the air and tradition rings with tenacity

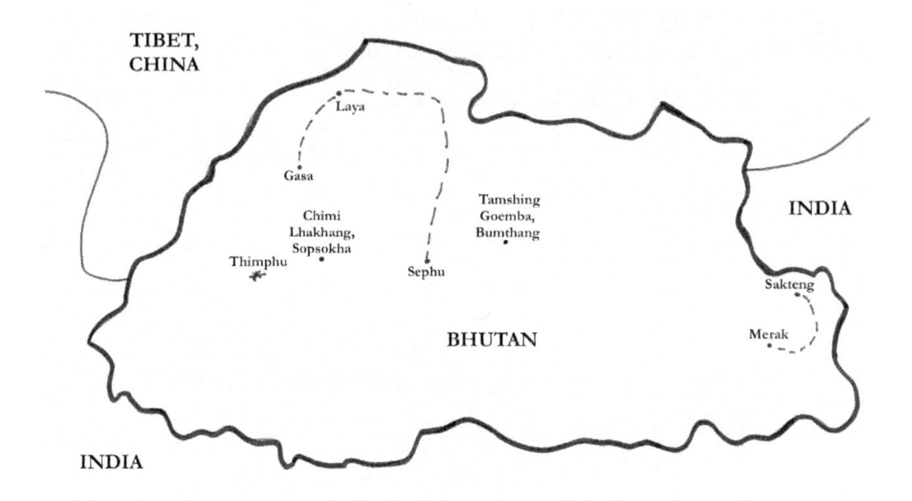

The Experience

Unfamiliar sounds hung in the air as I unlaced my boots and stepped inside the dim room. Ritualistic objects had been placed near three men who sat on the floor. It soon became apparent that they were monks, although it was not initially obvious from looking at their attire. One wore a down vest over a mustard-coloured T-shirt. The other two wore ordinary jackets: one a red down coat and the other a blue rain jacket—practical but not clerical. Rugs had been spread across the wooden floorboards. The three monks sat cross-legged behind three red chests that were organized into an L shape. Each chest looked like a mini garden, splashed with vibrant yellow, blue and pink painted flowers. My friends, husband and I were about to watch an annual *Jalashi* ceremony held by the family that ran our guesthouse.

The annual Jalashi is conducted in households across Bhutan, sometimes with more than eight monks leading the practice in bigger centres. As every family holds its own private ceremony, the number of monks depends on the family's wealth and accessibility, which is why remote homes tend to have a smaller entourage. Ceremonies incorporate an array of ritualistic objects and musical instruments. At our guesthouse, the monks played the large *nga* ("hand-held drum"), a *tangti* ("hand-held knocker") and a bell. Horns and conch shells are also common additions to the ensemble. The music, mantra and ceremony together are believed to drive away evil spirits and any bad sentiments attached to the home. In Sakteng, most families seemed to be related to a monk who either lived in their own or a neighbouring village. The three monks at our guesthouse were family members, which explains the casual familiarity around the room.

We had reached the family's ceremonial room by climbing a set of ladder-like stairs above their shop. Like most stores in Sakteng, it was packed with the essentials: alcohol, noodles, candy and other local favourites. As we settled onto the floor mats, the monks began to chant. Their voices curled in a slow cadence around the room. They read a mantra from their sutras, pages containing the written teachings of Buddha and held dear by every monk and lama. Stories were captured on the narrow rectangular sheets of paper. Six rows of writing filled each page, written in the local Dzongkha language. Stacks of similar sheets rested atop each of the three chests and were protected by wooden planks. After the ceremony finished, the pile of loose-leaf paper would be bound between the boards, secured with ribbons and stored inside a protective box. For now, the wooden covers acted to prop up the pages.

A large nga leaned against one of the trunks. Its skin, stretched decades ago, was likely originally from a local sheep. Striations tarnished with age and dust did not taint its sound. The drummer monk used a thin S-shaped baton to rap the giant nga at regular intervals. The monks sang. Sheets were flipped, and the nga's beat resonated across the room.

As I sat beside one of the monks, he motioned for me to move closer to integrate into the ceremony. Despite the symbolic chanting, the mood was relaxed. People smiled and joked. Family members entered the room; some sat down to join us while others popped out again. The monk beside me held up his mobile phone and slowly scanned the room with it. Afterwards, he replayed his video as a slight distraction between mantras. Soon another chant started, the nga gonged and the monks' glasses were refilled. The wife running the guesthouse handed a beer to one monk. She poured masala *ja* ("spicy tea") for another.

Soon after we sat down, we were handed porcelain cups. The wife immediately filled these with the family's potent *arra* ("homemade whiskey"), all while keeping a straight face. In the town of Sakteng, every family brews their own version and serves the clear, fiery liquid from a special canister. This family's one-litre flask was made from a hollowed slice of bamboo stalk that had been decorated with red paint and gold embellishments. It was evident the drink was popular when a five-gallon plastic jug was brought in to refill the more refined bamboo serving canister. Arra is part of their culture, a fun custom that people enjoy, but a custom nonetheless. I attempted the delicate art of evading large mouthfuls of the punchy liquid with its stark flavour. My friends tried another strategy: if you finish your glass, it will indicate that you have finished drinking. After the third refill, they attempted to convince me to try the same tactic—surely their cups would not be refilled a fourth time. The owner retained her stoic face, although I might have caught a modest grin slipping through as she circled the room, jug in hand.

Plates were passed around, covered with a handful of popped rice kernels that propped up a tight ball of rice. Next to the rice ball rested a larger raspberry-coloured sphere of sweet bread-like dough. I had seen similar food as offerings at shrines. The most curious was a long phallic-shaped breadstick with a curl on its tip. Everyone nibbled on these assorted edibles, but few ate everything. I sensed they were more symbolic than a food source, too bland compared to Bhutan's typical chili-infused cuisine.

The eldest family member attending our guesthouse's ceremony was referred to simply as Aunty. Her smile never ceased. It wrapped her entire face in a glowing warmth and sense of serenity. I had often seen her around the house, swaying back and forth while gently talking to herself or whoever would listen. When we were around, she chattered to us even though we could not understand her words and she did not know our foreign language. We still engaged in a sort of communication that lacked specific words but expressed a shared appreciation for one another. Her feet were clenched in uncomfortable-looking crescents from some affliction, which caused her to wobble when she walked. Yet she had somehow managed to climb the rungs, likely with someone's help, and join us in the ceremonial room. Throughout the ceremony, I do not think her hands left the prayer beads that hung around her neck, caressed out of habit and for reassurance.

Near the end of the evening, Aunty rose alongside her niece and a male relative. Side by side, the three approached the lead monk and offered stalks of incense, the arra flask and a plate of food. Words were spoken. Blessings were made. Then attention turned to a platter that had been sitting in the centre of the floor. Miniature figurines moulded by hand and made from a homemade dough filled the tray. These were *tormas*, or ritualistic offering cakes. The tallest figure looked like Buddha with a red-dyed robe and arched helmet shaped onto its head. A circular candle burned at the dough statue's feet, near which three kneeling figures leaned. The imprints from the fingers of whoever had shaped their bodies remained. One figure had large rabbit-like ears, so I suspect the youngest child might have crafted it. Two rows of tiny shapes were stuck on the tray and arranged around the central Buddha.

At the end of the Jalashi, these ritual cakes would be removed from the house. A lama would instruct the family which direction to take them and where to place them. The cakes went to various places based on the lama's advice and guided by astrology. This practice intrigued me. Did they scatter the pieces, like feeding bread crumbs to pigeons, or bury them beneath one of the countless pine trees that surrounded their village? I never saw any remnants during our walks, so perhaps birds or the rare red panda found them first. If a family did not observe the lama's instructions, bad luck was believed to follow. Even the date for each family's ceremony was set only after consulting a lama and made according to his astrological reading.

A separate *Lo Che* ceremony was also held on this same evening. The husband and wife who owned the guesthouse sat in the centre of the room. Each put on a yak-fur hat decorated with golden embroidery. These peculiar pieces had caught my eye earlier when they hung from a nearby ceiling beam. The wife also held an ornamental bowl heaped with rice and topped with a decorative panel as long as my forearm. Their young son sat between them, licking his fingers as he sampled some of the treats with one hand and held a smartphone in the other. Earlier, he had been randomly recording video clips of the ceremony. The husband held five shoots of bamboo that had been decorated with multi-coloured ribbons. At regular intervals in the music he swung the sticks around his head three times. It was believed that this action would wipe away ill forces from the family's house. The couple was then blessed. After the ceremony closed, we offered a donation. This collection was done whenever visitors came to the house and was linked to the Lo Che's blessing of good fortune. The money would be saved for years, similar to an insurance policy.

We stayed in Sakteng for two nights. While walking through the streets, we would often hear a gong or clang of symbols emanate from someone's home. Streets in Sakteng are not much more than a metre wide. As the town is accessible only by foot, these lanes are not intended for vehicles. Stone houses are built right up to the side of the path, while a few homes have a fenced garden area that abuts the walkway. A sense of community and sharing is strong in this remote enclave. On one afternoon walk, my husband and I were unexpectedly invited into one of the family's homes. We had just stepped around a curve on the path when a man waved at us. He stood on the second-storey balcony and motioned for us to come upstairs. Cedar branches smoked in a small shrine beside the gate to his home. We noticed a few pairs of shoes sitting on the veranda, so we slipped off our hiking boots and stepped inside. Shards of light cascaded through the windows, and it quickly became clear we had entered a spiritual room. The family was soon to start another phase of their Lo Che ceremony.

The man who had invited us spoke a couple of words in English and seemed keen to practise his language skills. He was the brother of the owner of the house. Although conversation was limited, fragmented sentences and smiles flowed freely. A third brother was a lama and had travelled from a nearby town to conduct the family's service. An older woman, who I assumed was the wife or grandmother, walked into the room with a broad smile. She grabbed two cups and a two-litre plastic soft drink bottle. The soda had long disappeared, and the family's special arra swirled from the bottle's spout. Thankfully, this family's concoction was less potent than some I had tasted.

I noticed several recognizable objects placed around the room. A large nga rested against a low table. The table was covered in a familiar red, blue and yellow satin table cloth in a style we had seen frequently across Bhutan. Unsurprisingly, a golden pot of holy water and stack of sutras sat on top. This lama's collection of mantras was protected by red-painted wooden covers, which acted like weights to keep the well-used pages in place. The lama wore distinctive attire, a rose-coloured velour shirt beneath a traditional maroon robe slung across his shoulders, more cape than robe. I noticed a conch shell and uniquely Bhutanese bronze bell with a gold thunderbolt for a handle resting on the table in front of him. In Bhutan, the thunderbolt represents harmony between secular and religious powers.

After the two men were seated, a plate of ceremonial food was brought in. Family members stood around or leaned against the wall. They encouraged me to try on their ceremonial yak-fur hat, and everyone seemed to have a laugh once I plopped it on my head. From there the ceremony began, mantras were spoken, ngas gonged and the sacred objects were waved in the air. When we returned outside into the sunlight, the mystical gongs and low mantras we had heard spilling out from random houses seemed less cryptic.

Ceremonial bell and tangti

Exploring this little town nestled in a valley of the low Himalaya was like getting a taste of another world. With every step, we uncovered more delectable sights. A creek trickled a few paces beyond our new friend's home, where a footbridge and little hut stood. Inside, a water prayer wheel spun, much like a regular prayer wheel except operated by the flow of water. Some of the creek water was redirected below the slightly raised hut along a duct made from a bamboo trunk sliced in half. We kept walking towards buckwheat fields that surrounded the town. It was harvest time, and clusters of men and women worked the fields. Women sat on the ground with hand-held sickles to slice the stalks. Once they were cut, a traditional yet effective thrashing technique was employed. A wooden pole supported by two Y-shaped structures offered stability for a man and woman to balance while they trampled the buckwheat husks. Their efforts tore seeds and blossoms from the grassy stalks, leaving the chaff to be collected in a flat woven basket by another lady. After it was filled, she shook the basket above a canvas tarp. The loose weave effectively filtered any unusable chunky bits. Eventually, a pile of dark seeds formed below the shaking basket. These were the buckwheat kernels. The process was repeated all afternoon.

We met more of the resident ladies later in the evening and experienced yet another unexpected sight. The *Tshogchang* is a traditional greeting performed to welcome visitors. The owner of our tour company is from the Sakteng region, and her connection helped garner us a personalized performance. I had expected a small dance, something minor compared to what we had already witnessed in this friendly village. I was in for a surprise. The four of us and our guide sat cross-legged in the ceremonial room, comfortably sitting in the same places we had on the prior evening. About twelve ladies filed into the room. One brought her young daughter to play with some other kids, but her little girl regularly snuck back into the room for a snuggle.

The ladies wore handwoven skirts and knitted sweaters with geometric designs stitched onto the fabric. Embroidered scarves hung around their necks. Their collars were further adorned with two and sometimes three necklaces made from shells, multi-coloured beads and stones. The owner of the guesthouse wore a traditional felt hat made of yak hair. It looked like a modified French beret with strings of wool twisted into long curly tail-like appendages that hung at regular intervals around the cap. This distinctive look is worn only by people from the Brokpa tribe of the Sakteng region. The tails drain rainwater away from the face.

Three of the ladies made the rounds, approaching each of us, one at a time. Our arra cups were filled and then refilled. Any attempt to receive just a little of the potent beverage was slyly ignored. Images of the prior evening's copious rounds tingled in our thoughts—and stomachs. Our friend was the first to receive the welcoming treatment. One lady bent over and pinched his thigh while another lifted and pressed the cup of arra to his lips. They giggled. This was part tradition and part game. The guesthouse owner stood watching with a glint in her eye. One sip turned into a splash across our friend's mouth, a little landed in his mouth and the rest was absorbed by his beard. He squinted at the familiar flavour. One mouthful was sufficient, and they moved along to their next guest.

When it came to my husband's turn, he pretended to enjoy the pinches, which only encouraged more laughter and more arra. The lady tipped the cup into his mouth; however, he managed to divert most so it dribbled over his clothing. It was an effective tactic to avert full consumption. When my turn came, I braced my lips. As with most homebrewed whiskeys, I found the arra's strong flavour rather unpleasant. Yet it was embedded in the culture and rather difficult to avoid—to do so would have been considered ungracious.

The pinch was more of a mild squeeze, done in fun. My cup was near overflowing, which played to my advantage. During the lively banter, more drops were spilled on my sweater than actually made it into my mouth. After I had swallowed a few swigs, the ladies moved on.

The arra flask was set to the side for the next phase. The women began to softly sing songs handed down over generations. They sang and shuffled in a smooth dance, slowly shifting around the room. The steps were simple but effective when synchronized in the small space. Hands shifted, wrists twirled. A few songs later, we were asked to join them. Our nonexistent Dzongzha-language skills meant that we could not participate in the song, so instead we attempted the dance moves. I linked my right hand with the lady to my right and my left hand with another woman to my left. After everyone was linked, we had formed a circle around the room. The ladies started to sing. We stepped forward, swaying into the centre of the circle and back, then stepped forward once again. The routine continued. Again, arms moved, wrists twisted and fingers curled into a gesture particular to this welcome dance. The lady on my right guided my hand as well as my footsteps. The pace was slow, an advantage for us novices. After the dance we sat down again. More arra was served, and more pinches were administered. We attempted to minimize our intake, not completely successfully. After all, we had to hike five hours the next morning to reach the nearest road and continue our journey through Bhutan.

The Basics

Most useful items to pack: Layers of clothing for warmth and a sweater that can easily be washed

Useful words and phrases in Dzongkha: *kuzuzangbola* ("hello"); *tashidelek* ("good wishes"); *mantra* ("prayer formula or chant"); *Chö meng gaci mo?* ("What is your name?"); *Chögi pâ ci tapge mä?* ("Can I take your photo?"); and *kaadinchheyla* ("thank you").[2]

For more, refer to visitbhutan.com/useful_words_phrases.html.

For further travel information: Bhutan requires most foreigners to travel with a government-approved tour company and pay a regulated day rate. The government's intent is to promote high-quality, low-impact tourism. For more information, refer to our tour company's website at rainbowbhutan.com.

To reach the village of Sakteng, we followed the Merak to Sakteng track. Refer to Chapter One for further details on the hike. No roads led to Sakteng, although one was in the works at the time of writing. Amenities are basic, as Sakteng received electricity only in recent years and residents' livelihoods have traditionally been yak herding, buckwheat farming and cheese making.

There is one guesthouse and one camping area in the town of Sakteng. The camping area is at the edge of town. When we were there, it had a stone building that was intended as a kitchen and a toilet building, but unfortunately both were in a horrible state during our visit. Open-aired roof structures were also scattered around the camping area and would have

2. Based on Lonely Planet's *Bhutan Travel Guide* (see Bibliography).

provided ideal weather protection for our tents if they were better maintained. Regrettably, the camp had no caretaker.

We hiked into camp in the morning and expected to stay in tents. While eating lunch, and luckily before we had set anything up, one of the wooden structures to our right suddenly crashed to the ground. The toilet stalls were overflowing. Our guide suggested we move to the guesthouse, which, considering the alternative, felt luxurious. Each couple had a room on the second floor. There was a shared bathroom with a flush toilet, a sink with running water and even an electrically heated shower—although none of us tested it. Our cooks and dzo herders had their own room. Sheets were fresh, blankets were warm and the toilet room was clean.

The ceremonies we watched were performed in early October 2017. Timing varies from year to year based on lama guidance and astrological interpretation. In Bhutan, many local events take place across the country, so ask your tour company for recommendations during your visit, recognizing that expected dates can change at the last minute. Also, refer to the Tourism Council of Bhutan's website for an overview of the main festivals across the country: tourism.gov.bt/activities/festivals.

~~~
~~~

BHUTAN—BURNING ARCHES AND MASKED DANCERS AT THE TAMSHING PHALA CHOEPA

Feel the heat of flames overhead as evil spirits are subdued at the annual mewang, *launching a masked-dance festival choreographed hundreds of years ago*

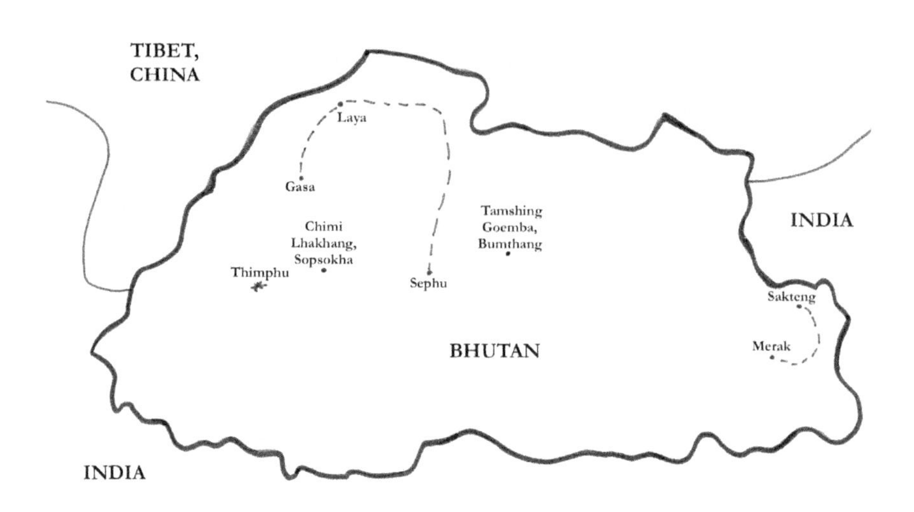

The Experience

Brilliant ceremonial dance costumes and mythical masks replaced the typical crimson robes of the monks. Their arms were bare, and their chests were covered only by embroidered vests that left their sides and stomachs exposed. Flowing material had been wrapped around their waists and legs to form a pant-like garment that still allowed for fluid dance moves. Yet this outfit seemed incidental compared to the wooden face masks tied with wide ribbons around their heads. Each disguise was carved into the image of a deity, evil spirit or character from local folklore. Deep tones of ochre, black and grey coloured the masks.

My husband, two friends and I waited as long as possible inside the dry vehicle before joining the procession. As the van door slammed shut behind me, rain droplets exploded onto my face. I felt the air move while a swell of people quietly shuffled past. My boots slid sideways, carried by the ooze of the mud. Our cue came when a small group of monks walked forward, lighting up the darkened route. The persistent rain did little to diminish the flames of their torches. The monks walked from the direction of the Tamshing Goemba, an ancient monastery up the road to our left. They led the way to a field, and the crowd followed. We merged into the mass. Everyone sloshed through the muck, the brown puddles and the odd tufts of greenery. It was a road we were following, but a dirt road transformed at the end of the monsoon season. Our destination lay a couple hundred metres away.

Our guide had contacted local connections to confirm that the affair would indeed take place on this September night. It was to be held in a field behind the Tamshing Goemba in the tiny town of Jakar. The *mewang* ("fire blessing ceremony"), as it is called in the local Dzongkha language, is distinct to the Bumthang Valley in the Kingdom of Bhutan. Only three temples follow this practice, usually between late September and November. You cannot find a definitive schedule posted on the internet or a program advertised in advance on social media. The specific date for this ceremony fluctuates from year to year, as do most traditions in Bhutan. A local lama must interpret lunar signs and ascertain the right time for such a cleansing ritual. The day must be considered auspicious according to the cosmos, local signs and other religious indicators that shape the lama's guidance.

When we arrived in the field, an arch made from the branches of cedar, cypress, pine and other local trees stood almost hidden in the gloom. It was just after nine thirty. Two monks beat drums, creating a unified pulse that moved across the audience. Fellow monks joined in with a melody of horns, and a rhythm formed. The masked monks then started to dance. The enlarged features of their masks glowed under the light of the fire and, at certain angles, disappeared completely into the shadows. This *cham* ("dance") is believed to rid the area of evil spirits, to purify the scene. Soon, the head monk touched his torch to the dangling branches of the arch. Their dry needles grabbed the flame and carried it higher.

At first, only a few audience members dared to step forward and tentatively run under the flaming arch. Participants believed that their sins would be cleansed as they passed under the blazing structure. This would earn them a second chance. Such acts of purification are common in Bhutan, where the predominant religion is Buddhism. The good that you do in this life is believed to affect what form your soul will be reborn with in the next life. After the first brave devotees dodged beneath the flames, the crowd galvanized. People ran. Friends watched. Couples huddled together. More people jumped into the activity. Others returned to the sidelines to watch. The rain was forgotten.

Throughout, people smiled, laughed and recorded the scene on their smartphones. I could not help but mentally compare the scene in front of me with how I imagined ancient pagan rituals unfolded. However, it also felt strangely comforting. At that moment, standing amid chanting monks and people participating in a purification ritual below a burning arch in a muddy field felt completely normal. The words to describe the spectacle may make it sound eerie and mysterious—darkness, fire, spirited believers, masked dancers and haunting music—yet the feeling was entirely different. It was like a Halloween party, a completely natural diversion for many North

Americans between summer and winter, yet a strange sight for newcomers.

Just fifteen minutes before, the sky had been dark, and people had been cloaked in obscurity, hiding beneath umbrellas. How the night had transformed. Specks of carrot-coloured ember flitted into the sky and formed a swirling crown above two pillars of fire. The flames glowed coral, orange, crimson and white. I felt a rush of heat, even though I was standing five people back.

My thoughts were interrupted when a camera shot upwards: click, image captured. I ducked left to get a better view, away from the phone that had popped up in front of me. Flames reflected in the wet smudges along people's arms, which stretched up all around to record the excitement, not only by us few foreigners but by the young twenty-something-year-old Bhutanese who composed the majority of the crowd. This soggy field at the southern edge of town was certainly the place to be on this drizzly night.

The crowd developed a natural ebb and flow. Some left the close clutches to walk, then run beneath the burning arch. I imagined how it would feel. As the participants got closer, the heat would intensify; perhaps they intuitively dodged a cluster of ash as it broke free from a too-close-for-comfort cedar branch. As they passed the centre, the crowd would seem to disappear, replaced by a sense of otherworldliness. Darkness and light diverged like the heat of the flames against the cool night air. Another step and they were past the most precarious section. The fire obliterated their transgressions, however big or small, and their sins floated away, mingling with the smoke to drift across the valley. Did they feel cleansed, as if they were entering a rejuvenated reality? Certainly they would feel light and invigorated, if from nothing else than from the energy of the crowd. I watched people smile and laugh as they emerged from the darkness and out through the other side of the burning arch. It was contagious: after one person went through, more dashed around to do their own circuit.

The pyre spread up the branches. Bursts of white fire danced higher as smoke and steam puffed outwards from both sides. Another person ran underneath the burning arch. Arms waved, people shuffled, flames twisted and the branches shifted. Policemen and policewomen stood among the crowd. They smiled and enjoyed the performance, but they were also watching. As the fire progressed, the arch beams cracked, burned and bent. When the arch began to crumble, the officers gently raised their hands to stop the eager runners. The white-hot flames subsided into orange flickers, which then fell away. Embers spewed upwards in one last attempt to light the sky. Soon, smoke plumed around the fallen structure, and the field darkened. The hopeful anticipation that people had brought with them turned to worthwhile satisfaction as they walked away.

Most attendees would soon return to the monastery, as would we. The fire ceremony was over, but it marked the beginning of another celebration. The next day was the start of the Tamshing Phala Choepa festival, held inside the nearby temple grounds. Its highlight was an array of chams performed by masked dancers, tossing their heads and spinning around an open courtyard.

To appreciate the significance of these ceremonies, it helps to know a little about the history of this temple. Its stone foundation dates back to 1501. The temple was constructed by Pema Lingpa, a key figure in Bhutan's Buddhist upbringing. He is famed for locating sacred texts and stimulating Bhutan's appetite for Buddhist artistry. The inner sanctuary walls are said to have been painted by Pema Lingpa himself, and their darkened facades seem to corroborate an ancient past.

In Bhutan, Pema Lingpa is known as the blacksmith and a *terton* ("treasure finder"). It is said that a local king once questioned Pema Lingpa's authenticity, whether his enlightened prowess was in fact true. In response, Pema Lingpa picked up a lit butter lamp and walked into a pool of water. He continued to walk deep into the basin until he could no longer be seen from the surface. After some time, he re-emerged holding the butter lamp still alight and carrying what had been previously thought to be lost treasure. This was not just any hidden cache, but a bundle of ancient relics hidden by the esteemed Guru Rinpoche, considered the Second Buddha. The king understood that only someone with divine knowledge from a past life could have found this treasure. He was humbled and sought retribution for his earlier disbelief.

Being a highly skilled blacksmith, Pema Lingpa responded through his hands. Link by link, loop by loop, Pema Lingpa created a twenty-five-kilogram chain mail. His Majesty donned the physical atonement like a cloak, a burden to be worn for the rest of his life. That same cloak lay on a table within a dimly lit corridor in the Tamshing Goemba where we stood. It is said that if you perform a *kora*—walking clockwise around a sacred site—at least three times while wearing it, you will accumulate merit for your soul's next life and be absolved of sins from your current and past lives. Our guide confirmed that this practice is conducted to this very day. In fact, he had worn the venerate chain and walked his own kora a few years back.

Upstairs from the chain mail, monks prepared for the cham. Masks sat under windowsills as final costumes were tied into place. From here, the monks could look down onto the courtyard. It was surrounded by the monastery, a one-storey structure with a series of doors and rooms making up the monks' residences. The wood panels and beams were decorated in Bhutan's traditional style, a dark orange or grey background covered with detailed painted figures. Flowers seemed to be the most common design; the monastery looked like a giant painted garden.

As it had on the previous evening, the rain continued to fall when the festival was due to start. Bystanders dodged the wet by standing beneath the building's overhang or by sitting on plastic chairs under a canopy. The performers were not so lucky. Puddles swelled on the sandy ground of the open-air arena. A handful of locals with thatch brooms swept the accumulated water as if it were a pile of dust. An occasional gong from a massive bronze drum echoed across the area. Around us people shuffled, waiting for the event to begin.

One man sauntered out from the red-curtained entrance. He walked purposefully into the courtyard wearing the traditional Bhutanese *gho*, the national dress for men, a handwoven jacket-like wrap that hangs to the knees. He held a stick over his shoulder, and a red cloth covered his head. A black face mask with a tuft of hair for a beard had been tied overtop of the cloth and topped with a red balloon that stood straight up. In his right hand, he carried a wooden phallus. It was carved with all the physical contours one might expect and hung from his waist to his knees—at least when he was not swinging it around and taunting the audience. Giant penises are not uncommon sights throughout Bhutan. They are often painted in grand murals across houses or hung from the eaves as iconic decorations. They signify protective power.

Three other masked jokesters skipped out from the red curtain. One mask was the colour of burnt auburn, and another looked like a butternut squash carved with eyes and a hooked nose. The third was a pasty face finished with a carved grin. Each clown had a different-coloured balloon bobbling above his mask. The jokers danced and laughed, teasing each other and audience members with their toy penises. They moved across the stage in a silly routine filled with hugs, mock arguments, pelvic thrusting and much prancing. I was one of many audience members who attracted the jokers. Thankfully, a small donation prompted them to move along to the next innocent bystander and eventually return to the central area.

After this vigorous introduction, the festival began. The mood turned more sombre as a row of lamas and young monks sat cross-legged at one end of the monastery, from where they led the ceremony. The head lama started to chant a mantra into a microphone. The others played large *ngas* ("hand-held drums") and ancient horns in a melodic tune. A distinctive cadence floated over the crowd. The festival progressed with a series of dances, each lasting from fifteen to twenty minutes. The masks matched the theme of each dance. One showcased a stag with the dancer's mask larger than his head. The mask had a carved tongue curled as if to say "laaa." Under the curl hid an opening through which the performer peered out. The mask's shiny eyes swept across the audience, and flared nostrils brought its enamel expression to life. Green ropes tied to its horns flailed as the dancer swung and dipped his head, nearly touching the ground. A circle of similarly costumed dancers twirled, mimicking one another's moves. The clowns ran through the middle, adding a lighthearted distraction while the dancers carried on, indifferent to the comics' antics. Bright layered skirts and hand-embroidered frocks flowed, creating their own spectacle. It was a whirlwind of movement. Heads pivoted, bodies turned and waists dipped.

Masked dancer at the Tamshing Phala Choepa festival

Masked dancer at the Tamshing Phala Choepa festival

Sadly, our schedule allowed us to spend only one day at this small yet action-packed ceremony. My memories are overlaid with a feeling of community; the monks and the townsfolk—both young and old—all came out to participate in the annual festival. I felt like I had fallen into another world, a valley where arts, tradition and a little bit of modern technology blended together. It was not so different from any other day in this enigmatic country of Bhutan, yet it felt surreal compared to our Western world, which seems to be on fire in an entirely different way.

The Basics

Most useful items to pack: Shoes that can be submerged in mud and an umbrella

Useful words in Dzongkha: *kuzuzangbola* ("hello"); *lhakhang* ("temple"); *goemba* ("Buddhist monastery"); and *tsechu* ("religious dance festival").[3]

For more, refer to visitbhutan.com/useful_words_phrases.html.

For further travel information: Bhutan requires most foreigners to travel with a government-approved tour company and pay a regulated day rate. The government's intent is to promote high-quality, low-impact tourism. This was our second visit to Bhutan using Rainbow Tours & Treks, who I highly recommend. Ask the company about festivals taking place during your visit to Bhutan, and they can incorporate them into your itinerary. See prior sections on Bhutan or refer to Rainbow's website at rainbowbhutan.com.

3. Based on Lonely Planet's *Bhutan Travel Guide* (see Bibliography).

For more information on Tamshing Phala Choepa's festival, refer to bhutan.travel/events/tamshing-phala-choedpa.

Further information on the Bumthang region is found on the Tourism Council of Bhutan's website at bhutan.travel/destinations/bumthang.

~~~
~~~

BHUTAN—TRANSLATING SUTRAS INSIDE THIMPHU'S BUDDHA DORDENMA

Step inside a giant Buddha statue where monks use golden ink to restore sutras over three hundred years old

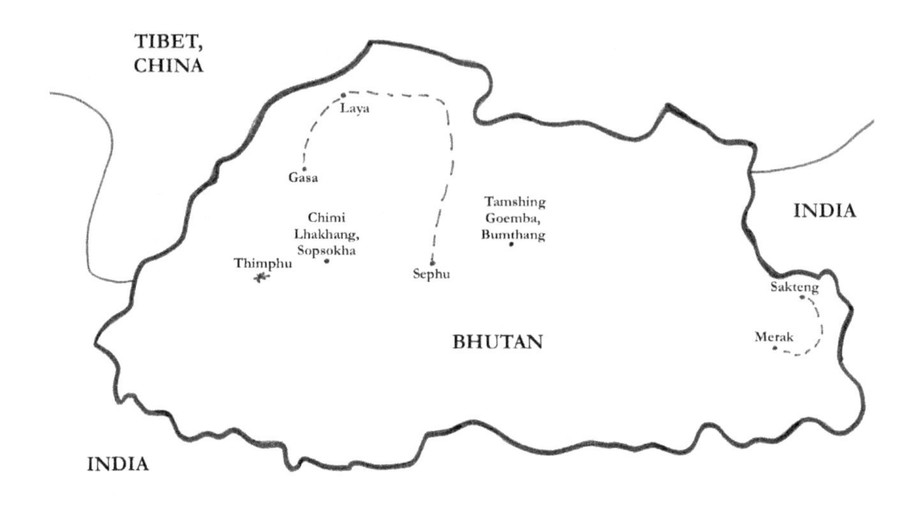

The Experience

Grass, dried by the sun, pointed upwards in millions of spiny stalks along the road. Hardy pine trees dotted the hillside around Thimphu. We continued to drive higher. The sprawling city stretched out below us, looking like a tiny town tucked inside Himalayan grandeur. I gained a different perspective every few seconds as our vehicle wound around yet another switchback. Cars were parked here and there along the edge of the pavement. Farther ahead, their numbers condensed and hinted that we were getting close to the top. Then our van curved around one final twist, and a mass of golden forms stole my attention. Banners hung across the road. Tables had been set up to welcome guests and help manage the volume of visitors. Cars were parked in any spare space available in the small parking lot near the main entrance. We had reached the 51.5-metre high Buddha Dordenma, built in 2014. The statue itself was impressive, but the atmosphere was even more compelling.

Couples and families meandered around the base of the giant Buddha. Tents filled the lower level, radiating a completely different ambience even though they were separated from the statue only by about ten stairs. These temporary shelters formed a massive semicircle around the statue. The outer tents served water, tea and meals. A central pavilion shaded hundreds of monks who looked like an ocean of maroon robes. A few lay people sat along the outer edges. Everyone sat cross-legged—there was no need for chairs. Their chant flowed in unison, the mantra curling through the air like a lonesome melody. The words were all in Dzongkha, Bhutan's national language, and were led by a head lama seated on a golden throne. His gravelly voice churned across the congregation. There was a cadence to his mantra, but a very monotonous one. Rather, his throaty tone exuded a hypnotic quality that took over the hillside.

We had arrived during a ceremony called the Translation of the Sutras. Lamas and monks had congregated to perform the delicate task of preserving their ancient scripts. Because it is so arduous, it is done only every nine to ten years. On the day we visited, the Buddhist association that our guide belonged to was providing lunch for everyone in attendance. Different groups assumed this role in rotation, and it helped to sustain the monks' dedicated efforts, which would proceed for months.

Initially, we remained on the upper platform. A lotus-flower base, above where we walked, supported the massive Buddha statue. Its petals acted as more than a foundation, as they represented rebirth and purity. Below the flowers, images of dancing horses and stomping elephants, double the size of the real animals, decorated a gold-painted wall. A young girl stood underneath a horse figure and stretched as tall as she could. The tips of her fingers just scratched the horse's belly. This exterior embellishment was only part of the grand display. Two sets of golden doors revealed a temple glittering in gold tucked inside the great statue. Shelves swept across the entire interior. Some were vacant, but most held rows of miniature golden Buddha statues; 125,000 of these figures adorned the temple. My eyes first went to the centre of the room where, as in every temple, a statue of Buddha rested. Everywhere I looked, the space seemed to shimmer and shine as if I were inside a giant golden ornament turned inside out.

In one corner, a small group of monks sat on the floor. Their maroon robes brought a sense of earthliness to the sublime space. Piles of papers lay on the ground around them. Calligraphic script filled the narrow rectangular sheets. Only about six rows of scripture fit on each leaf. They contained sutras, which are written mantras of Buddha's teachings passed down to new followers and repeated by lifelong devotees. Some of the pages were over three hundred years old.

One monk hunched over a low wooden table in the middle of the team. A pot of liquid gold ink was perched dangerously close to his yellowed strip of paper. The exposed sheaf was separated from the jar's contents by a thin bamboo stick, carved into a delicate point. His second tool, a thin paint brush as sparse as a feather, had been pushed to the side. All the monks shifted ever so cautiously. Arms moved with care. Hands manoeuvred even more diligently. The monks glanced up as we approached, and a grin immediately curved across each of their faces.

The stacks were arranged in a system that allowed the text to be checked, passed along for correction, given time to dry and then assembled once more. Monks reviewed the pages one at a time, searching for faded letters or smudged words. Once complete, the sheets would be stored between slats of wood and then wrapped in a yellow satiny fabric before being placed back in their allocated cupboards. Every monastery had its own copy. Lamas recite the mantras contained on these pages as lessons to their followers. The lama outside was doing exactly that. He would continue for a period of three months until every sheet had been read.

The teachings had been translated from their original Sanskrit into Bhutan's Dzongkha tongue only over the last century. Part of this year's preservation process entailed checking that the translation was done correctly. Mistakes were frequent before a common dictionary existed to help Bhutanese monks decipher the foreign script. I leaned forward to watch. The monk rarely dabbed the bamboo tip back into the pot. He seemed to knead a practically endless dribble of mustard-coloured ink to perfect the side of a letter or rewrite an illegible word. Line by line, page by page, the sutras were meticulously revised and restored to last another ten years.

We left the monks to carry on with their work. Outside, golden *Tara* statues greeted us in the sunshine. Taras are considered similar to angels, and statues of these mystical beings circled the entire platform. As we walked away, the throaty voice of the lama followed us to our vehicle. Almost every family in Bhutan has at least one member in a monastery, either a monk or nun. So it was not surprising that the site was filled with visitors, mostly from Thimphu or the surrounding countryside. It was at times like this when I truly grasped how engrained Buddhism is in everyone's daily life. Here in the largest city of the country, traditional Buddhist practices were inherently incorporated as just another layer to everyone's daily routine.

Buddha Dordenma

The Basics

Most useful item to pack: Binoculars to scan the city of Thimphu, which lies far below the Buddha Dordenma statue

Useful words and phrases in Dzongkha: *kuzuzangbola* ("hello"); *lhakhang* ("temple"); *kaadinchheyla* ("thank you"); and *Pâ tabney chokar la?* ("Can I take a photo?").[4]

For more, refer to visitbhutan.com/useful_words_phrases.html.

For further travel information: Bhutan requires most foreigners to travel with a government-approved tour company and pay a regulated day rate. The government's intent is to promote high-quality, low-impact tourism. This was our second visit to Bhutan using Rainbow Tours & Treks, who I highly recommend. See prior sections on Bhutan or refer to Rainbow's website at rainbowbhutan.com.

We visited during September 2017, so the next Translation of the Sutras should be in 2026—give or take a year or two. However, the Buddha Dordenma can be visited outside this ceremony at your leisure. For more information, go to bhutan.travel/attractions/buddha-dordenma-statue.

~~~

4. Based on Lonely Planet's *Bhutan Travel Guide* (see Bibliography).
~~~

CHINA—UNROLLING TIBET'S OLDEST THANGKA AT THE GYANTSE FESTIVAL

Sit side by side with locals as lamas light fire pujas, monks create colourful sand mandalas and Black-Hat dancers whirl in centuries-old costumes

The Experience

The third-largest city in Tibet is a muddle of clay-brick houses, a fifteenth-century monastery and an esteemed *chorten* ("Buddhist monument") holding a hundred thousand images, all overlooked by an aging fourteenth-century fort that rests high above them. These muted ochre and white buildings remain as they have for hundreds of years. As we had wandered the town's central maze of streets earlier in the day, we found that the houses followed a standard style. Homes were one-storey, made from mud brick and painted white with a distinctive band of black and maroon at the base of their flat roofs. From a higher vantage point, their unpainted, sand-coloured tops blended into the barren terrain around the walled city. Rough mountains scratched at the sky and framed a storm of colours that drenched Gyantse's centre during the four-day Saga Dawa festival.

Anticipation hovered over the crowd as we waited in Gyantse's central plaza, where we sat shoulder to shoulder with locals on cement steps. Some bystanders stood between pillars of the surrounding buildings. A trickle of movement passed through the group as pilgrims arrived or residents left to complete their personal *kora*—a circumambulation, usually of something sacred—or to pray at one of the adjacent temples. Most women had braided a coloured ribbon into their hair and twisted the plait around their head. It reminded me a little of the traditional Ukrainian hair style. The men's hats looked like cream-coloured fedoras. It was a cool climate, so both men and women had bundled up in layers. Many of their coats were made of a yak-hair felt or woven wool, typically hand knit with intricate patterns. There were also those who chose a less-than-traditional option from the racks of Western jackets and sweaters that had filtered into local stores.

We sat beside two young children who wore track suits and baseball caps and giggled indiscriminately. They told us they had come from school, a few streets from where we sat. The ten-year-old boy studied English in school and was keen to practise. He pointed to our shirts and the photos on our camera and proceeded to spell out the English words for practically everything he saw. One image in particular caught his attention. My husband had captured an outdoor assembly of school kids we had watched that morning. While we stood on top of the nearby *dzong* ("fort"), dozens of children marched in concentric circles below us in what looked to be a schoolyard. Most wore sky-blue track suits and held out their arms as if they were pretending to be airplanes. A few seemed less focused and instead waved at friends as they passed each other. At the time, we were not sure if this was part of the Saga Dawa festival or a regular school activity. It turned out that the boy sitting beside us had been among the children we saw. When we asked whether he had had fun, he quickly shook his head no. For the moment, however, he was clearly enjoying himself.

Our attention was diverted as a row of monks slowly walked into the central arena. Their chanting resonated across the open area, guided by a sombre harmony. One monk gonged two brass cymbals. Two others blew into silver-crusted conch shells while another duo sounded horns. These jagged sounds somehow merged to create a wistful melody that had a surreal effect on the audience. At the other side of the open space, the head lama wore robes of gold, red and black. He closed his eyes in concentration. Golden serpents lunged out from either side of his headpiece. Above them, five flowery panels stood vertical like a crown the size of a footstool. He sat on a wooden throne painted burgundy and decorated in gold leaf. A rug offered some cushioning on his chair, which had been wrapped in white prayer flags. Beside him, peacock feathers adorned a silver flask of holy water. The lama started the fire *puja*, or ritual, from a pile of dried yak patties, incense and other assorted items. Low flames fluttered in front of him but were protected by a low white partition. While singing a mantra, he added ladles of butter oil to the burning embers. Then, one at a time, he tossed dollops of yak butter, sticks of incense, a sprinkle of spice and a handful of rice onto the flames. Beneath the chunks of fuel, a circle of sand slowly emerged.

The sand sphere, a mandala, had taken hours to create earlier in the morning. First, a layer of black sand had been poured over the base, followed by a layer of white sand. We had watched as a monk, bent over, drew an outline with a narrow stick. Another monk leaned in to pinch sand from a silver bowl. A variety of basins were scattered around the area, each holding a different colour of sand: orange, cyan, yellow and green. The sand was made of graphite, collected from the surrounding mountains and ground to a powder. The white layer of the mandala ultimately disappeared. Overtop, circles and arches emerged to form a three-dimensional representation of the world. During the fire puja, flames scorched the image and transformed this colourful world to match its black base. Sparks surged. Flames climbed. At one point, burning tentacles reached as high as the lama's crown, albeit a metre in front of him. When the flames subsided, only curly ash fronds of burnt incense remained.

A band of elderly monks sat in a row nearby and waited for the right moment to lift their musical horns. They too had donned golden crowns, just not as tall or ornate as the one the head lama wore. Their horns were decorated in gold, silver and ebony. Conch shells trimmed with silver rested in front of two younger monks. Like the audience, they watched the puja sombrely. Men from the audience shifted prayer beads in their hands. A few women twisted their hand-held prayer wheels, causing the tassels to spin with bobbles that knocked the silver centrepieces. These were hard-working folks. Their skin was drawn taught from the sun. Grooves lined their faces like the fine striations that spread across a frosted pane of glass in the winter. Tradition meant a lot to these people. You could see it in their eyes, a soft acknowledgement that this is the way things are done, no questions, no uncertainty. The ceremony is believed to eliminate negative intentions and harmful thoughts from all those attending. This cleansing introduced a four-day festival, held annually and called the Saga Dawa. This sacred time represents Buddha's birth, enlightenment and *parinirvana* ("death").

Elders at the Gyantse Festival

Similar to the mandala that had been set alight, three additional sand wheels had been prepared. They lay inside the nearby Pelkor Chode Monastery's main assembly hall. The monastery had been founded back in 1418. Inside, murals blackened with age covered the walls. Bulges and dips in the paint's finish had developed over time from humidity and temperature fluctuations. Daily smoke from butter lamps added a thin layer of carbon that matched the mood of pious austerity. The ambience deepened as devout worshippers prostrated themselves at the foot of the Buddha statues and carved deities located around the temple and inside alcoves. At this temple, prostrating oneself meant the person kneeled on their knees and touched their forehead to the floor in prayer. Some of the more ardent devotees did a full prostration, stretching out flat on the floor so that the entire body touches the ground in devotion. They then tucked small notes of *renminbi*, the Chinese currency, onto the hands of statues or placed them alongside the base of effigies. Hope and devotion rang strong in this region.

We were drawn to the centre of the temple where the trio of sand mandalas had been placed. Each wheel extended more than two metres in diameter. Again, intricate scenes had been created using coloured sand. Animals, trees, flowers and mystical creatures intermingled with swirls and bands of colour. It looked like a Persian rug made from dyed powder. Monks placed daggers on the mandala to represent the severing of evil forces and cleansing of the area for the Saga Dawa. Bowls of rice and holy water covered nearby tables. They shared the space with earth-toned *tormas* ("offering cakes") and burning butter lamps.

Back out in the courtyard, monks performed a series of traditional masked dances that brought energy to the festival. They re-enacted scenes of birth, life, death and rebirth. Bright outfits and carved masks transformed the monks into characters from Buddhist folklore. Many of the costumes were over five hundred years old yet somehow stayed intact despite the dancers' continual motion. A dusty stuffed doll, a rather dire icon symbolizing death, was tossed on the ground. It had no clear features besides a raggedy and frizzy tuft of hair. It was made from blackened leather and had a rope tied to its legs and neck. The monks did not have to touch it but instead tossed it around and dragged it across the ground. It was intended to symbolize the connection between death, bad deeds and karmic consequences.

On the third day, another fire puja was conducted. This time, an older lama oversaw the ritual. It represented the dismantling of one's soul as a new beginning to follow the end of the festival. The lama had a spectacular headpiece and dramatic robe similar to the one the lama had worn on day one, but today's leader added a touch of the twenty-first century by wearing gold aviator sunglasses.

We stepped back in time again on the fourth and final day. Gravel crunched under our feet as we climbed a path leading above town. The sun had just begun to creep over distant hills. Pilgrims had been walking this circuit for hours, performing their personal kora around the old town wall. This clockwise circumambulation is customary in Buddhist practice, whether it revolves around chortens, temples or other spiritual places. This particular kora passed the base of a cliff. Its sheer face looked down on Gyantse like a caring parent. From its peak, a 490-year-old *thangka* ("painted or embroidered Buddhist banner")[5] had been unrolled so it covered most of the cliff face. Monks gathered at its fringe. Pilgrims carrying butter lamps shuffled forward. Some elderly folks were so hunched over when they walked that their face was level to their waist. They pressed on. Everyone paused at the base of the thangka, and many donated a white prayer flag to the swiftly growing pile. Butter lamps were lifted in prayer. The people's effort was rewarded with a well-deserved blessing.

The centre of the thangka was covered with an image of Buddha, which was surrounded by smaller Buddhas in different postures, all composed from countless tiny knots. It was handmade, likely by hundreds of hands. Eventually devotees carried on down the other side of the rocky cliff, their place continually refilled by a stream

5. newworldencyclopedia.org/entry/Thangka

of people eager to reach the thangka's base. The monks remained sitting nearby, as they would for much of the day. This moment was certainly the pinnacle of the festival. The atmosphere exuded devotion and passion for their Buddha and all he offered the people of Gyantse. As we walked away and returned to town, we carried this sense with us. From our travels, it certainly seemed like the people of Gyantse were free to practise their religion and propel their traditions forward. Although I understand the friction that exists between the Dalai Lama and the government of China, its effect was not apparent during Gyantse's timeless festival.

The Basics

Most useful items to pack: A couple of layers of clothing, as temperatures can be cool in the early morning and heat up as the festival progresses

Useful words and phrases in Tibetan: *tashi dele* ("hello"); *tujay chay* ("thank you"); *Kayrâng injikay shing-gi yöbay* ("Do you speak English?"); *gonda* ("sorry"); *kadü* ("when"); and *Par gyâbna digiy-rebay* ("Is it okay to take a photo?").[6]

A helpful reference can be found at tibetantrekking.com/culture/language.

For further travel information: Roger, the owner of Snow Jewel, both coordinated our stay and acted as our guide when we explored Tibet in 2010. Most years, Roger runs a tour specifically to attend the Gyantse Festival and hike around Mount Kailash; on his website he describes the tour as having "many highlights in terms of religion pilgrims and people of

6. Based on Lonely Planet's *Tibet Travel Guide* (see Bibliography).

Tibet…in short my favorite trip." The Mount Kailash trek is covered in my first book, *Dust in My Pack*. For more information about current tours, refer to the company's website: snowjewel.com.

~~~
~~~

MALAWI—DANCING THE MALIPENGA ON THE SHORES OF LAKE MALAWI

Cheer on your favourite team as they shuffle to the whistle of their drill sergeant and a melody of gourd horns under the warm African sun

The Experience

The drill sergeant stuck the blue plastic whistle between his teeth. Its shrill cry cut through the crowd. Troops leapt into form. They bent at the waist, leaning in with focused eyes and poised legs, ready to start their march. The sun blazed so strongly that the clear skies had become a dull haze. The island's sparse mango trees offered coveted shade to us and the residents alike. The soldiers' feet kicked up dust as they shuffled forward. About half wore running shoes while the others went barefoot. Their formal white T-shirts and khaki shorts were eclipsed by feathered headpieces. Bands cut from old newspapers or magazine pages had been glued onto rectangles of cardboard and curled into rings. A half-metre-long green feather was then attached to complete each helmet. Imagine rows of men, all wearing similar handmade hats with emerald plumes blowing in the breeze while they grooved in a systematic shuffle. This group called themselves the American BOMA (British Overseas Military Authority), and they were one of the teams competing in Likoma Island's Malipenga competition.

The residents of the small island of Likoma, midway along lengthy Lake Malawi, have devised a novel competition. It draws on Malawi's colonial past by poking fun at the British military's fixation on marching. A century ago, many Malawians had joined the Queen's army and trained under what they viewed as strange practices. Since gaining independence, the locals have taken these foreign conventions and turned them into a parody. The competition leverages a natural rivalry that brewed between the close-knit communities of the island. This spirit only enhances the intensity of the games. Fans jump into the dance for their respective team, usually adding a sense of vigour to the otherwise methodical rhythm of the shuffle. Elders retain a more composed and focused demeanour.

The American BOMA drill sergeant took on a persona all his own. This captain had donned a traditional British sergeant's hat and a bulky navy sweater adorned with red scarves draped over his shoulders, held in place with big bobby pins. A thicker red, black and green striped scarf—the same colours as Malawi's national flag—criss-crossed his chest in a giant X. The predominant colour, red, signified the people's struggle for independence, which they eventually achieved in July 1964. The sergeant never cracked a smile.

I am not sure how he managed to bear the heat beneath a T-shirt and sweater, but he led the dance in fine form.

Beyond the costumes, the musical accompaniment was truly unique. Dried gourds with long curved stems acted as horns. Their sound reminded me of a kazoo, with the same piercing quality. Between the shrieking whistle and vibrating vegetables, anticipation swelled across the audience. My husband and I attempted to clarify the rules with some of the locals. We asked what makes a winning Malipenga team. Their response was rather vague. It seems few rules restrict the judging process. Likely, the team that gains the most audience support would claim the winning title. Admirers often joined the shuffle and donated scarves to their favourite dancer. By the end, two of the dancers had accumulated armloads of the cotton wraps.

Malipenga dancers

We relished the afternoon along with everyone else. Some of us stood back under the shade of the mango trees. Others joined in the dance and swung their arms to the beat of the gourds. A handful of entrepreneurial kids brought plastic baskets filled with bananas or iceboxes of water bottles to sell. However, when I glanced over at two of the young boys, they both sat on the sand transfixed by the performance, their wares unsold and ignored at their sides. A few other children joined the ensemble. They had rolled scraps of paper into their own horns, the paper tubes making a surprisingly similar noise to the squealing gourds.

When it was all over, we walked back along a dirt road to the main town of Chipyela. Our favourite restaurant, the Hunger Clinic, had promised to serve us their staple dish, *nsima* and beans. After all, it was on the menu every day. Nsima is a simple dish made from maize flour and tastes much like polenta.

The best aspect of the Hunger Clinic was its location. We sat beneath a thatched roof, chatted with the staff and watched the town's main attraction, the central market, unfold on the beach in front of us on tarps set up on the sand. Piles of tree branches collected from the island's baobab and mango trees were a popular item. The kindling was carefully laid out on display, each stick neatly parallel to the others. Most people rely on wood fires for cooking, as diesel is expensive and electricity unreliable. Sellers typically have small stashes, which they display with pride in a tidy array. Each of these similar shops claimed a small patch on the sand, yet individual vendors took charge of their space. Bags were organized and stalls were lined up in straight rows. We watched as sellers sat amid their stock and waited for customers, unconcerned by the blazing sun that beat down endlessly.

Sacks of maize flour and ground nuts covered large sections of the beach. Men used one-gallon buckets to fill the bags from their supply of dried kernels piled on canvas sheets. Nearby, tarps strewn with tiny fish, left in the sun to dry, attracted an occasional buyer.

More permanent shops lined the main street leading to the beach. This road passed the other side of the Hunger Clinic, so we could watch it as well. Here, barbers worked from single chairs that sat in the middle of their tiny huts. If they had sufficient diesel, men could get a cut with an electric razor. Otherwise, an old pair of scissors was pulled out for a less precise trim. Farther down the street, vegetable stalls sold what was available; most vendors displayed one, or at the most two, types of produce.

Likoma Island is not overly fertile. Much of the ground is dry and dusty, making it difficult for locals to cultivate crops. This explains why most meals consist of nsima and beans, two of the few staples consistently available. Somehow mango and baobab trees cope and even flourish in the higher central region of the island. Their shade allowed for the second most appealing aspect of visiting the island: exploring relatively untouched communities. Since the island is only seventeen square kilometres, we covered much of it on foot.

Friendly children ensured our travels were not lonely. As we walked past the old Cathedral of Saint Peter and out of Chipyela, the soft patter of feet caught up to us. The steps were rapid and light, the sound of youngsters running. Their voices yelled with delight in the local dialect: "*Mzungu, mzungu!*" ("White person, white person!"). The sight of us triggered a fresh dose of exhilaration and adrenalin, as if they had just conquered a new game. Within seconds, each of my fingers was snatched up, and four or five school kids clung to each hand. They wore green and white uniforms. We did not speak more than a couple of words in their language, and they knew only a few English words. Sometimes we all just walked in a contented silence.

Other times we joked or raced with them. The later part of our walk to their home village of Khuyu turned into a series of one-hundred-metre dashes.

I could not help but feel like long-lost neighbours with the people of Likoma Island. When walking into town, we were certain to receive greetings from everyone we passed or, at the very least, a nod and a wave. Lifestyles were basic. Many homes were made of mud brick with tin roofs. But it was clear that education was a priority from the number of children wearing school uniforms. Parents sold fruit or vegetables or offered their services as barbers or police officers. Most earned enough to enjoy the occasional Kuche Kuche (pronounced "coochy coochy"), a Malawian beer. Our days were filled without much effort. If you are looking for a relaxed getaway and are tempted by a completely different culture, Likoma Island might be your answer.

The Basics

Most useful items to pack: Sunscreen and a hat

Useful words in Chichewa: *moni* ("hello"); *zikomo* ("thank you"); *inde* ("yes"); *iyayi* ("no"); *kuvina* ("to dance"); *abambo* ("sir"); and *amayi* ("madam").[7]

English is the official language in Malawi; however, Chichewa is the prominent dialect used across the country. For more useful words, refer to chichewadictionary.org/learning-chichewa/mini-course/20.

For further travel information: The Malipenga we attended took place in October 2010. I understand that it is a regular

7. Based on Lonely Planet's *Southern Africa Travel Guide* (see Bibliography).

event, so check with your accommodation for their local knowledge about its timing.

We stayed at the quaint Mango Drift. They cater to budget-conscious travellers and offer beachfront camping, dorms and private bungalows. Our chalet with a private ensuite was tucked away from the dorms and very quiet. It had views towards nearby Chizumulu Island. Their website has a comprehensive description of options to get to Likoma Island. For more information, refer to the website at mangodrift.com.

If you are coming from Mozambique's nearby mainland, you will likely clear customs at Cobue's one-room immigration office. Be warned, its corrugated metal roof and windowless construction turns into a sweltering hotbox. Even the duty officer must have felt the warmth; beads slipped down his temples as he wrote down our details in a half-metre-long ledger that held the particulars of every foreigner who passed through his watch. All foreigners coming and going from this remote corner of Mozambique are recorded here. When we arrived on Likoma Island, the duty officer had left Malawi's required forms inside his briefcase at home. So our customs intake included a diversion to stop by his house before our details could be processed.

One of my most memorable experiences was leaving Likoma Island on the infamous *Ilala* ferry. Not only did the crew leave the captain behind but the resulting backtracking led to a fuel shortage. This adventure and more are covered in my first book, *Dust in My Pack.*

~~~
~~~

5

Fallen Kingdoms

This chapter takes two utterly distinct regions and leaps back in time to look at their older selves. We started our trail in the medieval centres of Eastern Europe's Baltic countries, where stone-block castles and cobblestoned streets mingled with modern conveniences. Then we ventured farther back in history to the foundation of Sri Lanka's early civilization. The country's central highlands are referred to as its Cultural Triangle, with each corner representing one of the country's three paternal cities: Anuradhapura, Polonnaruwa and Kandy. Kandy has transformed into a modern hub of commotion, leaving the preceding capitals with their mossy bricks and tilted towers as far more evocative sites.

The first three sections of this chapter delve into the most memorable places from each of the Baltic nations we visited. Estonia's conflicted heritage showed its face in Kuressaare Castle on Saaremaa Island. In Latvia, the less-touristy Cēsis Castle captured the essence of its people and offered a glimpse into the country's past. Lastly, Lithuania's capital city of Vilnius exuded a passion and personality that normally evades urban centres. The final two sections of the chapter step through Sri Lanka's archaeological cities of Anuradhapura and Polonnaruwa, where the people and their stories extended our experience beyond merely walking through ruins. Despite the differences across all these locations, one common element trickled through their core: water. This fluid allowed societies to flourish, from its elemental life-giving properties to hosting ports along long-distance trade routes. Water led to growth, and growth meant greater power.

The Baltic Sea acted as a gateway allowing ships to travel from Europe to Asia and vice versa. It is therefore not surprising that the largest medieval cities lay on the coast. For those located inland, rivers supplied their illustrious liquid. Vilnius is situated on the Neris River, and its water-filled moats carried ships right up to Cathedral Square and the Royal Palace. Inevitably, the quest for power and its resulting conflict brewed within such pivotal centres and even seeps into the present day. We walked through medieval villages updated to appeal to twenty-first-century tourism but fortified with bygone quarrels. Power-hungry overlords might don a different cloak, but similar tensions remain. During our recent visit, a NATO alliance clustered along Baltic borders to discourage Russia from overstepping its bounds. Similar disputes have raged across these lands for hundreds of years, even before the Soviet Union's control. Back in feudal times, families battled for this territory in a persistent back-and-forth struggle with Russian kingships that seems to have amplified people's sense of identity.

Since the Baltic countries broke free from the Soviet Union in the late 1990s, their economies have blossomed. Beneath their outer shells and after approximately thirty years of solidarity, the three countries in this chapter have spun their own unique story. Estonia is the high-tech haven with a touch of reserved personality. You may have heard of the well-known communication software named Skype—its technology was developed by Estonians. Latvia feels comfortable in its own skin, sincere without having anything to prove. Lithuania has an effortless style, a contemporary chic with depth drawn from its past.

Jumping over to Sri Lanka in Southeast Asia, we explored the centre of the island, where most of the country's ancient cities are located. We started exploring the oldest and largest site, Anuradhapura, built in the third century BC.[1] Anuradhapura grew for over 1,300 years, in large part due to the city's industrious water management techniques. Massive tanks and canals were constructed to carry fresh water throughout the city, to royal baths and to a public hospital. However, these ancient wonders did not flourish indefinitely. Foreign forces crept too close and eventually compelled the royal families to shift their cosmopolitan homes elsewhere. The kingdom relocated farther south, to the site of Polonnaruwa, around AD 993,[2] where it thrived for approximately one hundred and fifty years.[3]

Sri Lanka's former urban powerhouses have now become archaeological sites. Their foundations are vacant except for inquisitive travellers and a few caretakers wandering among the tumbled stones. Although their ruins lie dormant, a vibrant urban sprawl beating with life sits adjacent to these aged centres, not unlike the capital cities that surround the Baltic's medieval cities. Stories from both ancient cities are captured in this chapter.

Since Sri Lanka's thirty-year civil war ended in 2009, people have been able to relax in relative peace. Their strong will is evident across the country. New hotels, tour companies and businesses have

1. whc.unesco.org/en/list/200
2. whc.unesco.org/en/list/201
3. britannica.com/place/Sri-Lanka/Conversion-to-Buddhism#ref278850

sprung up in every town we visited. More were under construction. Everyone seemed to know a driver for hire with our choice of taxi, tuk-tuk or private sedan. These networks earned them money and brought opportunity for a better future for their families. It struck me how much people can achieve if only their environment is free of violence and war. In both regions we visited, new growth sprouted during times of peace, unearthing an old narrative from a new beginning.

~~~
~~~

ESTONIA—UNRAVELLING TRAGEDY AND MYTH AT KURESSAARE CASTLE

Walk through the arched hallways of a captivating medieval castle that lured not only Nordic nations, but also Germany and the Soviet Union before Estonia gained independence in 1991

The Experience

For almost seven hundred years, the island of Saaremaa was yanked from one country to another until it finally joined with mainland Estonia in 1918. Its attractive location is partially to blame since the island sits in the upper west side of the Baltic Sea, offering the perfect portal through which to monitor ships travelling between Europe and Russia. It all started in 1227 when the German Brothers of the Sword seized control of this tranquil island. The Brothers arrived in the name of the Livonian Order on a crusade to conquer and spread Christianity. For three hundred years, they balanced the roles of monk and soldier. Their stronghold, Kuressaare Castle, was constructed on the protected southeastern edge of the island and took on the personality of both cloister and fortress. This odd coupling proved successful, as the Brothers of the Sword maintained relative peace while they reigned over this region until the sixteenth century.

Skipping forward to 1559, Russian forces were advancing across the Baltic region, and the Brothers' bravery was slipping. The governing bishop sold Kuressaare Castle to the King of Denmark and fled to escape the feared Livonian War, led by the infamous Ivan the Terrible. This move inadvertently kicked off a series of unintended consequences. The Russians did not actually arrive at Kuressaare for another hundred and fifty years, but the Danes soon handed the fort over to Sweden to settle a separate skirmish. Eventually Russian forces did show up. They took control from the Swedes in the early 1700s by virtually annihilating the fortification. German troops also occupied it for a short period during World War I before the Estonians finally regained their land.

With Estonians back in control of their island, local farms flourished and community life recovered. However, this liberty was short lived, a mere twenty years long. In 1940, forces from the Soviet

Union arrived and took over the island. In 1941, Nazi Germany began a three-year occupation. At the end of World War II, the Soviet Union jumped in and annexed the island along with Estonia. They turned the agricultural island of Saaremaa into a military restricted zone. Locals were forbidden to even speak with foreigners. Eventually, in the early 1990s, the Soviet Union dissolved, and Estonia, with its beloved island of Saaremaa, emerged as a sovereign nation once more.[4]

When our bus rolled out of Tallinn, Estonia's capital city, I did not fully appreciate the imprint left from this country's past, an ambiguous enigma developed over generations. Its culture still seemed shadowy, and its edges had only started to materialize in my mind. We ventured to the smaller community of Kuressaare on the island of Saaremaa in hopes of finding a truer reflection of local life away from the city's bustling sprawl. Saaremaa enticed us for two reasons: our Lonely Planet travel guide described the island as having "forested coastlines and [a] languid lifestyle" and Kuressaare Castle as "the Baltics' best-preserved medieval fortress."[5] When we arrived, we found the town's streets lined with cement buildings, painted in pastels of lemon chiffon, alabaster and pale pink. Clay roof tiles tarnished with age added an element of gritty truth.

Farther down the main street, tall trees and green grass create a barrier between the town centre and the city's namesake castle. A star-shaped moat of murky water protects the fortress' grassy banks as it has for centuries. The castle is home to the oldest museum in Estonia, and its fully restored interior relays a feudal past. Stone walls, metres thick in some places, kept rebels out and secrets in. We climbed metal stairwells and traversed narrow passages to explore

4. www.saaremaa.ee/index.php?option=com_content&view=article&id=195
5. Based on Lonely Planet's *Estonia, Latvia and Lithuania Travel Guide* (see Bibliography).

various areas of the fortification, each revealing a different page of the castle's history. I stepped down a set of curving stairs into the basement. With no windows providing access to the outdoors, it appeared as if the curators had attempted to bring nature inside. Displays showcase stuffed local birds such as the grey plover. This specimen, an oldie that had not flown for over a hundred years, is a member of Mierzeyewski's 1908 collection, which composes much of the museum's exhibition.[6] Although intended to convey nature's beauty, the Department of Natural History's subterranean exhibit felt more gloomy than celebratory.

In the northeastern wing, connected rooms form a chain of exhibits that reveal a local perspective during and after World War II. The feeling of oppression that Estonians must have felt during this period rings vehemently through the hallways. Stills from Soviet propaganda films and posters hang on the walls. The desk belonging to the first collective farm's chairman stares across one room at a tiny wooden rowboat balanced in the opposite corner. The boat is not much larger than the desk. Refugees had once used this small vessel to try to escape the Soviet Union's iron fist by paddling through rough waters to Sweden. It is a poignant display of cause and effect. The scene effectively screams the dissent of the people of Saaremaa over the Communist domination of their previously autonomous livelihoods. Black and white photos of local Communist Party leaders and their rallies line the walls. Local farmers who resisted and sabotaged the Soviets became local heroes. Stories from these "Forest Brothers," named after their forest hideouts, are retold in the museum's displays.

The most dramatic exposition is located in the Gunpowder Cellar. In 1941, Soviet troops killed ninety people inside Kuressaare Castle,

6. www.saaremaamuuseum.ee/en/castle-and-fortress/permanent-exhibition/loodusosakond

thirty-one of whom were found buried in a mass grave below this very cellar. Their wrists had been tied with barbed wire. The perpetrators clearly hoped this act would never be detected and blew up the Gunpowder Tower to destroy the scene. However, their actions were later unearthed. The museum exposes the horrid event through photos of victims discovered underground and of their executioners.[7]

Another section of the museum cultivated an entirely different ambience, a lighter tone requiring an abrupt shift of mindset. Abstract artwork covered one room's gothic arches. Tiny spotlights lit up cream-coloured stone and shone across pretty framed paintings. From there time shifted as we climbed the watchtower, one of the oldest structures in the castle. In an attempt to recapture an air of time-worn realism, the sound of growling lions played from hidden speakers as we crossed the upper bridge. I looked down and a pitch-black hole stared back with one impenetrable eye. At one time, prisoners were apparently thrown down this dark cavern. Ahead, an empty room indicated we had reached the top of the tower and the end of our walk. The museum's collage of themes felt unsettling at times but, in retrospect, it illuminated the diversity of issues influencing this region.

The island of Saaremaa also has a quirky side. Where else would you find a Tree of the Year? We spotted the lush one-hundred-and-fifty-year-old oak in the middle of a pasture, after our bus rolled past the town of Orissaare. There was no need to return for a closer look. It was simply that, a tree in the middle of a field. The second peculiar sight came on the same bus ride, as we passed another field just as nondescript as the first. In this case, a yellow signpost stood in the

7. www.saaremaamuuseum.ee/en/castle-and-fortress/permanent-exhibition/commemorative-exhibition

grass. It was a diamond-shaped kangaroo crossing sign and reminded me of those I had seen in Australia. I presumed the landowner must have taken a very memorable trip to Australia and decided that this cautionary notice was the best souvenir he could find.

Although members of Kuressaare's most recent generation live in a peaceful environment, their parents and grandparents know a very different past. Gaining an understanding of the island's tumultuous history has helped to frame my impressions. The community's trust of outsiders has certainly suffered, and at times I sensed a not-so-veiled aura of constraint. It came across in a stoically stern grocery-store clerk and in the unseeing eyes of a passerby who smacked shoulders without slowing. Casual conversation was not given; it was earned. This cool persona might not be the warm welcome that travellers crave, but it reflects the region's true self. After all, travel is about more than just a fun holiday. The experience illustrated the many layers of Estonia's cultural reality and exposed a new perspective that I might not have understood without visiting that world myself.

The Basics

Most useful item to pack: An internationally recognized driver's licence to rent a car and explore more of the island

Useful words and phrases in Estonian: *tere* ("hello"); *tänan* ("thank you"); *jah* ("yes"); *ei* ("no"); and *Kus on bussijaam?* ("Where is the bus station?").[8]

For further travel information: Kuressaare Castle houses the Saaremaa Museum. For more information, refer to their website at www.saaremaamuuseum.ee/en.

8. Based on Lonely Planet's *Estonia, Latvia and Lithuania Travel Guide* (see Bibliography).

A number of bus companies travel throughout Estonia and south into neighbouring Baltic countries. Lux Express was my preferred company, but they do not cover all routes. Further information can be found on their website: luxexpress.eu/en/routes-within-estonia. I recommend purchasing tickets at the bus station rather than online. Schedule boards and staff working in the ticket kiosks provided useful information about route options.

Bus connections allowed us to reach key centres across Estonia, but more remote parks and less-visited sites without direct bus routes were out of reach on our relatively short schedule. With hindsight, I would recommend renting a car for at least a few days to give yourself more flexibility to explore. If hiking and the outdoors are of interest, consider Lahemaa National Park or Karula National Park.

~~~
~~~

LATVIA—FINDING RUGGED SIMPLICITY AT CĒSIS CASTLE

Wander partial walls and climb defensive towers without the crowds at one of Latvia's most influential medieval sites

The Experience

I quickly forgot the modern glass panels of the Cēsis Tourism Development and Information Centre after stepping outside its doors and facing a scene that drew me back in time. Remnants of a once foreboding fortress lay ahead, refreshingly vacant of the amber gift shops and T-shirt vendors that had invaded Riga's and Tallinn's medieval centres. Instead, the walls of a four-storey cloister stood—at least partially. The roof was missing and only two sides remained. Arched doorways led to bygone kitchens, and stone bricks rounded from weather and jagged with age looked much like a craggy mountain peak. A few original slabs lingered, but most had been restored into place using traditional techniques with mortar and dolomite. Green lawns and bushy trees completed the remaining space around the old convent.

The main structure was built in 1214 for the Livonian Brothers of the Sword. This fortified monastery housed members of the brotherhood, some of whom were knights and others were priests, as well as servants, artisans and general workers. The self-contained society even had its own brewery, which might have implied a dynamic atmosphere of love, war and merriment, except that members of the brotherhood vowed to abstain from any sort of entertainment, leaving the fun to their weary crew.

The ascetic lifestyle might have continued unabated if it were not for the area's prime location. What was considered greater Livonia at the time, including parts of Latvia and Estonia, offered access to the precious Baltic Sea. Its waters connected ports across northern Europe to Saint Petersburg, so it was a valuable trading passage that drew Russian interests. Nearly thirty years of conflict ensued. Cēsis Castle, an important base for the Teutonic Order that ruled Livonia, became embroiled in the messy Livonian War. Tsar Ivan the

Terrible sowed his wrath upon this stronghold. In 1577, the Russian military besieged the Cēsis community. Three hundred civilians fled to the fortress. Its stone walls were insufficient, and historians surmise that the group chose to blow themselves up rather than suffer imprisonment by the Russians. So they set fire to the gunpowder storage room, creating a massive explosion that killed everyone inside.

A signpost at ground level tells of three women and two children whose remains were found in 1974 one level beneath the explosion's core. They were thought to have hidden in the basement chambers to avoid the mass suicide that their neighbours above had chosen. Unfortunately, the explosion obliterated the floor of the gunpowder cache and thereby destroyed their shelter in the process. A reconstructed photo of what the lady is thought to have looked like, based on archaeological and historical data, adds a sense of poignancy to the story. Her daughter's bones were discovered lying next to her. When I looked up from the placard, the partial walls and ancient past seemed less distant. A breeze blew, stirring leaves fallen from the same trees that would have witnessed such devastation.

Conflict between this region and Russia continues to ferment to this day, more than four hundred years later. In just the few days we were in Latvia, we spotted Canadian troops twice. They were members of a NATO coalition aimed to deter aggression from Russia towards Eastern European borders under Operation REASSURANCE.[9] We felt this shadow of unease throughout our travels in the Baltic regions as former feudal wars and struggles over land rights continued to percolate. People seemed tense, and they avoided casual banter between strangers. It makes sense when you

9. forces.gc.ca/en/operations-abroad/nato-ee.page

consider the backdrop against which they have lived and endured for hundreds of years, compared to our temporary visit as strangers.

Cēsis Castle

A whirring buzz startled me back to the present moment. A white square darted overhead, weaving like a seagull after eating bad fish. I decided the drone must be capturing photos for next season's tourist brochure, despite it being distinctly out of character for this antiquated site. I looked around for the gadget's owner but saw only a couple of visitors striding out of the northern tower's doorway. They carried candlelit lanterns, a much more appropriate device for the castle's setting. The drone flitted away, and I turned my attention back to the northern tower. My husband and I had climbed without the helpful lamps. Clips of sunlight had filtered through window openings on each floor, shedding just enough triangular rays to allow us to see inside the curved stairwell.

On the third level we had found a medieval drop toilet, unused for centuries. It had been built into a stone antechamber off the king's bedroom. This might have been one of the earliest ensuite bathrooms and much more convenient than stumbling down those dim stairs in the middle of the night. For now, a narrow window let just enough light into the lavatory that we could recognize its purpose. If you prefer more modern amenities, the newer and adjacent Cēsis manor house showcases what life was like after the old castle was abandoned. The von Wolff family stayed in the newer mansion until the 1770s and then sold their luxurious home to Count Karl Eberhard von Sievers. It remained in his family for five generations. Its present style recreates the von Sievers' lavish home life. Rooms include two in-house libraries and even a coffee room, as coffee drinking was a popular social activity back in the early 1900s for those who could afford it.[10]

Overall, Cēsis Castle stood out from many other fortresses scattered across the Baltics. It had been renovated enough to give a sense of its scale and the different chambers, but not so much as to appear artificial. The surrounding town carried on with its quiet life and

10. cesupils.lv/en/the-castle-complex/cesis-castle-manor-house/interior-exposition

seemed rather uninterested in redefining itself for the tourism industry. When we left the castle and headed back towards the town's bus station, a small mini-market showed the only sign of activity. One teller processed a queue of about six people, who practically filled an entire aisle of the wee shop. We decided that we could survive without snacks for our return bus trip. Our decision paid off, as a bakery closer to the bus stop offered doughy goodness to fill the gap in our stomachs—without the lineup. On schedule, our bus rolled into its designated stop at the depot, and we settled in for a relaxed ride back to the big city of Riga.

The Basics

Most useful item to pack: Walking shoes that can handle a bit of rough ground

Useful words and phrases in Latvian: *sveiks/sveika* ("hello" to a male/female); *jā* ("yes"); *nē* ("no"); *paldies* ("thank you"); *Lūdzu rēkinu* ("The bill, please"); and *Kur atrodas autoosta* ("Where is the bus station?").[11]

For further travel information: Cēsis can be visited as a day trip from Latvia's capital city, Riga. Buses take one and a half hours and, when we were there, cost €2 to €4 each way, depending on the direction. For some reason, it cost more to leave Riga than it did to return. The buses were in good condition and even offered Wi-Fi on board.

For more information on visiting Cēsis Castle, refer to cesupils.lv/en.

11. Based on Lonely Planet's *Estonia, Latvia and Lithuania Travel Guide* (see Bibliography).

LITHUANIA—MINGLING WITH THE OLD AND NEW IN REFINED VILNIUS

Stroll through a city where European comfort fuses with the medieval past to form a medley of arts, culture and contemporary urban venues

The Experience

The streets were deserted. Had we fallen into a fairy-tale city decorated like a fancy wedding cake but without any guests? The morning felt oddly serene as we wandered the cobblestoned lanes and wound our way to Vilnius' central Cathedral Square. The square's liveliness from the night before had turned sedate. There were no tour groups, no hawkers or people rushing to work. Only a couple of people strolled the silent expanse. Our first clue of what was happening was the chorus that drifted from Vilnius Cathedral. A weekday mass at a time when people would normally be grabbing a coffee and rushing to work seemed abnormal. We left the spacious square to explore the narrow and windy streets—all to ourselves. Every block seemed to house an ornate church topped by a spire with a golden fringe reflecting the rising sun. Brilliant crosses and bulbous domes glittered against muted walls and stone carvings. A few more people drifted about, many carrying a small bundle of dried wildflowers. Desiccated petals softened by purple and yellow hues created a delicate country chic look. We turned down another narrow street. Men, women and young ladies walked with their petite bouquets.

Ahead lay the Gate of Dawn, which housed a shrine above the only surviving gateway to the old city. We caught a glimpse of the tiny chapel through an open archway visible from the street below. A bridge-like walkway formed a sanctuary that connected buildings on either side of the street. Two rows of people scrunched in its narrow hall and prayed. They stood by a golden plaque of the Virgin Mary from the sixteenth century. Rays emanated from her bowed head, heavy under a head scarf of gold. We listened as psalms reverberated from the window and down the street. Under the Soviet Union's control, religious services at this shrine were prohibited. It was not until Lithuania gained its sovereignty in 1990 that they could recommence, turning this place into an icon of independence. Many now consider this image of the Virgin Mary to be the guardian of Lithuania.[12]

We walked beneath the elevated chapel and soon uncovered the source of all the bouquets. Elderly women sold bunches of blossoms from square tarps set on the cement sidewalk in front of the old city gate. This makeshift market conveniently caught anyone headed to their favoured sanctuary without an offering. Bunches of lavender and wildflowers of yellow and cream concealed the grey cement beneath the women's feet. Between serving customers, the ladies rested on plastic stools, munching bread filled with what looked like slices of Spam. We bought a couple of small bundles of flowers for €0.50 each from an elderly lady hunched over her wares. She had tied a paisley kerchief around her head and wore a navy and white striped sweater, unlike the contemporary styles worn by younger generations. Her eyes squinted in the sunlight, veins burst from her tanned forearms and wrinkles crimped her skin.

It took some navigating, as the ladies spoke no English and we had not yet mastered the words for numbers in Lithuanian. My meagre handful of change was not sufficient, evident after one lady picked through it and gently pushed my hand away with disinterest. When I handed her a €5 note—not sure what, if any, change I would get back—she gladly went to her money bucket and pulled out €4.50. After I handed back a €0.50 coin and picked out a second bunch, the mood shifted and smiles surfaced.

12. ourladyofsiluva.org/visiting/shrines/dawn

Flower seller outside the Gate of Dawn

As we walked away, feeling good about our small purchase, Crustum Bakery and Café's array of baked goods and vacant tables caught our attention. Their plum and custard pastry was flaky and delicious, and the staff explained why so many people had picked up flowers to leave at churches and shrines on a weekday. It was August 15, Assumption Day and a national holiday. Re-energized, we walked past the Church of Saint Casimir, which was tucked off the road leading to the Gate of Dawn. Jesuits built the church in 1604, and it had taken seven hundred people to haul the cornerstone block into its present position. The building could be considered ahead of its time, for it changed careers over its lifetime as much as millennials tend to switch roles in the modern era.

Ill fate welcomed the church into the world, as fires burned it down three times during its first one hundred and fifty years. After each, the church was rebuilt. In 1812, Napoleon's army came through on a bid to topple Russia. They used the structure as a granary and then passed the dusty building on to missionary priests a few years later, by which time, Napoleon's troops had proceeded so far into Russia that their supplies had run out and many had perished.[13] The Russians returned, kicked the priests out and switched the building over to a Russian Orthodox church. They even made some impressive renovations in 1868, only to have the Germans take the building over during World War I, when their soldiers used it for Lutheran services. After the Germans left, the building was returned to the Catholics and then specifically to the Jesuits. During World War II, the Russians re-entered the scene, and the building reverted back to a granary until the 1960s, when it was curiously transformed into a museum of atheism.[14] Perhaps it was divine intervention, but in 1988 the building was once more returned to the Catholics, and in 1991 the cycle ended when it was returned to the Jesuits to become a working

13. bbc.co.uk/history/ancient/archaeology/napoleon_army_01.shtml
14. baltictimes.com/news/articles/3011

church once again. Sadly, many of the original Baroque frescoes and statues were destroyed during its turbulent past.

The tension between Russian and Lithuanian national forces has brewed for centuries. This became particularly noticeable at two sites: a palace and a university. At the central Palace of the Grand Dukes of Lithuania, the region's history unfolds with tales of marriages, alliances and power struggles. It is as if the present and the past are stuck rolling and tumbling in a repetitive loop, feeding the cliché that history certainly does repeat itself. Battles for land have raged in this region since fiefdoms first appeared. The palace's exterior of white walls, rigid corners and a slate roof establish authority and control. Inside, its softer stance becomes evident. Partially restored walls, cellars and remnants of the fortified and frequently renovated palace transform from its archaic foundations into colonial opulence on higher floors. Tales from the past are retold in museum displays. Marriages, births and battles can be followed from room to room as family ties and political power surged, abated and re-emerged years later.

After gaining a historical perspective on the region, we moved on to explore the intellectually inspiring Vilnius University. It was founded as a Jesuit college in 1570 and became a university nine years later. Access is gained through an imposing brick gate, behind which the school grounds open up into a world far different from life outside. Only a few other visitors walked the ancient cobblestoned corridors with us. Street sounds faded inside this compound. Through a pillared gateway, the magical courtyard of the Astronomical Observatory greeted us. Two grey pillars stood three storeys tall. From the structure's outer wall, four windows peered down on us like square eyes. The sun's glare prevented any insight into what might lay within this mysterious building. So I focused on what was visible. Zodiac signs made from white plaster formed a band across the upper level. Beneath the astrological icons, Latin words invoked my imagination, encouraging all those who read its message to push themselves beyond their perceived bounds: "Courage illuminated the old world with new light. This is the house of Urania: begone, everyday cares! We turn our backs on humble Earth, from here we rise to the stars." Sadly, such dreams and inspiration have been feared throughout history by certain people with power.

At times, education in Vilnius was banned entirely or at least reshaped to the will of the particular governing entity. Tsar Nicholas I of Russia closed the university's doors in 1832. They were reopened by Polish authority in 1919 and then closed once more by the Nazis in 1943. The Soviets reopened it in 1944 but under Soviet principles of higher education. In 1990, Lithuania was able to ratify the University Statute under its own sovereignty. I left with the distinct impression that Lithuanians pride themselves on their educational prowess and advanced ideologies. Having jurisdiction over their university and all it represented gave citizens freedom of mind.

Vilnius was a captivating city, artistic yet absolute, stimulating yet resilient. It was a city with energy enough to reawaken my passionate travel bug, which had been feeling dejected. Perhaps it was the cosmopolitan layers that somehow both protected and flaunted the city's treasures with one twist of a street. Its old centre had not been eclipsed by tourism. Restaurants and museums stood alongside business towers and shopping malls. It felt real, vibrant and savvy. Locals met friends, drove to work and walked children to school. They went to church and chatted at street-side cafés while visitors melded into the daily mélange of city life. Vilnius is definitely worth a visit so that you can unravel its delicate secrets and tantalizing tales for yourself.

The Basics

Most useful item to pack: A notepad to capture the endless stories from the past that are shared on informative signs at various sites and structures around the city

Useful words and phrases in Lithuanian: *sveiki* ("hello"); *taip* ("yes"); *ne* ("no"); *dėkoju* ("thank you"); *Kur yra autobuso stotelė* ("Where is the bus stop?"); and *kavos* ("coffee").[15]

For further travel information: We travelled from the town of Klaipėda to Vilnius with Eurolines. The bus company outsourced its service to the local Klaipėdos Autobusų Parkas, a top choice that rivalled Lux Express for comfort and timeliness. The trip took four hours with only a couple of stops along the way. The on-board Wi-Fi was strong and the seats were cushy. For more information, refer to the website: klap.lt/en.

We stayed in a one-bedroom apartment, centrally located and tucked into a quiet old stone building. Our specific unit on Klaipėdos Street no longer appears on internet searches, but this was a convenient location if you find another suitable hotel on offer.

Crustum Bakery and Café earned its place as our favourite coffee and bakery spot in Vilnius: crustum.lt.

As recommended by our apartment's host, Mano Guru served

15. Based on Lonely Planet's *Estonia, Latvia and Lithuania Travel Guide* (see Bibliography).

a tasty selection of salads and light meals at a reasonable price. Their coffee and fruit drinks were also noteworthy. For more, see their website at manoguru.lt.

~~~
~~~

SRI LANKA—DELVING INTO THE SPIRITUAL PAST OF ANURADHAPURA

Follow early morning devotions as pilgrims place offerings at a two-thousand-year-old bodhi tree and pray inside an equally ancient temple

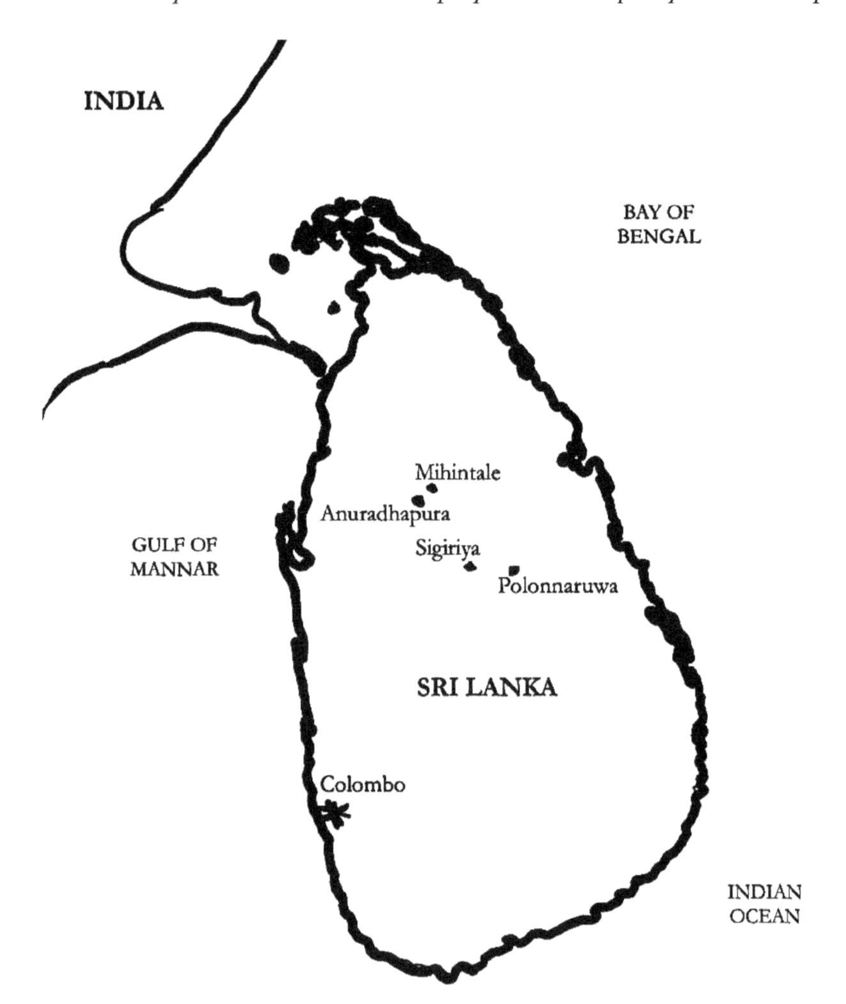

The Experience

We trod back in time to Sri Lanka's central archaeological sites, which seep with passion even in the present day. As the sun's early rays turned the sky from steely grey to a soft lemon colour, we stood alone near the ancient Jaya Sri Maha Bodhi, a tree in the southern end of Anuradhapura's archaeological city. Metal gates barred access, clamped together with a large lock that hung dejectedly until the key man arrived. It was not long before we realized everything was about to change. A band of people walked towards us—well, not precisely towards us, but towards their revered tree, which drooped overhead. Two monks led the congregation. One wore flip-flops and the other was barefoot. They looked to be teenagers, but their robes in the colour of raw sienna evoked a sense of earnest respect. Behind them, men and women followed, up to three or four abreast, holding a lengthy swatch of cream-coloured material above their heads. These pilgrims were dressed completely in white, making the monks' robes stand out as brilliant beacons against the white flow in their wake.

Every devotee would have risen at four or five o'clock. Any style of dress was fine, so long as it was modest and white. There were long skirts, pants, lace-sleeved tops and button-down shirts. Once at the gate, the pilgrims removed hats, shoes and socks. As worshippers entered the now unlocked gates, women stepped through a passageway on the left while men walked through the right side. Within a few steps they were back together and proceeded towards the central tree. Bare footsteps silently pressed the sandy earth into a smooth path that circled the grounds. The hushed calm was replaced by low chanting, which carried us through the morning's homage.

An old stone temple emerged from the same sandy bank as the ancient tree. I edged closer to the door, trying to meld into its thick panel so as not to block the surge of pilgrims headed inside. Bodies pressed together. Drumbeats grew into a crescendo so loud that their pulse tugged at my veins. I glanced backwards to see the crowd continuing to flood forward. They were led by eight men pounding either single or double handmade drums slung over their shoulders. Everyone pressed forward, restraining themselves just enough so as not to push the drummers. Initially they entered single file. More pilgrims arrived, squeezing through the doorway shoulder to shoulder to settle onto the increasingly cramped floor. The small sanctuary turned into a bundle of bowed heads. Worshippers stretched their arms and slid their hands through the slow-moving procession to sprinkle flower petals at the feet of the central Buddha statue.

The crowd ebbed, people following one another closely, even touching a shoulder or lightly clutching an arm. Some found space to sit cross-legged on the floor. A low chant reverberated across the room. Candles flickered in the dawn's sunbeams before their soft glow was obliterated by the flash of fluorescent lights switched on. Some folks brought baskets filled with lotus petals, while others carried bowls of rice. The scene turned into a finely connected mesh of activity, each person holding out their offering as they walked barefoot into the temple. Fellow worshippers reached to gently touch the incoming offerings while murmuring a prayer like a tidal lullaby that never ceased. The drums added their strength to the rhythmic cadence. Attendees seemed to become entwined during this morning ritual. They might not have known one another outside this service, but here they came together. It was as if a thread of the sacred bodhi's wispy root had woven a web around its followers.

This bodhi tree is said to be over two thousand years old. Guardians, typically monks, have tended to it over that entire period, generation after generation. It grew from a sapling brought to Sri Lanka in 236 BC, reportedly from the very tree that Siddhartha meditated under when he first attained enlightenment—referred to as the state of *bodhi*. Fig trees spread as they grow, and true to this trait, the Jaya Sri Maha Bodhi's limbs had grown too long and too weighty for its trunk to support. To compensate, golden posts dotted the temple grounds and propped up any branch that draped too low.

Every fibre of the esteemed bodhi tree is believed to be sacred. Nature, people, animals and life in general are believed to be connected through a circular life energy, like a shared kinship bound for eternity. Care for the environment is not a compartmentalized activity one should add to one's daily chores, but rather a fundamental slice of the Buddhist wheel of life. Buddhism considers everyone and everything around the world to be linked, life after life, birth after birth.

Only monks or approved caretakers entered the cordoned area that surrounded the tree. A picket fence painted gold marked the boundary. The people wearing white lined up and handed over platters mounded with lotus petals and jasmine flowers. It was powerful to see the wholehearted dedication in the men's and women's eyes as they walked, stooped or upright, towards their sacred tree and temple. Such devotion was routine for the people who kneeled with respect before heading to the office. By eight thirty, the sun was beating down and even the sandy ground emanated heat. In two days, the *poya* ("full moon") celebration would transform this same location into an even grander event. But not today. This morning's activities were typical in this ancient city, kept alive by both young and old generations.

Pilgrims at the Ruvanvelisaya Dagoba

Devotee at the Abayagiriya Stupa

The vast temple complex of Anuradhapura initially sprouted from the small Jaya Sri Maha Bodhi seedling. After it was planted, temples were constructed, administration took hold and political control reigned for 1,300 years. What remains is an assortment of ruins, many refurbished or partially restored but still used as active temples.

The adjacent urban sprawl of modern Anuradhapura makes for a convenient base to explore the archaeological site.

Nearing eleven o'clock in the morning, our tuk-tuk pulled up to one such temple, the Jetavanaramaya Dagoba. Its plain brick dome and tottering pillars attracted no one beneath the blue sky turned hazy with heat. After removing my sandals, my toes prickled on the rough brick base, and I imagined singe marks seared on my soles. I missed our tuk-tuk within four steps of leaving its shaded cover. After our five hours of exploring that morning, the oppressive heat had asphyxiated my curiosity. Anuradhapura's proximity to our hotel's air-conditioned comfort prevailed over the sun's rays, which had burned away any enthusiasm to appreciate another stupa.

When we returned a few hours later, Jetavanaramaya Dagoba felt like an entirely different place. The air had cooled, if only slightly. A family walked slowly around and talked in hushed voices, heads bent together. My husband stayed back to capture some photos while I circled the dome. A couple of men were working nearby, high on a set of scaffolding. One called out to ask where I was from. He then wondered why I was travelling alone. In Sri Lanka, women usually travel with friends or family, so my apparent solo travel seemed odd. He appeared satisfied to hear that my husband was nearby.

The country's thirty-year civil war had ended in 2009, only eight years earlier. Sri Lankans now seem galvanized to rebuild their country and prove its potential. They no longer feared driving between cities, at risk of being ambushed by a military outburst or showered by a grenade's explosion. Instead, new hotels were popping up around Anuradhapura and other tourist sites. People felt hope. They were energetic and motivated to build a better life. I felt this bloom across the country, making Sri Lanka an exciting place to travel. If we needed transport, a guesthouse staff would find a driver.

If we sought local knowledge, they might suggest a hidden temple or locally known ceremony. All we had to do was ask.

Even the monkeys treated us amicably. They did not steal the sandals we left outside of temples or snatch my hat thinking it was a sumptuous melon propped atop my head. I recall a surprisingly subdued monkey that I met at Jetavanaramaya Dagoba. I approached an offering table in front of the domed sanctuary. It was awash with lotus petals and jasmine buds strewn across its rough top. The tender flowers offered by devotees earlier in the day looked like a silk gown draped against an old woman's skin turned leathery after too many years in the sun. A grey langur sauntered over to the same table. The gleaming petals had caught its attention as well, but for a different reason. It glanced at me tentatively and then watched as the four other visitors walked away. It then took one leap and hopped onto the edge, surveying this scrumptious buffet. The lanky monkey looked straight into my eyes, reached out and unabashedly plucked a handful of petals. Soon enough, I was forgotten, and it leaned back on its hunches to stuff the delicate morsels between its lips. I have a feeling that this langur is a frequent devotee to such treasure piles around Anuradhapura.

Not every site around this ancient city was a temple. Palace remnants were scattered across the area, and the occasional museum showcased original artifacts. Former water reservoirs had transformed into algae stews, almost as thick as green-bean curries left simmering too long. Much earlier in the day, we had arrived at Isurumuniya Vihara before its ticket office opened. Like the Jaya Sri Maha Bodhi, this temple sold separate admission from the main Anuradhapura ticket. Two friendly guards waved us in, trusting we would pay before we left. We approached a cave temple built into an imposing boulder. Beside its dark entrance, steps had been chiselled into the rock's seam, and they enticed us to climb. We wound up the backside until we reached a small metal railing. From this first flat ledge, a bridge guided us towards a second rim. Glass protected a dip in the rock's surface, presumably a Buddha footprint, as coin offerings had been slipped underneath the clear cover. When I read about this temple, nothing mentioned this lofty spot. Instead, the site's more provocative element is a carving of a couple in love. Their image is embedded in the boulder, near the bottom of the stairs, where they look across a lime-coloured pond. Its waters are stagnant, covered in floating algae and guarded by a ring of elephants etched into the same rock face. Although the pair's effigy is beautiful, the furtive view from the top of the rock felt more magical.

Back on ground level, we turned our attention to the reclining Buddha tucked inside an adjacent cave. Initially, it had seemed dim, until we passed under the door frame. Massive body parts embellished in an onslaught of primary colours awoke our eyes like a caffeine jolt. Its paint must have been recently touched up, as the vibrant mustard-coloured skin of the statue seemed to dare the red robe to try to cloak its brilliant hue. The pillow and surrounding statues were covered in a similar collage of intense colours; green, yellow, pink, teal, orange and blue filled almost every inch of the cave. Only one corner remained dark. This space was overtaken by a flock of what I believe were swallows. They were truly early birds that rapidly flitted in and out of the same door we had entered. More than once, they came close to shaving our scalps with the purr of their wings. Eventually, we left them to carry on with their morning ritual.

Before the 1800s, Anuradhapura was overcome by jungle and laid dormant for centuries. It was later reactivated as a pilgrimage site and has since become a place to practise worship for locals who have enlivened its aged stones. We witnessed white scarves and clusters of flowers left as offerings at most structures. Yet what a massive shift compared to its days of grandeur, when it reigned over Sri Lanka from the fourth century BC to the eleventh century AD. Invasions from India ultimately pushed its leaders and residents southward, where they set up Polonnaruwa as their new capital. Surprisingly, Polonnaruwa is now a similar archaeological masterpiece but has not been re-engaged as a place of active worship like Anuradhapura. See the next section for more on this second ancient city.

The Basics

Most useful items to pack: Sunscreen, a hat and slip-on sandals

Useful words and phrases in Sinhalese: *aayu-bowan* ("hello"); *owu* ("yes"); *naha* ("no"); *istuh-tee* ("thank you"); *vihara* ("temple"); *Ehika kiyatada arinneh* ("What time does it open?"); and *Bahth denna* ("I'd like a rice and curry, please").[16]

For further travel information: A small entrance fee is collected at the Jaya Sri Maha Bodhi gatehouse. For more information on the site, refer to srimahabodhi.lk.

UNESCO recognizes the archaeological city of Anuradhapura as a World Heritage site. It sweeps across a large track of land and is hugged by the present-day city with the same name. We used our guesthouse's tuk-tuk to travel to the main site and between temples for a fixed day rate. Be specific upfront in what you expect, such as the ability to return to the hotel for a break during the day. The volume of history and the seemingly endless temples can become overwhelming and lose their impact after a few hours, so I recommend taking a midday break. The tuk-

16. Based on Lonely Planet's *Sri Lanka Travel Guide* (see Bibliography).

tuk was perfect with its ever-so-nice breeze that kicked up as we drove between temples. Alternatively, you can rent bicycles or a car.

Site-wide tickets are valid for only one calendar day. Fees were US$25 when we visited. Guards regularly asked to show our tickets at the many temples spread across a vast area, so keep them handy. The most informative website I found on the ancient city is at lanka.com/about/destinations/anuradhapura.

Our guesthouse, Kutumbaya Resort, was fairly new when we visited. They were midway through building an on-site café to supplement their shaded patio, at the time used to serve breakfast and dinner. The owner told us that after completing the new café, he planned to install new doors and windows to reduce street noise, which could be mildly heard inside the rooms. The owners and staff were fantastic, particularly in fine-tuning our itinerary, arranging transport around the city and to and from the hotel and sharing their knowledge of lesser-known sites nearby. Rooms are minimalistic, modern and comfortable. For more information, refer to their Facebook page, @kutumbayaresort, or search on Booking.com.

~~~
~~~

SRI LANKA—SHIFTING WATERS AT THE KINGDOM OF POLONNARUWA

Wander back in time through ancient temples and grand sculptures that have been reconstructed just enough to portray a sense of their grandeur but without pretense

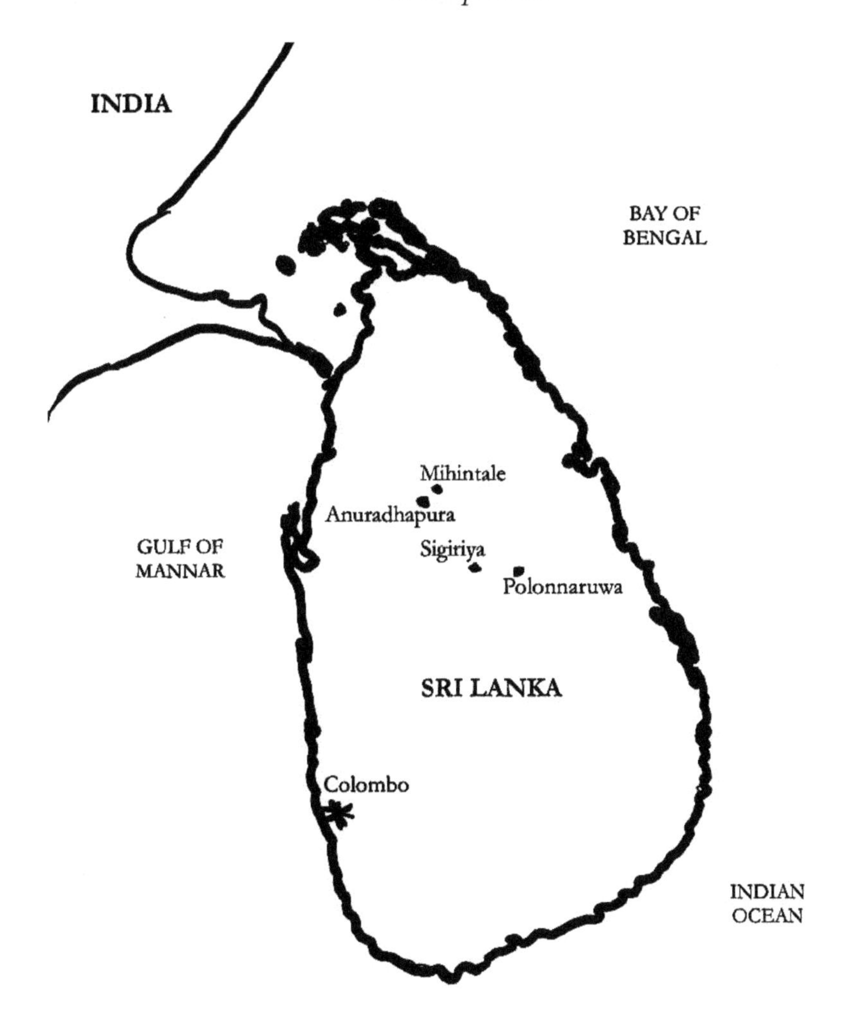

The Experience

All that remained of the once opulent *kumara pokuna* ("royal bath") were the stubs of former drains and a puddle of green sludge, too gooey to evaporate. We stood in Sri Lanka's former capital city, Polonnaruwa, among sprawling ruins that fanned out beneath shady palms. The kingdom's name reminded me of a board game, and from what I saw, its remains matched this image. Pieces of ancient ruins dotted the ground, and a winding trail enticed us to navigate farther around its terrain. For the next five hours, we explored its vast treasures. In some places, we found only traces of brick foundation or a few standing pillars to remind us of its distant past, whereas other sections were flush with history.

Between the eleventh and thirteenth centuries, Polonnaruwa would have been a flurry of activity. Agriculture enjoyed a golden age, when crops were kept lush by irrigation genius. The Sinhalese had devised impressively progressive technology for this era and built massive tanks that fed the city through a series of water ducts. One such massive basin funnelled fresh water into the kumara pokuna, a basin large enough to bathe a parade of elephants, but actually used only by the royal family. Standing nearby, a stony pavilion would have offered a convenient changing room to prepare for the regal scrub. The king and queen lived in a seven-storey palace, which has since collapsed, so only three levels remain. Its windows have crumpled, leaving crooked gaps peering through the surviving brick wall. Spread before us lay a honeycomb of rooms created by partial walls and vacant doorways.

We left the palace to head north towards the densest section of ruins. Pathways and structures merged like a downtown grid, and information plaques deciphered their present stillness with descriptions of what once prevailed. Memories poured from this cluster of temples, known as the Sacred Quadrangle. Unlike in Anuradhapura, few pilgrims left offerings in Polonnaruwa's ancient sanctuaries. Sri Lankan tourists walked along its brick pathways and, like us, admired the workmanship while trying to imagine what life would have been like close to a thousand years earlier.

The most notable temple was the circular Vatadage, which seemed to smile down on us like an eccentric aunt. Its wild expression showed through in the rounded brick walls cut off at the entrance to expose teeth-like edges. Its burgundy tint was defined by grout, whitened with age and spotted black from mildew. Beneath this jagged grin stood an ornately inscribed platform and a pair of guard stones that framed stairs leading into the upper temple. A life-sized deity had been carved into each guard stone along with smaller mythical beings that stood on either side. The stairs' risers were engraved with twelve figurines on each step, all bent in the same oddly contorted position. Their rotund bellies and raised arms somehow did not feel out of place, but rather welcomed us to explore inside.

Before climbing, we crossed a semicircular stone, positioned where a mat would normally sit at the base of a stairwell. This moonstone was covered in carvings of elephants and prancing ponies in concentric rings. Although the exterior base was covered in wild animals, the temple's interior was much simpler. My eyes relaxed after being pulled in so many directions outside and now gravitated to the centre of the platform. There sat a white stone Buddha with his hands folded and legs crossed. His placid face brought an aura of serenity to the otherwise animated design. The temple's message seemed to imply that all life would eventually unite, reminding me of the Buddhist belief in reincarnation and the release of desires. Outside, the temple was covered with rows of carved lions, chubby bodies and swirling flower buds. Inside, these identities were discarded and replaced with one simple source of energy.

Moonstone of the Vatadage

This distinctively designed structure is also thought to have once held a revered tooth of Buddha, the symbol of Sinhalese sovereignty. As I continued to walk around the Sacred Quadrangle, I learned that many of the temples once held the sacred tooth. It was not clear whether new shrines were constructed over time or if the tooth was simply passed around according to the seasons or at the whim of a royal command.

The Hetadage, another shrine, was also said to have held the Buddha's sacred tooth. King Nissanka Malla is said to have built this structure in an incredulous twelve hours during the twelfth century. Its walls have collapsed, leaving a long corridor lined with large stone blocks. At the end of the walkway, we met two men repairing its floor. One man perched on a stool that propped him about four inches above his cobblestone work. His pan was half-filled with a muddy paste, which he incessantly but delicately smeared on the floor with his metal spatula. The barefoot men grinned as we walked into their workroom. Sadly, we could not speak their language beyond our initial greeting. They continued to gently pat the mucky residue into place to, hopefully, grip the bricks for many years to come. Three unmistakably restored statues oversaw their work. A mess of lines tracked where their pieces had been fit together, making the statues look like human-sized jigsaw puzzles. Not every fragment had been recovered, and the central figure's face was left with no more than a mouth.

We smiled at the workers and moved on towards another shrine. It was named the Atadage and was also said to have housed the sacred tooth. This oldie is the grandfather of the Sacred Quadrangle, built in the eleventh century. Only pillars and a partial floor survive. Inscriptions found here disclosed the tooth's private guards were none other than the king's sentries, a direct linkage between royalty and religion. We walked on through domed stupas and random colonnades that had lost their roofs. It would have seemed lonely except for the grey langurs, guests who had recently made the pillars their home. They had decided to flop on the peaks of the pillars for an afternoon siesta. Apparently, the heat of the day had sapped their energy as well as ours. One sandy-coloured monkey had curled his legs up on the top of the pillar and let his arms, head and tail droop down. I do not think he would have even twitched his full-body loll if I had held out a tempting banana.

I brushed my sweaty brow, thinking how tasty a cool lassi, a yogurt-based drink, would feel at that moment. We ducked into our vehicle once again and drove a few more minutes to the second-last stop, Gal Vihara. A paved trail led us around an embankment where we found a crowd gathered in front of four massive beings. The statues filled the entire side of the hill. Gal Vihara had been carved eight hundred years before from a granite block embedded in the hillside. The larger-than-life creations stood four to five metres tall, making me feel rather small. Toes the size of my head peeped out from a brick robe. The hard rock was shaped into soft waves across the Buddha's legs. None of the statues were painted, just bare rock carvings oozing purity. The grain of the creamy granite swirled and swayed, almost lifelike, across the seated Buddha, though his eyelids had been shut for centuries. His neighbour, a reclining Buddha, had been etched in grey tones and meditated on a stone pillow, oblivious to all the onlookers.

Our last stop was the Tivanka Image House. For some reason, the crowds did not venture the extra kilometres to reach this temple of fine paintings, one of the few in Polonnaruwa. Clouds coalesced above its grandeur, and the forest tried to creep close, but the gardeners were diligent in their trimming. A mass of statues and pillars consumed the brick walls and gave a sense of ancient wisdom. As I walked around to the rear of the temple, I saw that a family of monkeys had wedged themselves into any available nook or ridge among the carvings. Eight eyes peered down at me for a second before returning their attention to plucking bugs or nibbling their fingernails. One plucker lounged comfortably on a corner ledge and rummaged through its sibling's hair and around its ears, periodically nibbling at bits. Another lanky rascal had fit its body to arc alongside a curvy figurine chiselled into the wall and rubbed bare over time. Many of the inscriptions had lost their original precision where details had blurred or eroded, giving me a jolt when I did come across a few carvings that still revealed intricate headdresses and elaborate jewellery.

Inside the temple, shadows dominated. An occasional beam of sunlight cut through narrow openings in the stone walls to light up images from an ancient past. Fine lines and deep colours danced along the walls, depicting vibrant stories from Buddha's journey to enlightenment. Some sections were worn off, perhaps crumbled during an earthquake or rubbed away over time. A buzzing sound overhead divulged rotund bees who occasionally flitted through a ray of light. They were nearly the size of a walnut shell and zipped in and out of the temple to visit their favoured forest flowers. They ignored me and my lack of pollen, useless in their industrious community. As I reached the far end of the enclosure, a Buddha statue eclipsed the final confined chamber. The figure's hips, shoulders and knees were bent in a way that reminded me of a feminine *apsara* ("celestial nymph") more than a traditional Buddha stance. Accordingly, the temple's name, Tivanka, signifies "thrice bent."

The variation between barren and bold seemed to highlight how history often chooses one perspective over another when retelling the past. Emptiness and vitality both reflected down on me as I walked through Tivanka's hallway. Perhaps the unanswered question of what else happened here is why the Tivanka Image House is often the first image that comes to mind when I think of Polonnaruwa. Was the king's version of truth, that which was deemed worthy of being inscribed into stone for eternity, fact checked as an objective rendering of reality? Or was it just one person's view from his rock palace, missing the hundreds of other lives lived, fought and loved? What stories merged into a solidary rendition hinted at by the mere crumbs that remain for us today in the walls and etched over doorways?

Buddha statue at Polonnaruwa

Like Anuradhapura in the previous section, the great city of Polonnaruwa was also abandoned in order to evade attacks from southern India's troops. The reigning powers that had governed central Sri Lanka from this site for over two hundred years shifted their domain westward. Warring factions moved in. Money was directed towards military spending rather than maintaining the water tanks. Perhaps the new residents did not understand or just chose to ignore the importance of the advanced irrigation system. It soon fell into disrepair and agriculture suffered.[17] This was certainly not the first time in history that a community's downfall was triggered by notions of power and war.

The Basics

Most useful item to pack: Bottle of water

Useful words in Sinhalese: *aayu-bowan* ("hello"); *owu* ("yes"); *naha* ("no"); *istuh-tee* ("thank you"); *vathura* ("water"); and *vihara* ("temple").[18]

For further travel information: Polonnaruwa is recognized by UNESCO as a World Heritage site and can be visited as a day trip from either Dambulla or Sigiriya. Each of these base cities has its own ancient sites to explore during your stay. I recommend taking a car to visit Polonnaruwa, as the drive takes a couple of hours each way. We read that bicycle rentals are available for exploring the ruins; however, we only saw people using tuk-tuks, tour buses or cars when travelling from site to site.

17. britannica.com/place/Sri-Lanka/The-fall-of-Polonnaruwa
18. Based on Lonely Planet's *Sri Lanka Travel Guide* (see Bibliography).

Entrance tickets are sold at Polonnaruwa's museum reception desk. One ticket grants access to the entire site, including the well-organized museum with many original artifacts on display from the surrounding region. Virtually every ruin and temple across Polonnaruwa has its own sign that explains relevant historical details specific to each structure, making it an informative visit even without a guide.

~~~
~~~

6

Modern Metropolises

Where does a city's mystique lurk? The soul of a great cosmopolitan city can often be unclear, between speeding vehicles and swaths of flashing neon all vying for attention. Admittedly, I typically prefer to escape cityscapes in search of more remote parts of a country in which to unravel its persona. Yet some cosmopolitan cities leave an imprint, drawing me into their web of delectable corners. From living on five continents, I have realized that you see a completely different side to a city when you live there versus passing through as a visitor. The same perspective that captures the locality of a place beyond the tourist highlights and must-see destinations spurs the stories in this chapter. I have tried to look deeper into the heart of urban centres, to glimpse what residents experience. Three of the four cities are located in Asia, with the outlier being Cuba's Caribbean city of Havana.

Starting in Asia, Bhutan once again captivated my attention. Its capital city of Thimphu ensures tradition thrives at its weekly market of local wares, despite the growing influx of foreign conveniences that have begun to cross the country's borders. Trade with India and

Japan has increased, bringing new bridges, road construction and jobs. When we visited in 2017, I noticed that since I had last visited the country in 2010, public notices warning of drug abuse and health concerns had started to creep onto Thimphu's streets. Citizens are trying to balance a tricky road, merging a secluded society with the modern world. To an observer, the city throws a maze of old, new and something completely different down every street.

Bandar Seri Begawan (BSB), the capital city of the tiny country of Brunei Darussalam—an Asian country that seems to straddle the Middle East and Asia—showcases a subdued urban culture. The country lies in a northern enclave of the island of Borneo. It attained riches through its oil and now faces the challenge of diversifying its economy away from its declining reserves, especially with recent lower oil prices. BSB reminded me more of the Persian Gulf cities with its grand mosques and wide boulevards, except that BSB streets were nearly vacant of cars. But the resemblance ended at the Gadong Night Market, where the people's personality shone as brightly as their spices burned boldly.

We then shift to the Caribbean nation of Cuba, a long narrow island angled like a spear towards the Gulf of Mexico. Before we visited Cuba, the country was like a fuzzy bubble in my mind that then burst into shards of piercing clarity once we landed on its soil. Not only was Havana a cosmopolitan centre, but its diverse neighbourhoods displayed a depth of artistry, daily struggles and beautiful architecture. Since Raúl Castro relaxed certain laws in 2011, entrepreneurship has exploded. New restaurants, *casas particulares* ("bed and breakfasts") and sights fill every inch of this amazing city.

Lastly, we return to Asia, to the enigmatic country of Myanmar. It is emerging from decades of conflict between the militaristic regime and feuding tribes, but it is emerging with poise. Even in the city of

Mandalay, with a population of over one million, tranquility hid in plain sight. Across a jumble of buildings, shrines, bikes and activity, its urban identity united into a mass of contrasts waiting to be peeled apart, one cryptic piece at a time. In this bustling city, we challenged ourselves to explore its most defining sights. We awoke for a daily ritual in which monks washed the golden face of a Buddha statue at 4:00 a.m. and tread the longest teak bridge in the world while locals waded through waist-deep water to catch their daily fish.

The vibes from the urban wonders in the following sections grabbed my attention. They were unique and inviting places that wrapped a rare blend of captivating urban hubs in unfiltered expression.

~~~
~~~

BHUTAN—A TRICKLE OF CHANGE ENTERS THE SECLUDED CAPITAL OF THIMPHU

Wander through local markets and explore traditional shops unchanged for decades

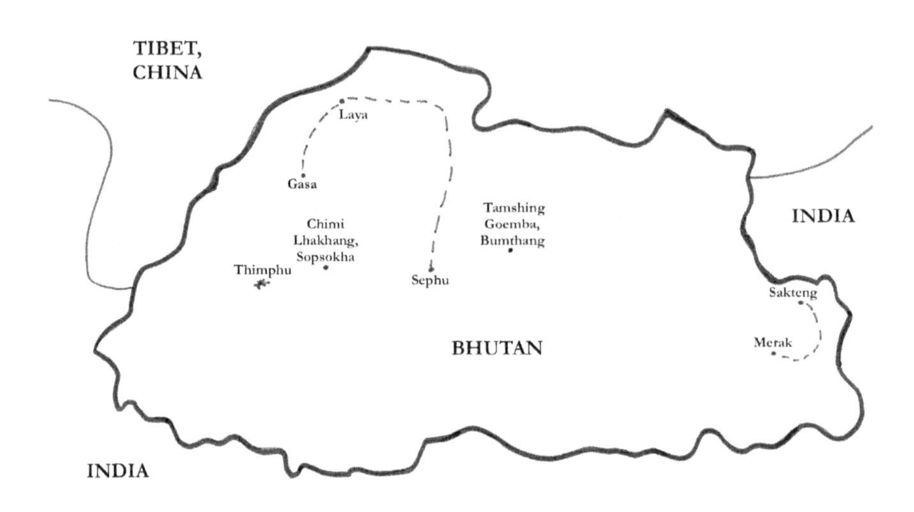

The Experience

What is the secret behind Bhutan's capital city of Thimphu, the essence that so delicately balances the city between its past and present? Go where locals go and stroll through their market. In these ordinary scenes, cultural obsessions trickle to the surface. The very treasures that grab a stranger's eyes are simply part of the traditions and culture that make up everyday life for the residents. When I meandered through the rows of foodstuffs and household necessities at Thimphu's Centenary Weekend Market, I felt as if I had snapped on a pair of swimming goggles and dunked my head beneath Bhutan's societal waves. Everyday objects became magnified before me, and the market was like a picnic blanket loaded with handed-down family recipes.

Take the betel nut, a Himalayan addiction steeped in mystique. I had seen the red stains on cement sidewalks. An elderly lady revealed their source; she smiled as she stepped out of a truck, with gums looking as if they oozed blood, and then spat, adding her own red splotch to the footpath. Inside the market, the time-worn betel practice was simplified into its elements. Areca nuts were cracked open to bare their kernel's quality. Piles of betel leaves, each the size of my palm, crowded tabletops. Nearby, a whitish paste made from boiled limestone was sold in small bags or metal canisters. It would be smeared onto the betel and nut concoction like a secret sauce.[1] Once the contents were arranged, chewers would roll them and stuff them into their mouth for the anticipated hit. They would tuck the fibrous mass between their cheek and molars, allowing saliva to gradually tenderize the wad. I had heard locals refer to the dangers of betel, the increased risk of mouth cancer that chewing the nutty treat brings. Yet many people still crave this traditional practice. The addiction's three ingredients were readily available at Thimphu's market, proving that the nut's grip held tighter than any medical warnings. Its appeal was lost on me, so I continued my search for other native treasures.

Some type of cube with rounded corners and concave sides had been strung onto white, yellow or blue cords. Strings of these slightly askew nuggets hung from the corners of plywood tables. They reminded me of Turkish delight candy coated in confectioner's sugar, but these would have had a distinctly different flavour. Our guide referred to them as Bhutanese chewing gum, lumps of cheese so hard that people sucked on them for hours since they were too tough to

1. himalaya.socanth.cam.ac.uk/collections/journals/jbs/pdf/JBS_08_03.pdf

bite. This dairy-laden table displayed more than just cheese bites. The adjacent wooden shelf was neatly piled with clear bags filled with fresh cheese, banana leaves that had been carefully wrapped around some mysterious snack and trays of eggs stacked on the floor.

Strings of dried Bhutanese cheese

Breezes blew across the tables, swirling with the scent of produce and vague echoes from the street before settling into a comfortable atmosphere inside the market. Even though the weekend sales had just started, many of the vendors already looked bored. It was a comfortable boredom, for they knew buyers would come and it was only a matter of time before their supply would be drained. There were no fake smiles or wild claims to con potential patrons. Mutual respect hung in the air between buyer and seller, each knowing what was on offer and what it was worth. Nevertheless, vendors' eyes expressed a longing to return to their mountain villages, away from the city's bustle.

An elderly man working at one stall sat back and gazed across the market. I could almost see his mountain village reflected in his eyes beneath a well-worn, blue wool toque. He sold sacks bulging with what looked to be sawdust but was actually barley flour. It was used to make the *tormas* ("offering cakes") we had seen so frequently at ceremonies around Bhutan. They were not what you might imagine a dessert to be, but more like Play-Doh shaped into people or intricate ornaments and placed in front of Buddha statues. At certain ceremonies held inside family homes, tormas were placed in the centre of the room for rituals and later removed to designated locations outdoors, as directed by a lama. The elderly vendor at the Thimphu market also displayed cellophane-wrapped incense sticks piled on an adjacent table, adding to the religious overtone of his wares.

On the market's ground floor, sacks as high as my waist lined the aisles. The rims were folded open to display various types of rice. Bhutan's renowned red rice was the most popular, but the less expensive white grains also attracted buyers. Corn was also sold, usually dried and crushed in a form similar to Kellogg's Corn Flakes. It was probably manufactured in Bhutan's far eastern regions the same way it has been for years. Production is kept simple, often just a couple of roadside stalls run by a single family. The only change is that the corn is now packaged in cellophane bags. They keep the roasted corn fresher for longer, but the empty bags end up littering roadsides.

The corn in the market reminded me of a factory we had seen in eastern Bhutan; a single family grew the crop, baked and pressed the kernels and sold their product all from a one-hundred-metre plot.

Their roasting hut housed two key pieces of equipment: a fire pit and a well-used, homemade machine. The owner's son dumped raw corn kernels into a blackened wok so large it could have held an adult goat. Its metal base was propped above burning logs. He then grabbed a smouldering cinder and tossed it onto the dirt ground outside the hut. This was the only way to manage temperature consistency.

Using a wooden spoon the length of a small child, the young man slowly stirred the seeds. It smelled like popcorn, but this was not the popping type. After becoming nicely browned, the kernels were transferred to the second contraption. The father took over and revved the decrepit engine. Its belt whirred to life, spinning a shallow cavity beneath a puff of diesel fumes. Flattened flakes—identical to those nicely packaged at the Thimphu market—spewed out of a spout and into a bucket. Behind the production scene, the open-aired hut looked onto terraced fields of corn plants and shady palms. Somehow, the operation flourished on this steep ravine located in a remote part of the countryside.

We moved along to the fruit and vegetable section of the Thimphu market beside other shoppers as they bantered with shopkeepers. Buyers clearly knew their favourite tables. Carefully piled cobs of tender hearts of palm, a popular ingredient for local dishes, were protected by their bluish-violet husks. Bags of fiery red chilies and platters of piquant green ones were sold at nearly every stall in this section. One of the most favoured dishes in Bhutan is *ema datse* ("chilies with cheese"). In this meal, chili is not a seasoning but the main ingredient. A little yak, goat or sometimes cow cheese simmers with the chilies to build the dish's distinctive flavour. Ema datse was served with nearly every meal of our five-week trip through the country. Often another vegetable—perhaps a handful of beans or a pile of mushrooms—was mixed in for variety in an attempt to accommodate our Western palates. But the Bhutanese people clearly preferred the classic chili-only version.

Chilies are dried on rooftops in Thimphu and on virtually every house across the country. The tin roofs work double duty by conducting the sun's heat, much like an oven, and keeping the chilies out of the reach of scavenging dogs. I had not thought the spicy peppers would appeal to dogs until one day when four strays devoured our lunch leftovers. After filling their bellies, two of the dogs slurped from a nearby stream to cool their mouths. The remaining pair had truly Bhutanese taste buds and immediately settled in for an afternoon nap without any cooling gulp of water. Outside Thimphu's market, a few tan dogs reminded me of that quartet as they lounged on a patch of sun hitting the sidewalk. We had noticed that for some reason, dogs here seem to prefer to sleep during the day and howl through the night, resulting in our catchphrase, "I slept like a Bhutanese dog in the daytime."

There was one critical item we needed to buy while in Thimphu that was not available at the central market. It related to our upcoming Snowman trek (see Chapter One). A notable characteristic of mountain passes in Bhutan, Tibet and virtually anywhere across the Himalaya are the lines of prayer flags strung across their highest point. These colourful swatches of cloth are covered with scribed mantras, or prayers, intended to scatter positive thoughts and compassion in the wind. Prayer flags represent a deep connection between nature, people, the afterlife and rebirth. The colours—blue, green, red, yellow and white—correspond with the five elements: sky, water, fire, earth and air. The concept originated with Tibetan soldiers who showcased their allegiance on flags hung during battle. Later, the banners were adapted by Bon shamans to reflect the five elements and then absorbed into Buddhist practice. Unlike with a country's national flag, the frayed edges and faded cloth of prayer flags are embraced and thought to represent the natural life cycle of all living things. This wear and tear reflects the inherent flow of energy between birth, aging and reincarnation. New flags offer renewed wishes. And we intended to add our own mark as we crossed many mountain passes during the upcoming weeks.

In search of prayer flags, we entered a dim, narrow shop off Norzin Lam, Thimphu's main street. Shelves reached the ceiling in this timeless store, stacked with scrolls and a miscellany of dusty articles. I could have spent three hours in that small space, flicking through ornaments and brass trinkets, and still not uncovered a third of the stuff stashed away. The most popular items were within a hand's reach of the saleslady. She confirmed that a lama had indeed blessed each of the five prayer flags inside the sealed bag she was showing me. Our friends, my husband and I together wanted a couple of bags, so I instinctively asked for a volume discount. The saleslady looked at me directly, emphasizing the *we* as she spoke: "We do not ask for discounts for these. They are prayers for a longer life." That was the most effective shutdown to bargaining I had ever heard. I even felt a little dubious for asking the question. But all in all, she did not seem overly fussed. As visitors, we were excused. We paid our bill in full, and she handed me a cotton woven bag, thick and sturdy to carry our holy scrolls.

In this musty store off the main street, it felt as if nothing had ever changed. Even in the capital city of Thimphu, residents held dearly to their old ways as the new world rushed in. In the centre of the town's only traffic circle, a policeman stood inside an elaborately painted gazebo, manually directing traffic. We left the shop and returned to the busy street, silently wondering how we would cope at elevations of over five thousand metres. The streets of Thimphu were sunny and pleasant, a contrast to the wind swells we were sure to meet, which would not only batter these flags but numb our fingers as we tried to affix them to rocks or boulders.

The Basics

Most useful item to pack: Reusable shopping bag to blend in or just in case you find something interesting

Useful words and phrases in Dzongkha: *kuzuzangbola* ("hello"); *Dilu gadeci mo* ("How much is it?"); *Gong bôm mä* ("That's too much"); *ing* ("yes"); *mê* ("no"); and *kaadinchheyla* ("thank you").[2]

For more, refer to visitbhutan.com/useful_words_phrases.html.

For further travel information: Bhutan requires most foreigners to travel with a government-approved tour company and pay a regulated day rate. The government's intent is to promote high-quality, low-impact tourism. This was our second visit to Bhutan using Rainbow Tours & Treks, who I highly recommend. See earlier sections on Bhutan or refer to Rainbow's website at rainbowbhutan.com.

Thimphu's Centenary Farmers Market takes place on Saturdays and Sundays and is an easy place to spend an hour or so. Beyond the market, the Changlimithang Archery Ground, Jungshi handmade paper factory and the miscellany of shops along the main street are worth a visit while in the capital city. For more information, refer to the government's tourism website at bhutan.travel/destinations/thimphu.

2. Based on Lonely Planet's *Bhutan Travel Guide* (see Bibliography).

For an introduction into Bhutanese art, head to the National Institute for Zorig Chusum. Wander through classrooms as students learn how to create Bhutan's distinctive handicrafts. Skills include carving, embroidery, woodworking, painting and sewing.

~~~
~~~

BRUNEI DARUSSALAM—DISCOVER BANDAR SERI BEGAWAN'S PULSE BENEATH ITS FORMAL FACADE

Ease into a country where everything is within a day's reach and savour sambal that lights up your senses

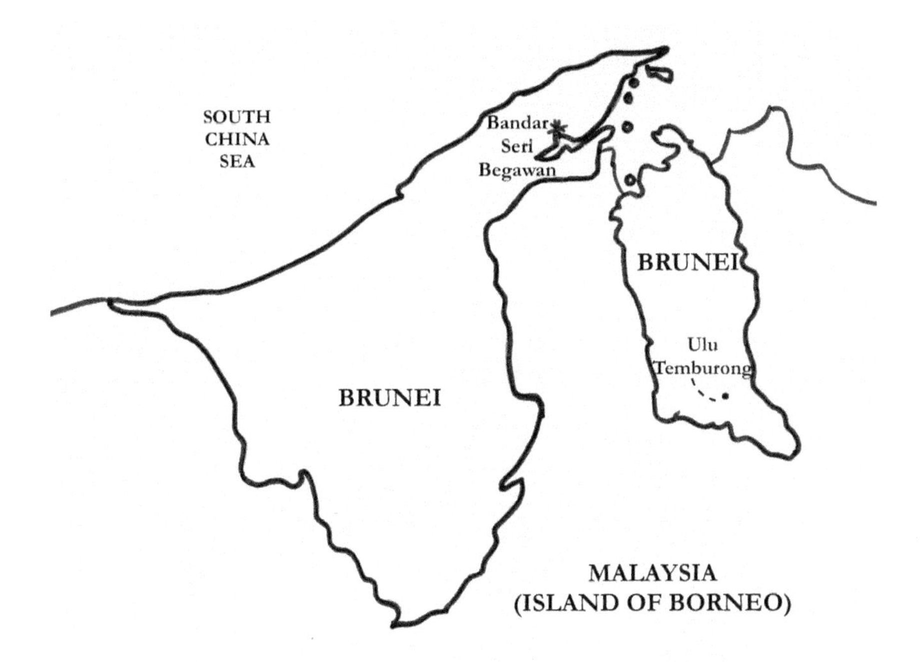

The Experience

The open-air structure across the road vibrated with activity, contradicting the seclusion I felt from inside our van. The lively atmosphere was the opposite of every other street we had seen in this capital city. Bandar Seri Begawan, usually referred to as simply Bandar or BSB, initially seemed stiff compared to neighbouring capitals such as Bangkok and Hanoi. I recalled our walk earlier in the day; sidewalks had been deserted, the waterfront lacked the typical barrage of hawkers and coffee shops were missing their usual buzz.

Yet this spot surged with life as the sun set. Fans whirred from the ceiling of the structure across the street to partially disperse plumes of smoke that drifted from one section to another.

We left the quiet vehicle to explore the arcade's wide corridors. Families walked between the stalls. Young office workers weaved through the crowds as they assessed their options, somehow remaining dry in their crisp button-down shirts despite the heat that lingered even into the evening. Women wore head scarves in whatever style they preferred, in bright pink, paisley blue or earthy tones. Beside them, men in ball caps and tennis shirts turned skewers on blackened grills. I noticed that most of the staff joked among themselves, smiled at customers and generally appeared to enjoy their evening shift. This ambience was standard for the Gadong Night Market, where BSB's personality blossomed away from the otherwise desolate sidewalks and quiet streets.

Young, old and everyone in between came to this venue. Prices were low and flavour was intense. The heart of Brunei's Malaysian-based cuisine danced across these market stalls. We had two hours to grab a freshly grilled meal before our hotel's shuttle bus returned from its routine loop. To our right, table after table of fiery barbecue attracted hungry diners. Lines of people three or sometimes four deep waited to place their order. It was difficult to tell who was queuing and who only strained to catch a peek. On first glance, it appeared a chaotic cluster of bodies, but as we stood back to watch, the flow became apparent. A gap opened at another stall where rolls of grilled banana leaves lined a plastic box soon to be emptied. Orders of three, five or ten quickly depleted the stash of steaming morsels. I slipped in towards the man selling these popular treats. In English, he explained they were filled with sticky rice and either beef or prawns. By the time we had circled the entire market, the man had sold out of the beloved rolls. I learned my lesson: grab them while you can. The next evening, I nabbed one of each. The beef roll was superb, but both nicely mixed the gooey rice with tender flesh so delicately spiced.

Farther down the aisle, a flat grill looked more like a French crêpe pan than Asian cookware. The chef smeared a thin layer of batter across the hot metal. As the edges crisped, she sprinkled roasted peanuts evenly across the pan. I had seen something like this before on mainland Malaysia, a sweet peanut pancake treat that was slightly addictive due to its sugary goodness. A canvas sign hung above, describing this delight as *kuih malaya babu cantik*. Canisters of sugar and ground nuts sat within reach so the aproned cooks could add a touch of flavouring depending on the order. This stall was one of the most popular, with a steady stream of hungry patrons. Other people stood back and watched, seemingly fascinated by the endless flow of batter and toppings poured onto the steaming pans before getting flipped, wrapped and handed over to the next person in line.

A collection of less popular stalls congregated at the far end of the market. The row of mini-supermarkets interspersed with stalls of ready-to-eat food lacked the drama of the fiery grills. Along the aisle, baskets brimmed with a selection of papayas, some still young and green while others had started to turn a ripe yellow. Beside them, plates piled with juicy limes and trays of mandarins tempted passersby. My favourite finish to a spicy meal is a plate of fresh papaya drenched in lime juice, which turns the otherwise bland fruit into a flavourful sensation. A whole array of local fruits and vegetables spread out before us, including bunches of lemon grass tied so tightly they looked like celery stalks. Bundles of crisp long beans looked fresh and tasty. Lady-finger bananas and curved red chilies added their exuberance to the selection, but were still not enough to compete with the sizzling grills on the far side of the market, where most people hovered.

As we turned to leave this aisle, I was surprised to see a barbecue stall selling American-style hamburgers. It seemed distinctly out of place. The lack of patrons implied they had lost favour with their choice of flavours—or perhaps we just walked past during a rare lull. Farther along, I smelled a familiar aroma before I spotted the source. Cobs of corn seared to crispy perfection neutralized the fishy scents of nearby grills. We passed vendors selling nothing but vibrantly coloured fruit drinks. The limeade version was doused in sugary syrup, tasting much like a soft drink after its fizzle has worn away. By this point, we were back where we had entered. Out of all the choices, a simple sambal dish enticed us. Styrofoam plates filled with rice and sliced meat swimming in sambal sauce had been stacked on a table in front of two women. They were likely the chefs who had now switched gears to sell their creation. The plates could not have been sitting long, as steam condensed inside the plastic wrap that sealed each serving.

Nearby, at the north end of the market, we settled at a picnic table with our meal. The cling wrap peeled off to reveal sticky slices of chicken, so dark with sauce they could have been mistaken for beef. The rice was standard steamed rice, not the sticky glutinous type from Thai and Laos cooking that I have grown to love. Then I bit into the chicken. Shots of flavour curled around my taste buds, a zesty, fiery and smoky goodness all at once. My eyes snapped wide open as the intensity of the chili exploded through every taste bud. We had not bought any water, no liquids to dilute the seething heat. Breathe in and then breathe out. Slowly, the raging blaze subsided, and the embers eased their exotic frolic inside my mouth. And that was only the first bite. Strangely, the sambal flavour was like a tease, a spectacular tease. I wanted more. Its heat was inconsequential to its incredible flavour. To this day, that sambal chicken is like nothing I have tasted elsewhere. It alone might be reason enough to make a side trip to Brunei.

One aspect remained consistent despite the variety of food offered—the Gadong Night Market was impeccably clean. Floors were swept, counters sparkled and grills were devoid of the usual crusty, burned-on splatter. This new structure had opened earlier in the year, leaving a barren bunch of former night-market stalls standing just across the street. The original venue housed a collection of circular huts, like mushrooms clustered in a cement forest. A stray cat caressed one of the vacant bench legs and then morphed into a darkened shadow, which only made the former site appear more desolate.

We walked beyond these obsolescent domes and headed towards the river. Farther still loomed a large shopping mall. Its air-conditioned shelter offered refuge from the hot outdoors but held little else of interest unless you were seeking the latest local fashion or an iced coffee. When we retraced our steps back over the bridge, the same fisherman we had seen on our way over stood along the bank. He reeled in a tiny fish from the murky waters. It looked no bigger than bait fish and certainly not big enough for a meal. We were invisible to his quest, and within a minute his rod had flicked the line back into the black oblivion of the river's water.

The Basics

Most useful item to pack: A stash of water for spicy dinners or sunny afternoons

Useful words and phrases in Malay: *helo* ("hello"); *ayam penyet*

("fried chicken smashed and served with sambal"); *terima kasih* ("thank you"); *maaf* ("excuse me" or "sorry"); ya ("yes"); and *tidak* ("no").[3]

For further travel information: The Capital Residence Suites offers spacious and clean apartments. After a sweltering day, the in-suite washing machine is particularly useful. Staff are friendly and helpful. The hotel's regular shuttle runs between the main sights and simplifies travel around the city of BSB. For more information, refer to capitalresidencesuites.com.

In Brunei, weekends fall on Thursday and Friday. Do not be surprised if shops close between 12:00 and 2:30 p.m. on Fridays while the predominantly Muslim population attends midday prayers.

It may be damp and rainy, but if you want to experience Brunei outside of BSB, the city is surrounded by rainforest, with Ulu Temburong National Park its crown jewel. Head over to the friendly team at Borneo Guide, and they can arrange accommodation and tours to places like Sumbiling Eco Village. Their office is in central BSB. For more, go to borneoguide.com.

~~~

3. Based on Lonely Planet's *Southeast Asia on a Shoestring* (see Bibliography).
~~~

CUBA—LOSING YOURSELF IN HAVANA'S TANGLE OF ART, HISTORY AND AUTHORITY

Find your flow in Cuba's city of marbles, where each district offers its own swirling ball of history, grit and artistic soul

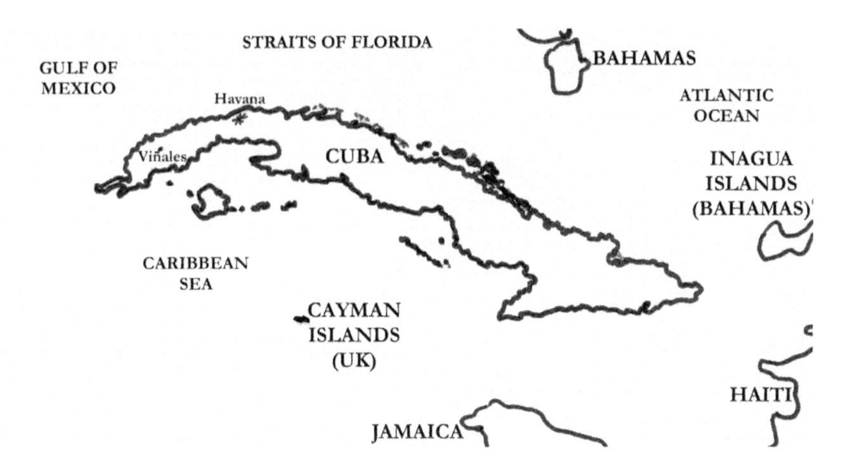

The Experience

Our senses flickered under a storm of contradicted reality. We had walked only three blocks and had already been passed by 1950s-era Buicks, Chevrolets and Cadillacs painted in faded mauve and brilliant turquoise. In comparison, dented Ladas pointed their snout-like hoods down the road and beeped at pedestrians who might be looking for a lift. They bid adieu with a plume of carbon puffing from their exhaust pipes, either from burnt oil or just cranky age. Somehow both varieties remained operational, made necessary because few new models are able to pass through Cuba's strangling trade embargoes, bureaucracy or a combination of both.

Mechanics prevailed in this country. Every family knew someone who could jury-rig an engine or wring another week of life out of a car that might otherwise be sent to an automobile morgue elsewhere in the world. Drivers passed bronze statues of warriors proudly facing battle and ornate buildings either freshly painted in pastels or peeling under the salted air. On occasion, a vehicle less than half a century old rolled by, usually of Korean or Chinese origin. I felt we had stepped inside a bubble from some alternative world, locked inside a lost timepiece fallen from an old man's tweed coat. Cuba's urban Havana felt like a peculiar tug-of-war world caught between a mid-twentieth-century socialist era and a gradual privatization movement. Amid all this clutter, she emerged as a beautiful diva full of bold corners and evocative idiosyncrasies.

On this particular morning, we were on a mission to secure Wi-Fi access cards. Beyond an occasional high-end hotel, internet access was available only in designated public parks across Cuba. In the city of Havana, with over two million people, there were only six hotspots in 2016—including hotels. People huddled over their phones or plugged earbuds into laptops in these designated public spaces. Such a congregation was the telltale sign that we had found another connection point. For example, a signal radiated along the sidewalk of Calle 23 near La Rampa, an iconic movie theatre in Havana. Smaller cities around the country usually chose their central square to host the one and only Wi-Fi signal available to residents. In theory, and at times in practice, it turned out to be fairly convenient—just walk to the designated curbside or park and log on. On the plus side, controlled access ensures people do not become obsessively attached to their device or crave a social construct woven from constant connectivity as we see elsewhere in the world.

In our case, we first needed to acquire an access card and wanted to see how the locals did it. We could have walked into a big hotel and paid triple the price for a card, but that foreigner's tack would have evaded the challenge of the quintessential Cuban puzzle. And we were stubborn. We were perplexed by this country and wanted to peak beneath its layers. Not everything fit into the expected mould, whether it was when we lunched in a Chinatown restaurant strangely absent of any Chinese or when we passed a bronze statue of a naked woman hoisting a human-sized fork over her shoulder while riding a rooster who balanced on one leg—not the image you might expect from a restrained population. These oddities captured Havana in all her quirky appeal.

Three blocks from our *casa particular*—a bed and breakfast in a private home—a government-run ETECSA communications office conveniently sold Wi-Fi cards. On the morning we arrived, three people sat on a bench outside its office. On instinct, we headed for the glass entrance doors, where we were quickly intercepted by a lone security guard. He asked our intentions. After a relatively brief exchange, he directed us to wait outside along with the others. Our Spanish was sufficient to confirm that the office was indeed selling Wi-Fi cards on that day. They were available in five-hour blocks, with a maximum of three cards per person. People came and went but entered the building only with the consent of the security guard. His role was paramount, and we wanted to remain on his good side. Most people, like us, joined the line. It was not so much a physical line, as a mental placement of who arrived when. Some sat on chairs while others leaned against posts in no particular order.

We waited. A man sitting beside me leaned over and spoke a few words in English. I answered back in Spanish. From there, the conversation unfolded. He practised his English, and I worked on my Spanish. Our topics of conversation were broad. While waiting in the shade, I was transported to the days of Caribbean pirates. Back then, Spain would not allow trade between its colonies, so ships laden with gold, silver and pearls hauled their cargo east towards their mother country. Havana was the last Spanish port before heading out into the expansive Atlantic Ocean, and the city's protective harbour was an essential stopover. Prized cargo of gold and porcelain from the Aztec colony of Veracruz often sat in the harbour. These riches lured pirates and rogue states, making for a dangerous onward voyage. My newfound friend explained the resulting war and plunder faced by the Cuban population. French privateer Jacques de Sores set the city of Havana alight in 1555 as part of his campaign to seize some of the treasure. His aggression motivated Spain to build the impressive fortress of Castillo de los Tres Santos Reyes Magnos del Morro, which still gazes down on Havana's port.[4]

Havana's enviable position at the entrance to the Gulf of Mexico continued to tempt those in search of power. A few hundred years after the de Sores' disaster, Britain and Spain began tussling. Britain wanted a piece of Havana's optimal location to tap into the lucrative trading route between the Americas and Europe. In 1762, the British seized control for a not-so-long eleven months, until they traded Cuba back to Spain in return for Florida. The Spanish king was understandably disgruntled and was once again motivated to build a fort. This is why Havana can now claim to be the home of the largest Spanish fort ever built in North, Central or South America. The Fortaleza de San Carlos de la Cabaña dominates ten hectares on the banks of Havana, just down from the older Castillo de los Tres Santos Reyes.[5]

After Spanish-Cuban history, we moved on to more recent topics. We talked of travelling through Africa. After training to become a doctor, the man had been sent to work in Zambia. From there, he visited Victoria Falls in Zimbabwe and rafted down the very same

4. http://theageofpirates.com/places/havana/
5. Based on Lonely Planet's *Cuba Travel Guide* (see Bibliography).

turbulent Zambezi River that my husband and I had followed. Our wild ride was about ten years ago, whereas this man's excursion was likely much earlier. I realized Cuba was not the isolated bubble that I had believed it to be, if their doctors were sent abroad to share knowledge and gain experience. For me, small moments like this encapsulate the value of travelling. A flicker of truth gained from personal interactions sheds more insight into a place than any preconceptions I might have before arriving. The man then passed me his card and offered his counsel if we were ever in need of anything during our stay. His card revealed that his current profession was taxi driver, making me curious about the rest of his life story. What had changed his position from doctor to cabbie? Maybe it was a government mandate or maybe a personal choice. Regardless, those twenty minutes spent talking about history, travel and other bits of our stories coloured in another piece in Cuba's eclectic puzzle.

Eventually, the security guard waved my husband and me inside, where we waited on a wooden bench. From there, we watched an office performance with Cuban flare. Three women sat behind their desks. Two of them worked through the flow of customers, filling the role of efficient civil servants. The third lady was less effective and instead took on the part of distracted lover. Her co-worker, or perhaps a visiting beau, sat on her lap and nuzzled her neck. No one else seemed to notice or care. Kindly, the security guard did not send anyone to her desk. In time, her boyfriend went to a back office, but he soon returned and promptly resumed his nuzzling. Occasionally she tapped at her computer, and we waited patiently.

Then we watched the preferred-customer shuffle. The security guard opened the front door and quietly conversed with someone outside. He interrupted one of the ladies helping another customer and relayed a handful of bills. She slid him a few cards in exchange, which were delivered back to the mysterious client. Connections were clearly useful. We, unfortunately, had none. The security guard broke into song. He then wandered over with another wad of cash from another friend outside. By this point, we had deduced the process and waited patiently. Someone unseen in a back room began singing. Time passed, then three Wi-Fi cards were handed to us for thirty Cuban convertible pesos, or CUCs. All in all, our purchase took ninety minutes and allowed us to once more connect with the ubiquitous web.

Curious about daily life, we decided to wander through a *supermercado* ("grocery store"). I wanted to see what sort of ingredients locals had available. Raúl Castro had eased business restrictions in 2011, allowing private citizens to open cafés, bakeries and casas particulares. The bland beans and rice that Cuban cuisine was renowned for have since been replaced. We headed towards the Malecón, a popular esplanade that follows the waterfront and just a two-block walk from our casa particular. We entered a shopping mall with little else besides a jazz restaurant and a supermercado and climbed the giant circular staircase. As we neared the upper-level store, clerks slowly rang customers through at least three tills. Shelves ran deep towards the rear of the shop, hinting at a wide selection of food before we could see what actually lay ahead. Rows of frozen meats, jugs of cooking oil and cans of vegetables filled most of the displays. There was little variation among the items on offer. Some shelves sat empty. Prepackaged cookies, soft drinks and alcohol filled any remaining space. Our quest to find a healthy snack remained unfulfilled. We left without buying anything.

We headed east and walked along Avenida 5, an austere street down the centre of the Miramar district. Hardly anyone passed us. Most buildings were either embassies quarantined by metal gates or grand homes in the shadows of lush palms. The Russian embassy stood like an air-traffic control tower monitoring for an inevitable onslaught of broken-down Lada taxis. Its sombre stucco edifice rose higher than any other building in sight and dominated the entire block. We carried on farther along the boulevard, wondering if the lonely atmosphere might soon give way to another of Havana's curious fringe destinations.

We came across the warehouse-sized Supermercado 70, which was aptly located at the corner of Seventieth Street and Third Avenue. I surmised that this enormous grocery store *must* be the secret location where locals stocked up on an array of produce. Outside the main entrance, fast-food kiosks dished out burgers and fries or pepperoni pizza to families who had made an outing of their shopping trip. The parking lot was half full, busier than any of the surrounding streets. We walked through the automatic doors and slid into air-conditioned coolness. Large displays of bagged cookies greeted us beside packages of instant coffee. Half of one aisle was submerged beneath bags of caster sugar. Soft drinks filled another aisle, while beer and alcohol fit onto a third row of shelving. Dried pasta, tomato sauce and locally packaged cereal took up most of the remaining space. Freezers were half full of meat. A single product often filled a whole section, with the all-too-familiar lack of variety. I walked five paces only to find identical jars of tomato sauce staring back at me. Food was clearly available, but the selection remained restricted. I wondered where the restaurants that had opened after the regulations had been softened sourced their ingredients. Topoly, a delicious Iranian restaurant we had tried earlier, had managed to find parsley and pine nuts, while we had trouble tracking down even a bag of peanuts.

On the corner of Príncipe y Valor in Central Havana

Wi-Fi cards and supermarket selection are certainly not all there is to the lovely Havana, but these stories demonstrate a small piece of daily reality for its residents. Other aspects of the city's beauty leapt from nearly every street. Old forts, churches, markets and restaurants cram the labyrinth of cobblestoned streets in Habana Vieja ("Old Havana"). Steps away, Centro Habana ("Central Havana") discloses a more eclectic persona with theatres, museums, weathered apartment blocks and the dreamy Malecón. Farther yet, Vedado's stately homes and expansive cemetery-turned-national monument offer another layer of this intricate city. Havana has a vibe all its own, one that shakes and shimmers behind peeling paint and hidden cafés. Swirl it all down at the end of a day with a Cuba Libre as you watch the sun set from the Hotel Nacional—the same venue where Fulgencio

Batista's sergeants ousted the provisional government in 1933 and where, in 1946, notorious American mobsters gathered incognito during a Frank Sinatra concert.[6] You just might feel as if imagination and reality have collided to create fascinating Havana.

The Basics

Most useful item to pack: Printed bus tickets for pre-purchased Viazul trips and a prepaid credit card with a balance to cover ATM withdrawals

Useful words and phrases in Spanish: *hola* ("hello"); *gracias* ("thank you"); *sí* ("yes"); *no* ("no"); and *¿Cuánto cuesta?* ("How much?").[7]

For further travel information: Casa particulares are the bed and breakfasts of Cuba. Forget the state-run boxy hotels or all-inclusive resorts and instead immerse yourself in a truly Cuban experience when visiting Havana. Since Raúl Castro eased regulations for entrepreneurs in 2011, families have been able to legally open their doors to visitors. There is a wide range of cleanliness and quality across the casas particulares, so background research is recommended. When we went to Cuba in early 2016, many casas particulares did not have much of a social media presence because internet access was restricted. Email contacts can sometimes be found on TripAdvisor by reading comments and searching for vaguely encrypted addresses. We stayed at Villa Romera, a fantastic casa particular in Vedado run by a Cuban-Italian couple. Breakfast was excellent, especially the coffee and fruit platter. Rooms were

6. Based on Lonely Planet's *Cuba Travel Guide* (see Bibliography).
7. Based on Lonely Planet's *Cuba Travel Guide* (see Bibliography).

comfortable, and the location is handy to the Malecón, shops and restaurants. Villa Romera can be contacted at info@villaromerocuba.com.

Three varieties of taxis ply Havana's streets. As foreigners, we often heard the beep beep of the newish yellow taxis that tended to target tourists. They are privately owned, owner operated and the most expensive of the three taxi types. A trip from Vedado to Habana Vieja cost approximately CUC10, equivalent to US$10.

On the other end of the spectrum, black and yellow Ladas that had seen better days, depending on the mechanical prowess of their owner, also offered rides. From Vedado to Habana Vieja or to the Viazul bus station, they cost approximately CUC5 to CUC8, depending on your negotiating skills and the driver's inclination.

My favourite, although they covered a fixed route so were less flexible, were the old classics. These *colectivos* ("shared taxis") typically run between Vedado and El Capitolio Nacional. They can be waved down along the sidewalk of Calle Línea. You will more than likely share the vehicle with other passengers at a rate of CUC0.50 per person. Our fellow passengers were likely so used to the daily commute that it was nothing special to them, but that made it all the more impactful for us—we were not at some old car show but lost in a rush hour of to-do lists and demanding bosses like any other workers on any other day of the week.

Habana Vieja attracts most of the tourists and tour groups. Spanish forts, posh hotels, plazas and cathedrals connect windy streets with artisanal appeal. A cute haven is Dulceria Bianchini

II, tucked away off Plaza de la Catedral. Here, petite *cortados*—espresso cut with steamed milk—are served in old English tea cups along with a deliciously flakey quiche. Next door to this bakery-café stands the warehouse-style Taller Experimental de Gráfica. Once refreshed, take a moment to wander through its working display of vibrant local paintings and charcoal sketches.

For travel farther afield, Viazul is Cuba's well-run national bus company. Tickets can be purchased at the station or online up to thirty days in advance. Proof of online purchases must be printed; a copy on your smartphone is not sufficient. I recommend you print your ticket before arriving in Cuba, as local printing services do not normally connect to the internet, making it very difficult to print a document from an email without a USB stick. For more information, refer to viazul.com.

As a general caution, bring Canadian, euro or other non-American currency to exchange. US funds incur a ten percent surcharge when exchanging them for the local currency.

Cuba uses two currencies, the Cuban convertible peso (CUC) and the Cuban peso (CUP). The CUC is pegged to the US dollar and is used at most establishments. Alternatively, the CUP is worth far less and is typically used only at smaller local shops or street vendors. One CUC is equivalent to approximately twenty-five CUPs. So be sure not to confuse the two.

In Cuba, ATMs accept only Visa credit cards, not debit cards or Mastercard. To avoid excessive interest charges from your bank, transfer funds onto your Visa card before arriving in the country to cover anticipated cash needs. When we visited in early 2016, ATMs charged a three percent fee on all cash withdrawals.

If you prefer to stay connected, check the latest list of Wi-Fi hotspots before hopping on your flight. At the time of writing, these two blogs offered up-to-date lists: twoscotsabroad.com/internet-and-wifi-in-cuba and vagabondish.com/how-to-get-internet-wifi-in-cuba.

~~~
~~~

MYANMAR—MANDALAY'S SHIMMER AND SERENITY

Gaze at gold-leaf temples, watch a Buddha statue receive a face wash and walk the longest teak footbridge in the world while locals wade through waist-deep water to toss their morning nets

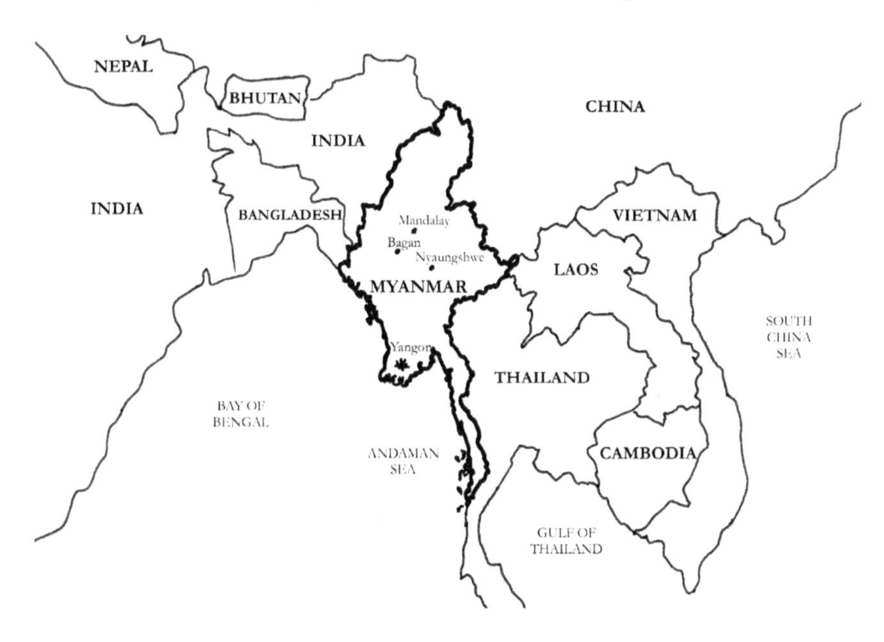

The Experience

Mandalay—the city's name embodies a sense of romantic melancholy oozing with Burmese tradition and a twist of British colonialism. Most visitors come to Mandalay to see its moated palace and the views from the top of the iconic Mandalay Hill. We wanted a deeper view, to strip the city's frantic overcoat and discover its quirky side, the ancient habits that spin around in their own orbit yet somehow blend seamlessly into Mandalay's discordant urban vibrato. Over three days, we followed several paths throughout the city. Each branch laid one more oddity before us. They initially appeared unfamiliar but were actually cornerstones of the daily routine for a handful of local residents. Between these diverse places, Mandalay's charm grew like a reef layered with individual bouquets of urban life. We watched as the city's spirit exploded in front of us into a hundred fragments of tiny moments that all fit together in an unexpected logic.

Forty-five minutes had passed since we had started our walk down Twenty-Sixth Street. It is a long street. Almost immediately after slugging back half of my one-litre water bottle, I felt a flood of droplets run down my back and soak my waistband. A neon sign read thirty-eight degrees Celsius, but I was sure that measure was inflated. It was hot, but not that hot. Perhaps the nearby air conditioner shop had fiddled with the display. Although the street was hectic, traffic buzzed past quietly without the expected onslaught of taxis plying for business. Motorcycles and open-backed pickup truck taxis swished past us with ease—they were accustomed to dodging foot traffic along the edge of the road. We heard the occasional "Hello, where are you going?" but never coinciding with when we actually wanted a ride. Only rarely would drivers call out in an attempt to generate a fare. Even rarer were pushy drivers. Most drove away after we replied with a simple "*No jày zù-ba*" ("No, thanks").

Our eyes skirted between the uneven ground and oncoming traffic in search of the optimal shady route—between parked motorcycles, under the occasional tree or up onto one of the intermittent cement slabs. Technically, a sidewalk did exist. Cement blocks concealed the city's drainage system and offered space to walk, in theory. However, tiles were often missing, broken or blocked by anything from women washing laundry to shops that had spread onto the walkway. We passed one woman crouched on the ground beside a water spout. She flailed a soggy pair of pants on the cement with a stick. "Out, damn spot!"—those pants were surely beaten clean.

We continued weaving between the road and pseudo-sidewalk. Our multi-day quest was to find a few of the more distinctive temples scattered across the city. Today's search was to visit the colourful Eindawya Paya,[8] while the previous day's target had been an aged-teak monastery named Shwe In Bin Kyaung. The third temple on our list was the Mahamuni Paya, which houses a four-and-a-half-metre-tall Buddha statue gilded with layers of gold-leaf swatches applied by the hands of countless devotees. Eventually, we approached our current destination's arched entrance after passing market stalls selling fresh mangosteens, sturdy rubber boots and random household necessities.

Today's aim, the Eindawya Paya, caught our interest because it is a relatively new temple, completed in 1847. It gained notoriety in colonial times when resident monks ushered a group of European visitors out of the temple. The foreigners had refused to remove their shoes and socks, as is customary practice, and therefore had insulted the Buddha. This was back when the country was governed by the British Empire. The pious monks faced retribution under the Crown's justice system, and the head monk received the brunt of the court's wrath with a life sentence. Despite the temple's conflicted past, locals did not seem to hold a grudge against the foreigners wandering through their temple. Rather, people greeted us with crinkly-eyed smiles or, for those lost in prayer, indifference.

We passed through Eindawya Paya's entrance gate and entered the temple's private market. Stalls lined both sides of the walkway for visitors to buy sparkly hand-held signs and bunches of flowers. The kiosks were part sales centres and part mini-factories. Half of the ground was covered with maroon signs left to dry after their sparkling golden letters had been glued on. These were an apparently

8. *Paya* is a broad term encompassing Buddhist temples, monuments or statues of Buddha.

popular item among devotees and rivalled some of the golden statues in brightness. Farther along the foyer, a golden Buddha sat in front of walls painted with bright blue, pink and green designs. Other surfaces had been covered with a mass of tiny mirrored tiles. Silver statues, bouquets of flowers and offerings of crackers, water and rice had been placed together on glass and brass tables. Bills of local kyat were stuffed into clear donation boxes. Between sunbeams and fluorescent lights, everything everywhere glistened. Smaller temples and shrines surrounded the main temple, all with equal measure of sparkle and decoration. In a back corner, I spotted a manmade cave encircled by niches carved into the cement wall and filled with statues.

This temple contained everything, from meditative caverns to Buddha statues adorned with more bling than I had thought possible in a religious setting. A colourful maze of corridors illuminated another world steeped in ritual and significance that seemed dizzying compared to the routine bustle of external streets lined with apartment blocks. I am sure there must be some thread of artistic cohesion across the sanctuary grounds, but I had trouble finding its serenity. Rather, every drop of luxury people could afford seemed to have been thrown at this temple in the belief it would build karma and improve their next life. Hardship can trigger extreme reactions. Perhaps the brilliance reflected the extent to which people had clung to hope as a counterbalance to their despair during Myanmar's unrest. That said, it was not so different to stained-glass churches and grand mosques built elsewhere over the centuries, all pursuing an image of power and reverence. At the very least, Eindawya Paya's golden sanctuary offered a pocket to escape the harsh realities from years of war and loss, which have only recently subsided in Myanmar.

In general, Mandalay's renovated temples bore no resemblance to the bare brick remains I had seen at Bagan (see Chapter Three). There, it had been rare to glimpse a bit of colour that still clung to the site's nine-hundred-year-old temples. Most chips of paint that had survived had dulled with age and blended into their surroundings. Another example of Mandalay's unpredictable temple style was the aptly named Skinny Buddha temple. Here, an emaciated Buddha stood twenty-three metres tall, its rib cage and vertebrae protruding. Statues of equally skinny disciples circled the Enlightened One. Perhaps it was the realness of Mandalay's temples that I had not expected, for they practically vibrated with modernity compared to Bagan's dusty shrines, which held a softer appeal.

My mind jumped back to the day before when we had found a droplet of serenity tucked within a mishmash of busy streets and the slow-moving Thinga Yarzar Canal. Tuk-tuks whirred past, and vendors sold daily necessities from carts or makeshift stalls. On our first walk by, we completely missed the monastery we had been searching for. It was missing the usual plethora of shoes around temple entrances, which may have explained our oversight. We walked beside a cement wall that ran down the sidewalk, shaded by mango and palm trees. Its smudged and mouldy surface nearly disappeared into the background and concealed the Shwe In Bin Kyaung, the ancient monastery we sought. On our second pass, two fellow travellers carrying their sandals stepped out from a narrow opening in the wall. As I slipped my shoes off, a local man leaned in and quietly suggested we take them with us; otherwise, they might get snatched along this busy street. I looked down at my dusty, formerly blue sandals. The heel straps had stretched out and grit stuck to the edges—hardly an enticing pair. We smiled and thanked the man, picking up our shoes as we walked through the gate onto a dusty path.

Traffic faded. Mango trees grew lush. I could smell the musty scent of the nearby canal water mixed with wood and damp earth. Around a bend, a sun-baked teak structure rose in front of us, looking much like a master baker's creation for the largest and most sumptuous chocolate-layer-cake contest. Above a three-tiered teak roof balanced a seven-layered pinnacle, itself topped with a golden spire. Nearly everywhere I looked, wood had been carved into the shape of deities, swirls, points, spires and other ornamental designs. Red roof tiles occasionally revealed themselves between pointy spindles.

The main sanctuary could be accessed by a cement staircase painted a soft yellow and moulded into gentle swirls. Fuzzy patches of mildew spread across its finish even though it had probably been repainted less than a year ago. Through the central doors, the wooden theme was carried through into a dim sanctuary. A donation box for renovation funds sat in the main upper hall; after all, the building had been originally constructed in 1895. An occasional old-fashioned lamp hung from the ceiling with pistachio-coloured metal that cradled a delicate glass shade. These antiques lingered, as did stories from the monastery's past. Dust gathered across the top of them and, in some places, dangled in strands like long spider's legs. Although lovely in its own way, the darkened room seemed to amplify the quietness that blanketed the monastery grounds. We walked in solitude, as the monks had either gone to their quarters or left the compound to help around the city. The only monk I saw in the entire complex lounged on a plastic chair as he read a newspaper, wearing his distinctive maroon robe.

Back outside in the sunshine, a couple of workmen remained. Their steady whittling reminded me that we were not completely alone. They sat in the shade beneath one of the buildings facing this aged-teak monastery. They were there to refresh the tender structure, or at least ensure the humid environment would not ravage it. Each man hunched over a long plank. One of the carvers smiled at us and said, "*Ming guh la ba*" ("hello"). They were copying a flower-like design onto a new panel using hand tools to etch the soft wood. Rosettes and other decorative shapes slowly emerged. A similar board laid nearby, warped with age. It was both their prototype and the piece to be replaced.

This temple's austere teak walls and serene garden diverged from the gold leaf and shiny walls found elsewhere. Its serene ambience confirmed the duality from which Buddhist followers can choose: the opulent, shiny shrines or the quiet, contemplative refuges. These places have offered a choice to generations of Burmese who have likely felt their emotions pushed to extremes over the years. To navigate the former militaristic regime, one moment could be passionate and determined while the next submissive and quiet. Although much of their past is hidden to foreigners, freedom of expression is something these sanctuaries have offered in a place where many had so little choice.

On our quest to see another slice of this eclectic city, we climbed Mandalay Hill. This landmark, 230 metres above the city of Mandalay, marks where Buddha once proclaimed a great city would be built. Most visitors climb the 1,729 steps from the southern entrance to reach the top and take in the expansive view across the city. Our Lonely Planet travel guide (see Bibliography) described a secondary entrance on the hill's southeastern edge as "more interesting for glimpsed views, albeit harder on the feet." Although this advice intrigued us, we discovered that our perspective of *interesting* differed from that of the guide's authors. As is local protocol, we removed our shoes and started the climb barefoot. The floor alternated between brick, cement and tile, all of which felt gritty. Dried bird droppings speckled most sections. We attempted to dodge them only to find discarded cigarettes, plastic wrappers and other garbage mixed with dust and dried leaves. Farther along, the stairs crossed a dip, which appeared to have taken on the role of garbage dump. We were flanked by plastic bottles, food containers and assorted filth.

In contrast, the hillside temples that we passed were delicately decorated. Tiny mirrored tiles encrusted the walls, and Buddha statues were lit up with neon lights and gold paint. Similarly bright and decorative figurines filled any free space. A few people hung about. They could have been vendors resting after the lunch crowd or pilgrims who had temporarily stopped en route. Pots, bamboo mats used as beds and other personal items were scattered on the ground.

We never reached the summit. Midway up the hill, dusty boards, cement barrels and bags of cement powder—remnants of construction work—blocked most of the passage. We lost our motivation to pick our way around them and headed back down, dismally taking the same joyless journey in reverse.

Following this disappointing climb, we sought a more endearing scene. At the ridiculously early hour of three o'clock the next morning, our alarm reminded us that our quest required discipline. We had an hour to reach the Mahamuni Paya, where the monks would be commencing their work at four o'clock. For them it was a daily routine; for us it was unusual and intriguing. The early hour convinced us that we would likely be among few foreigners to share in such an event. The monks' attention would be primarily focused on a four-metre-tall golden Buddha located within the Mahamuni Paya and believed to be over two thousand years old. It had been dragged by the Burmese army from Mrauk U in western Myanmar to Mandalay in 1784. Every morning, the monks bathed the face of this revered statue until it gleamed. We, along with about thirty other devoted early risers, came to watch. Women brought trays of offerings to donate to the Buddha and share with the monks. Water bottles, bags of chips, cups of rice and bouquets of flowers lined the area in front of the statue. Flowers were collected in large silver vases. Shortly after the ceremony started, the trays of food and drink were removed and presumably relocated to the monks' quarters. Male visitors could access the best view by passing through a metal detector to sit right in front of the sparkling statue. I remained behind the barricade and sat cross-legged with the women.

In addition to the Buddha's smooth golden face, everything around him looked like an intricate golden lace made of leaves, bells, lotus stalks and indiscernible shapes coated in gold. This effect was amplified by gold leaf pressed onto the surface of the statue, an act commonly performed by devotees across Myanmar.[9] Grand bouquets of flowers were carried into the room and placed on a table in front of the gold-encrusted Buddha. Big gold and silver bowls were then carried in and placed on low tables. The head monk redistributed the liquid from the larger bowls into several smaller basins. They held holy water and what looked like masala tea or butter tea but was likely tarnish remover. For the next hour, the monk daubed a white terry cloth into the milky liquid and gently smoothed it across the Buddha's face. With each rub, the surface dulled and then, after more gentle strokes, shone. Most people stayed to watch the entire production, and a few onlookers conversed in soft whispers.

When we left, the sun had not yet risen. Darkness cloaked the streets. Our taxi driver drove to Amarapura's U Bein Bridge, another of Mandalay's exquisite sites beyond its mélange of temples. U Bein

9. myanmarinsider.com/lending-a-golden-touch

Bridge is the world's longest teak bridge and stretches almost 1,200 metres across Taungthaman Lake. At this early hour, the market stalls remained shuttered. Our driver turned off the engine, and within a few minutes, we all nodded off for a morning nap.

About thirty minutes later, the sun emerged through a soft drizzle. As we neared the bridge, the scene could only be described as perfect serenity. A few long boats drifted through the water while fishermen laid nets. Many pulled themselves along using ropes previously set. Only after an hour or so did the rev of a motor pierce the air. In the distance, speakers blared a mix of eighties soft rock and local folk songs. The bridge was empty except for a handful of monks and the occasional fisherman. I offered one monk my poached eggs from the breakfast box our hotel had packed. His alms bowl was hidden beneath a tray of cups, which he readily lifted to pop the foil-wrapped eggs inside. With a nod to one another, we walked off in opposite directions.

Farther down the bridge, a lady approached on a sputtering motorcycle. She looked out of place compared to others who pushed their single-gear pedal bicycles or just walked. Abruptly, she stopped when she reached my husband and me, and we saw it was more than her motorcycle that made her stand out. She wore fishnet stockings beneath short jean shorts with an unzipped zipper. Her slurring mumbles did not make much sense. A monk who had been standing nearby stepped over and asked that she not bring her motorbike onto the bridge, for the structure was old and could not handle its weight. She babbled at him, a circular way of talking that comes after too many drinks or too many drugs. The monk's words turned to the topic of respect, spoken in English, which I found curious. Their discussion pivoted between his respecting her and her need to respect the monk and the bridge. After a few minutes, she revved the engine and drove off. The monk explained to us that motorbikes are illegal on U Bein Bridge, so he planned to call his "BFF" ("best friend forever"), who worked for the police. His English was impeccable, but the use of the casual term *BFF* seemed odd coming from a monk in Mandalay.

U Bein Bridge

To this day, I think there was something unusual in that entire interaction but cannot quite place it. Certainly, Mandalay is not a city to be bound by wide sweeps or ignorant assumptions. Inconsistent mysteries remain unexplained. For example, air conditioners spew cool air in abundance across the city, proving the reliability of the electricity's supply, yet in-house washing machines are nearly nonexistent, even at hotels. Mandalay showed us a medley of moments. Every site divulged another nuance that initially seemed contradictory, but somehow when stitched together, they formed an enchanting experience.

The Basics

Most useful items to pack: Slip-on shoes and small change for donations

Useful words and phrases in Burmese: *ming guh la ba* ("hello"); *jày zù ding ba de* ("thank you"); *hoh'gé* ("yes"); *híng ìn* ("no"); and *sàw rì nah* ("excuse me/sorry").[10]

For more, refer to worldnomads.com/explore/southeast-asia/myanmar/useful-burmese-phrases-for-travelers-to-myanmar.

For further travel information: Peacock Lodge is tucked among palm trees on a quiet street and within walking distance of the Mandalay Palace, Mandalay Hill and other central sights. The hotel is run by an informative family who also prepare tasty home-cooked meals at the on-site restaurant. The lodge did not have its own website at the time of writing, but reservations can be made through Booking.com and other hotel reservation websites.

Local knowledge paid off, and our hotel owner's recommendation for Unique Mandalay Tea Room led to multiple visits for an iced coffee. For more information, go to their Facebook page: facebook.com/uniquemdytearoom.

Few sites or temples in Mandalay operate their own websites. The best source of information is your favourite travel guide.

10. Based on Lonely Planet's *Myanmar (Burma) Travel Guide* (see Bibliography).

For general citywide information, refer to tourism.gov.mm/en_US/attractions/destinations/mandalay.

~~~
~~~

About the Author

Nancy O'Hare is the author of *Dust in My Pack*. She has travelled to over seventy countries and lived across five continents. Each move spurred her passion for diverse cultures and propelled her to seek out unique experiences. O'Hare's husband shares her passion to visit distant lands and captures remote scenes in his photography. Together, they have transitioned from a corporate career in finance to pursue their creative pursuits and explore our planet, one country at a time.

O'Hare captures moments from multi-month journeys to off-the-beaten path locations in her writing. Her love for nature and intriguing cultures is revealed in her stories from all seven continents. Inspire your inner traveller with her refreshing perspective on little-known destinations.

Discover more travel tales in O'Hare's first book, *Dust in My Pack*.

~~~
~~~

Connect with the author at:

Website: bynancyohare.com

Facebook: facebook.com/ByNancyO

Twitter: twitter.com/DustInMyPack

Goodreads: goodreads.com/bynancyohare

Book reviews help other like-minded readers discover O'Hare's writing, so please share your honest feedback on sites such as Goodreads, Amazon or other book-related websites.

Other Books by the Author

The best of O'Hare's earlier travels are available in her first book, *Dust in My Pack*. Like *Searching for Unique*, it captures little-known destinations categorized by travel interest. In her first book, themes include boat trips, multi-day treks, day hikes, temples and forts, ancient cities, getaway adventures, serene scenes, animal encounters and unforgettable accommodations. Tales range from adrenalin-inducing exploits to awe-inspiring sites across all seven continents.

Excerpt from *Dust in My Pack,* Chapter One: Malawi—The *MV Ilala*:

> Our intended itinerary was to travel from Likoma Island to Chipoka, a village on Lake Niassa's southwestern shore. Likoma Island is part of Malawi but sits nearer to Mozambique's shoreline and falls along the northern section of *Ilala's* circular route. The official schedule placed the journey from Likoma Island to Chipoka at twenty-four hours; however, the *Ilala* arrived at Likoma Island already fifteen hours late. Schedules are inevitably rough guides.
>
> The ferry eventually arrived late in the evening. The sun had long set. Awaiting passengers crowded the beach as the boat glowed in the moonlight and dropped anchor. When we boarded, the entire lower economy deck was filled with sacks of corn, ground nuts and other essentials. I walked very tentatively across the tops of these sacks in the

dark, carrying an eighteen-kilogram backpack plus a day pack hung on the front of my shoulders. My balance was further tested by the continual flow of people manoeuvring within the same corridor. They were headed in the opposite direction, eager to disembark from the very access point we had just entered. The secret was to give a brief smile to the passing voyagers, momentarily recognizing the challenge and humour in one another's journey, and to offer a hand or sway to the side to help each other pass. We were, quite literally, all in the same boat.

Despite sixty years of plying this route, organized chaos pervaded the boarding process. Climbing over and across bags was only part of it. First we had to climb up a rickety ladder balanced vertically between the *Ilala* and its overcrowded bobbing lifeboat. The lifeboat was well used, not for life-saving purposes, but as a loading shuttle because most destinations lacked a suitable dock. Passengers onshore shifted in a rhythm as they jostled to cram onto the lifeboat, often reaching for a child, bags, boxes or all such necessities. The owner of each sack and its specific destination was rather opaque. Yet in practice, bags were off-loaded, new ones filled their place and at times the entire bottom deck lay bare. It reminded me of a revolving door; each movement seemed small, but in their totality they were quite effective.

Our choice of a cabin was markedly advantageous, as the voyage ultimately took sixty hours—a mere thirty-six hours beyond its scheduled duration—and that excluded the fifteen-hour delay before the ferry even arrived at Likoma Island. Yet, with some planning, it is relatively easy to supplement the basic offerings of the ferry to incorporate a semblance of comfort into the wait. Bring a hammock to sway away the hours or reserve a cabin with two twin beds, a wash basin and a private toilet.

The first mishap became apparent when we headed to the upper deck for breakfast after a restful sleep during our first night aboard. Passengers who had expected to get off at the next stop remained on board lounging in small groups. One British university student readily explained, "Oh, have you not heard? We have turned around and are heading back to Likoma Island; they forgot the captain! It is absolute madness!"

Dust in My Pack is available as an e-book or paperback at most online bookstores.

~~~

Book reviews help other like-minded readers discover O'Hare's writing, so please share your honest feedback on Goodreads, Amazon or other book-related websites.

~~~

Bibliography

Bain, Carolyn, and Alexis Averbuck. 2015. *Iceland Travel Guide*, 9th ed. China: Lonely Planet.

Di Duca, Marc. 2015. *Pocket Madeira.* China: Lonely Planet.

Dragicevich, Peter, Hugh McNaughtan, and Leonid Ragozin. 2016. *Estonia, Latvia and Lithuania Travel Guide*, 7th ed. China: Lonely Planet.

Egerton, Alex, Tom Masters, and Kevin Raub. 2015. *Colombia Travel Guide*, 7th ed. China: Lonely Planet.

Mayhew, Bradley, John Vincent Bellezza, Robert Kelly, and Daniel McCrohan. 2008. *Tibet Travel Guide*, 7th ed. Singapore: Lonely Planet.

Mayhew, Bradley, and Lindsay Brown. 2017. *Bhutan Travel Guide*, 6th ed. Singapore: Lonely Planet.

Murphy, Alan, Kate Armstrong, Matthew Firestone, Mary Fitzpatrick, Michael Grosberg, Nana Luckham, and Andy Rebold. 2007. *Southern Africa Travel Guide*, 4th ed. China: Lonely Planet.

Ray, Nick, Isabel Albiston, Greg Bloom, Ria de Jong, David Eimer, Sarah Reid, Simon Richmond, Iain Stewart, Ryan Ver Berkmoes, Richard Waters, and China Williams. 2016. *Southeast Asia on a Shoestring*, 18th ed. Singapore: Lonely Planet.

Richmond, Simon, David Eimer, Adam Karlin, Nick Ray, and Regis St. Louis. 2017. *Myanmar (Burma) Travel Guide*, 13th ed. Singapore: Lonely Planet.

Sainsbury, Brendan, and Luke Waterson. 2015. *Cuba Travel Guide*, 8th ed. China: Lonely Planet.

Ver Berkmoes, Ryan, Stuart Butler, and Iain Stewart. 2015. *Sri Lanka Travel Guide*, 13th ed. China: Lonely Planet.

CPSIA information can be obtained
at www.ICGtesting.com
Printed in the USA
LVHW031554141118
597116LV00005B/693